Albert Bushnell Hart, Ralph Curtis Ringwalt, Walter Du Bois Brookings

Briefs for debate on current political, economic and social topics

Albert Bushnell Hart, Ralph Curtis Ringwalt, Walter Du Bois Brookings

Briefs for debate on current political, economic and social topics

ISBN/EAN: 9783337134334

Printed in Europe, USA, Canada, Australia, Japan

Cover: Foto ©Suzi / pixelio.de

More available books at **www.hansebooks.com**

BRIEFS FOR DEBATE

BRIEFS FOR DEBATE

ON

CURRENT POLITICAL, ECONOMIC, AND
SOCIAL TOPICS

EDITED BY

W. DU BOIS BROOKINGS, A.B.
OF THE HARVARD LAW SCHOOL

AND

RALPH CURTIS RINGWALT, A.B.
ASSISTANT IN RHETORIC IN COLUMBIA UNIVERSITY

WITH AN INTRODUCTION BY
ALBERT BUSHNELL HART, PH.D.
ASSISTANT PROFESSOR IN HARVARD UNIVERSITY

NEW YORK
LONGMANS, GREEN, AND CO.
LONDON AND BOMBAY
1896

Copyright, 1895
BY LONGMANS, GREEN, AND CO.

All Rights Reserved

PREFACE.

In preparing this volume the editors have had a threefold object in view. They have aimed: (1) to furnish a text-book for formal courses in public speaking and discussion; (2) to provide a manual for literary and debating societies; and (3) to give the ordinary worker, not a specialist in the subjects treated, suggestion and assistance. The value of the book for these three classes must lie chiefly in the fact that it states concisely the principal arguments, *pro* and *con*, on a large number of the important topics of the day; that it presents working bibliographies on these topics; and that it gives examples of logical statement, and may suggest a systematic method for the treatment of other topics.

The basis of the work has been a collection of some two hundred briefs prepared during the past ten years by students in Harvard University, under the direction of instructors. Of these briefs the most useful and interesting have been selected; the material has been carefully worked over, and the bibliographies enlarged and verified. A number of new topics, as well as a list of questions suitable for debate, have been added; and the whole has been made uniform in treatment. It should be said, however, that the lists of references are by no means exhaustive, and that many of the smallest subdivisions may be made subjects for separate and detailed discussion.

In the progress of their work the editors have become greatly indebted to many friends. Especially are they under obligation to Professor Hart, who, besides furnishing the Introduction, has given them unfailing counsel and assistance. They also wish to acknowledge the constant favors which they have received from Mr. Thomas J. Kiernan, the Superintendent of Circulation in the Harvard College Library.

W. DU B. B.,
R. C. R.

August 1, 1896.

CONTENTS.

INTRODUCTION.

THE ART OF DEBATE.

		PAGE
1.	Purpose of the Briefs for Debate,	xi
2.	Importance of Debate,	xii
3.	Selection of a Question,	xv
4.	Materials,	xviii
5.	Use of Materials,	xxiii
6.	The Brief System,	xxv
7.	Practice before Debate,	xxviii
8.	Management of a Debate,	xxx
9.	Rebuttal,	xxxiv
10.	Persuasive Speaking,	xxxv
11.	Criticism of Debates,	xxxix
12.	Bibliography of Debating,	xli

BRIEFS FOR DEBATE.

POLITICS.

SUFFRAGE.

I.	Federal Control of National Elections,	1
II.	Federal Protection of Negro Suffrage,	3
III.	Disfranchisement of the Negroes,	6
IV.	Woman Suffrage,	8
V.	A Property Qualification for Municipal Suffrage,	11

PARTIES.

VI. The Republican Party,	13
VII. The Populist Party,	16
VIII. The American Protective Association,	19
IX. Party Allegiance,	22
X. Party Allegiance in Municipal Elections,	24

POLITICAL METHODS.

XI. The Caucus System,	27
XII. The Choice of Presidential Electors,	30
XIII. Popular Election of Senators,	32
XIV. District Election of Congressmen,	36
XV. Cabinet and Congressional Governments,	37
XVI. Cabinet Ministers in Congress,	40
XVII. Civil Service Reform,	44
XVIII. The English System of Preventing Election Frauds,	47
XIX. The Executive Power of the Mayor in Cities,	49

INSTITUTIONS.

XX. Danger to Free Institutions in the United States,	52
XXI. The Jury System,	55
XXII. Capital Punishment,	57

NATIONAL POLICY (FOREIGN).

XXIII. The Annexation of Canada,	59
XXIV. The Annexation of Hawaii,	62
XXV. United States Ownership of the Nicaragua Canal,	65

NATIONAL POLICY (DOMESTIC).

XXVI. Restriction of Immigration,	68
XXVII. A Tax on Immigrants,	70
XXVIII. The Exclusion of the Chinese,	73
XXIX. The Pension Policy,	75
XXX. Increase of the Navy,	78
XXXI. An International Copyright Law,	80

PARLIAMENTARY PROCEDURE.

XXXII. Closure in the Senate,	83
XXXIII. The Counting of a Quorum,	85

CONTENTS.

ECONOMICS.

CURRENCY.   PAGE
   XXXIV. An International Gold Standard, ... 88
   XXXV. Bimetallism in the United States, ... 90
   XXXVI. The Tax on State Bank-notes, ... 93

TARIFF.
   XXXVII. Protection and Free Trade, ... 96
   XXXVIII. The Tariff and Wages, ... 99
   XXXIX. Reciprocity with Canada, ... 102
   XL. Free Ships, ... 104
   XLI. Shipping Subsidies, ... 107
   XLII. Free Sugar, ... 110
   XLIII. Sugar Bounties, ... 112
   XLIV. Duties on Wool and Woollens, ... 115

TAXATION.
   XLV. A National Income Tax, ... 117
   XLVI. A Single Tax, ... 120

SOCIOLOGY.

GOVERNMENT INTERVENTION.
   XLVII. Government Ownership of Railroads, ... 123
   XLVIII. Government Ownership of the Telegraph, . . 126
   XLIX. State Ownership of Manufactories, ... 129
   L. Municipal Ownership of Natural Monopolies, . 132
   LI. The Prohibition of Trusts, ... 134
   LII. The Prohibition of Railroad Pooling, . . . 137
   LIII. State Control of Education, ... 139
   LIV. Federal Control of Divorce, ... 142
   LV. Government Construction of Irrigation Works, . 144
   LVI. Federal Control of Quarantine, ... 146
   LVII. The Right to Prohibit the Sale of Oleomargarine, . 149

LABOR.
   LVIII. Labor Organizations, ... 151
   LIX. A Labor Party, ... 154
   LX. The Eight-hour Day, ... 156
   LXI. General Booth's Employment System, . . 160

CONTENTS.

	PAGE
LXII. A National Board of Arbitration for Railroad Disputes,	162
LXIII. The Contract System of Employing Convict Labor,	165
LXIV. Municipal Aid for the Unemployed,	168
LXV. The Housing of the Poor,	170

LIQUOR.

LXVI. Prohibition and High License,	172
LXVII. The Gothenburg Liquor System,	176

EDUCATION.

LXVIII. Co-education,	178
LXIX. A Three Years' Course for the A.B. Degree,	181
LXX. Intercollegiate Foot-ball,	184

MISCELLANEOUS.

LXXI. Irish Home Rule,	187
LXXII. Parnell and the Irish Cause,	190
LXXIII. The China-Japan War,	192
LXXIV. Nihilism,	195
LXXV. The Injunctions Against the Chicago Strikers,	197

ADDITIONAL TOPICS FOR DEBATE.

Politics,	200
Economics,	203
Sociology,	206
Miscellaneous,	208
INDEX,	211

INTRODUCTION

THE ART OF DEBATE*

1. Purpose of the Briefs for Debate.

To the building up of systematic discussion, intelligently conducted, Mr. Brookings and Mr. Ringwalt have given the labor and thought embodied in this book. They aim to aid debaters to choose interesting and debatable questions; they furnish a starting point for the collection of material on current topics; and they print a set of model briefs which may illustrate cogent statement. They had at the beginning a collection of about two hundred briefs which had been prepared by as many student hands, under the direction of elders; out of these they have selected the most important subjects, have condensed, restated, and added new topics, and have verified, corrected and completed the references. That work has been their own, and for the matter, arrangement and citations, they have full responsibility.

The set of seventy-five briefs is intended first of all to give concise information about the lines of argument which have been worked out by actual investigators on actual subjects; on each topic therefore the authors show the principal planes of logical cleavage. They have not attempted to make any statement of facts to be a groundwork, but through their panoply of painstaking references, they lead the inquirer to first-hand sources, and to the principal printed treatises and special discussions. This short cut will not release the truth-seeker from

* Copyright, 1896, by Longmans, Green, and Co.

the necessity of thinking for himself, but it will diminish the mechanical part of his labor, and set free more time for drawing the meaning out of the facts thus so readily found.

On the important subjects of proper statement, analysis and interweaving of argument, they have given not precept but example. Each of the briefs is made up by separating out the single detailed arguments, and then combining them into connected groups; it is the bookkeeping of argument, the journalizing and ledger posting. It is not expected that formal arguments will be shrunk upon these skeletons: the debater needs to make his own brief—but he has here working models, suggestive on the topics treated, and equally useful as showing the system which may be applied to any subject.

The briefs are therefore a guide to two of the essentials of discussion—control of the material; and marshalling of the arguments—but they contain no hint as to how a man may best phrase, speak and illustrate what he has learned. Though the experience of the authors would make their suggestions on such points valuable, they have chosen to ask one of their friends to prefix to their volume some consideration of this other phase of the matter—of the translation of the inner thought into an argument which will convince. That request is the occasion of this introduction.

2. Importance of Debate.

If there be a form of human expression which more than any other requires and calls out the whole force of him who employs it, it is the art of the persuasive speaker. He must put in practice grace of presence, bodily vigor, voice, memory, choice of words, logic, style, imagination, personal influence, sympathy with his auditors and quickness of retort. Of debating may be said as Thomas Hughes said, in *Tom Brown*, of boxing: 'There's no exercise in the world so good for the temper, and for the muscles of the back and legs.' Debate is older than language, and is in fact common among creatures which have no speech, such as babes and bees. Debaters have had both power and reputation as far back as

> 'Nestor, the master of persuasive speech,
> The clear-toned Pylian orator, whose tongue
> Dropped words more sweet than honey.'

Indeed the first book of the Iliad is little more than a record of a tumultuous debating society which sadly needed the restraints of Jefferson's Manual. Themistocles reached the climax of dramatic debate in his 'Strike, but hear me.' The Icelanders loved a wrangle and plied each other with the subtlest legal arguments over Burnt Njal; till the inevitable moment came when the crust over the Icelandic volcanic temper broke up, and the contestants clenched their arguments with battle axes. Cicero seems to have preferred those debates in which he had no opponent. For debatable questions the world has never found a lack. Religion has furnished an array of fatally attractive subjects, from the differences between Socrates and the Sophists down to the defence of Anne Hutchinson against the orthodox Massachusetts clergy; politics is, rightly construed, only organized discussion; and social questions have been the dividing wedge in families and communities ever since people became aware that they had neighbors with whom to dispute.

In the pleasures of open discussion, Americans have always been keen. What were Colonial town meetings and legislative assemblies but public debating societies? In a country like ours, abounding in town councils, synods, conferences, vestries, faculties and legislatures, persuasive speech is not only a pleasure and a power, it is a professional asset. Americans love a contest, even as listeners; and the good debater is likely to argue his way to success.

No treatise could classify or describe the endless oral debates of which the world is full; but it is possible to discuss those set and formal contests in which one or several persons, are pitted against an equal number of champions of the other side. This was a favorite diversion of the middle ages; and has left its tradition in the disputations which to this day every candidate for the Italian 'Laurea' (corresponding to our A.B. degree) is obliged to hold with his examiners. Luther enjoyed this kind of fray, as in the famous disputation of 1529 with Zwingli. Regular debating societies have long been a part of school and social life in this country; and in one of them Abraham Lincoln made the first of his recorded speeches. Most colleges have a machinery for such debates, taking its most effective form in two rival societies, such as the Whig and Clio at Princeton, the Philosophical and Dialectic of the University of North Carolina, the Philolexian and Barnard of Columbia, and the Union and Forum of Harvard.

Such practices and such opportunities need no discussion; every one knows that preparation for debate involves knowledge; that the logical arrangement of argument is good intellectual training; that the cut and thrust of actual contest is a type and preparation for life; that by discussion men broaden their own views and grow to respect those of their opponents. The effective use of one's mother tongue is stimulated by debate; and becomes an agreeable accomplishment, a valuable tool, the most important possession of the educated man. It even passes into proverbs and jocular quips. As Bacon says: 'It is good in discourse and speech of conversation, to vary and intermingle speech of the present occasion with arguments, tales with reasons, asking of questions with telling of opinions, and jest with earnest.' Or, as the poet of *Alice's Adventures* would less gravely have it:

> 'In my youth, said his father, I took to the law,
>   And argued each case with my wife,
> And the muscular strength, which it gave to my jaw,
>   Has lasted the rest of my life.'

For all the reasons just stated, the idea has for some years been gaining ground that argument, both written and spoken, is a proper subject for study in a school or a college; that the unravelling of the intricacies of a great, closely-woven speech, is as good a mental discipline as the analysis of a salt, or the solution of a spherical triangle. We begin to understand that the arrangement of material in clear and cogent form has the advantages of translation from a foreign language, or the deduction of a principle in philosophy; that discussion, and especially public discussion, is one of the best quickeners of individual thought and expression. The old-fashioned 'rhetorical exercises' of the schools often included set debates. A century ago disputations were a part of college commencements. It is only of late years, however, that there have sprung up formal courses in debate, in which the preparation and oral statement of argument 'counts toward the degree,' and is subject to the observation and criticism of regular instructors, expert in the questions under debate. This system is a substantial addition to the written themes, essays and forensics ordinarily required in colleges; and it differs from the usual courses in elocution in that it expects a man to put his thoughts into his own language, and not to attempt simply to give expression to the language of other people.

3. Selection of a Question.

Nothing is more essential, to make debates interesting and profitable, than the choice of a proper question. There must be, in the first place, two distinct and reasonably balanced sides. Yet even out of what appears upon its face a foregone conclusion, a question may often be made by limiting the conditions, by 'loading' the stronger side by such provisos as may take away its advantage. For example, who would undertake to argue the negative of the question: '*Resolved*, That the voter ought to be protected in his right to the ballot'? But there is good debating ground on either side of the question: '*Resolved*, That it is the duty of the Federal Government to protect the voter's right to the ballot,' or of the question: '*Resolved*, That a registry law is the best protection to the ballot;' or, '*Resolved*, That the Fifteenth Amendment was a mistake.' Skill in making a just balance in framing questions is very like the skill of the handicapper in foot-races.

In the second place, a question should be debatable: that is, it should include something important enough to be worth discussing, broad enough to lead to several different lines of argument, and near enough so that there is available information upon it. The old scholastic debate question: 'How many angels can dance on the point of a needle?' is the classical example of unreal subjects. Experience shows that general questions, not made too exact and specific, lead to livelier debates, because they give opportunities to come in with suggestive side-lights. Thus the question, '*Resolved*, That Canada ought to be annexed to the United States,' is more likely to be energetically debated than the question, '*Resolved*, That the best interests of Canada demand annexation to the United States.' The first form has plainly more material for four or six good speeches: and where there are numerous speeches from the floor, the broader topic gives each an opportunity to come in with some point not yet fully stated.

Next there must be some human interest at stake: the question must be one the actual decision of which would make a difference to the debaters. In the old-fashioned rhetorics are long lists of questions like, 'Is the hope of reward a stronger motive than the fear of punishment?' or 'Is revolution a natural right?' Who will lose his sleep if such questions be decided either way? The familiar biographical questions had a special value before the literature of current discussion was made available, because you could find out something about 'Was Cæsar justified in crossing the Rubicon?' or 'Was the execution of Charles I. deserved?' Yet where young men or young women accustomed to debate are allowed to choose for themselves, they are likely to prefer questions taken out of modern history and current social, political and economic problems.

In their selection of seventy-five topics, Mr. Brookings and

Mr. Ringwalt have recognized and accepted such preferences. Young people like to debate the questions which perplex their elders, and which they will be called upon to settle, on which they already know something, and wish to know more; questions which really affect the welfare of their friends or themselves. Modern conditions, especially in the United States, tend to bring out underlying differences of temperament or interest in hotly contested disputes; and some current topic can almost always be found which interests everybody—such as the tariff, silver, a navy, party nominations, or international politics.

Extending the same principle a little further, the spirit of a debate is much quickened if some or all the debaters have some personal knowledge of, or interest in, the question. The son of a railroad president will be certain to have very distinct ideas on pooling; a Pittsburgh girl knows what a protective tariff is; a Southerner can argue on the negro question; the worker in slums has an opinion as to the Salvation Army. Debates in actual life are always carried on by those who are convinced that they have the right opinion, and are determined to convince others; hence the value of debate-subjects on which the participants know enough to differ. Hence very good subjects can often be made out of school and college questions—marking systems, athletics, co-education, Greek letter societies, and the like. Any kind of actual personal contact with a question gives life to the argument.

No matter how good the question may be, the debate will be thin and dull, unless there be material available from which an argument may be made up. The intellectual training of debate is not to be had from hair-splitting—still less from general talk on an unfamiliar subject: for the object of debate is not to say something, but to have something that must be said. There must be preparation, and that involves the accumulation of material, and the throwing out of the unavailable. Preparation needs material, in books, or newspapers, or in the stores of one's own mind.

A glance at the table of contents of this volume will show how steadily the authors have kept these principles in mind. The seventy-five briefs are all on questions many times debated in Congress or Legislatures or Parliaments or Faculties. The list is enlarged by the 'Additional Topics for Debate:' (pp. 201-210) and may be further extended by using some of the bibliographies mentioned below (§ 12).

For intercollegiate and interscholastic debates, the choice of a subject has been a troublesome task: it was hard to state a question so that it seemed fair to both parties. But a system has been adopted in the Yale-Princeton-Harvard contests, and doubtless elsewhere, which prevents quarrels and puts the evenness of the question beyond doubt. The challenging (?) college selects and states the question; the challenged (?) has then the right to choose either side. No better plan could be invented.

4. Materials.

For such subjects as have just been suggested the materials are abundant and easily found. First come the previous recorded discussions, notably those of Congress and other national legislative bodies. The titles of the various official publications are given below (§ 12). On all questions which interest the government of the United States we have the nearly verbatim reports of the proceedings of the Senate and of the House of Representatives, which contain speeches, messages, and often quoted documents. The indexes to the annual sets of the *Congressional Record* are full and include three kinds of references—to names, subjects, and bills by their official number. In the *Congressional Documents* will be found valuable reports, both from executive departments and from legislative committees. These are arranged for each session of Congress into six groups: *Senate Executive Documents*, *Senate Miscellaneous*, *Senate* [*Committee*] *Reports*, *House Executive Documents*, *House Miscellaneous*, *House* [*Committee*] *Reports*. Each set has a poor index prefixed to each volume. In § 12 will be found titles of a few handier indexes. On the Constitutional Convention of 1787 we have the invaluable *Madison Papers*, reprinted in *Elliot's Debates;* and in a recent edition, bearing the erroneous title of *Journal of the Federal Convention*, edited by E. C. Scott. Remarkable speeches have, from 1775 down, been frequently printed in newspapers, in pamphlets, or in the collected works of the orator. Presidential messages and official proclamations will be found down to 1850 in Williams's *Statesman's Manual;* and from 1789 down in the fuller *Compilation of the Messages and Papers of the Presidents*, by James D. Richardson. The laws of Congress are in the *Statutes at Large*, and the decisions of the Supreme Court in the successive *Reports* of Dallas, Cranch, Wheaton, Peters, Howard, Black, Wallace, and 'United States.' Down to 1863 there are also the condensed reports of Curtis and Miller.

Newspapers are valuable to the debater for three kinds of materials: reports of speeches and messages; accounts of current events, and editorial discussions. Some newspapers have also a fourth department, of correspondence: the letters to the *London Times*, for instance, contain discussions of all kinds of pending questions; the *Nation* has sometimes very spicy letters. In all respects the newspapers most likely to help the debater are the great New York, Boston, and Chicago dailies. On the proceedings of state legislatures (which are nowhere reported in full) the leading dailies of the State are most helpful. Two newspapers have made it their special mission to collect and publish extracts from the daily press of the time, and hence they answer instead of a large body of papers; they are *Niles' Weekly Register* (1811–49) and *Public Opinion* (1885–96); the latter is one of the most useful sources for the making up of briefs. The *Nation* has since its first publication in 1865 made it a point to publish short editorials on topics of national interest: and it is not necessary to agree with the political views of the editors in order to avail one's self of their careful record of events and discussions which are likely to interest debaters. Of the foreign newspapers the most useful are the *Times* (London), *Temps* (Paris), and *Augsburger Allgemeine Zeitung*.

Of late years public men have got into the habit of putting their views before the public in the great periodicals rather than in speeches. Perhaps the first example was Stephen A. Douglas's article on *Popular Sovereignty* in *Harper's Monthly* for September, 1859; although Madison had contributed anonymously to the *North American Review* in 1830. Expert writers also choose frequently to discuss questions of public interest in the general, and even in the popular, periodicals.

Hence, among the most fruitful sources of information, especially on questions which have not yet been condensed into books, are the articles in periodicals. Especially to be mentioned are the *Forum* (1886–), *Atlantic Monthly* (1857–), *Scribner's* (1870–81, 1887–), *Century* (1881–), *Harper's* (1850–), *New-England Magazine* (1889–), *North American Review* (1815–; up to 1800, the best vehicle for intelligent discussion of public affairs), *Chautauquan* (1884–), *Arena* (1890–), *Review of Reviews* (1889–). Valuable articles are also often found in the religious reviews, as the *Methodist Quarterly* (1841–), *Bibliotheca Sacra* (1854–; Congregationalist, now changed in character), *Unitarian Review* (1844–91), *Universalist Quarterly* (1844–86), *American Catholic Quarterly* (1876–). The following periodicals are no longer published, though excellent on the period which they cover: *Magazine of American History* (1877–94), *Princeton Review* and *New Princeton Review* (1829–71, 1878–84, 1886–88), *Democratic Review* (1838–59), *American Whig Review* (1845–52), *De Bow's Commercial Review* (1846–70, Southern), *New Englander* (1843–72), *International Review* (1874–83), *Galaxy* (1866–77), *Andover Review* (1884–93).

Of foreign reviews the most serviceable are the *Contemporary, Fortnightly, National, Nineteenth Century, New Review, Quarterly, Edinburgh, Westminster, London Quarterly, Saturday Review, Spectator, Speaker* (the last three weekly).

In French, the *Revue des Deux Mondes, Revue Bleue, Nouvelle Revue, Correspondant*.

The debater will not fail to make use of the special periodicals on history, economics, government, and sociology. Such are the *Political Science Quarterly* (1887–), *Annals of the American Academy of Political and Social Science* (1889–), *Yale Review* (1892–), *Quarterly Journal of Economics* (1886–), *Journal of Political Economy* (1892–), *American Historical Review* (1895–), *American Journal of Sociology* (1895–), *New World* (1892–), *Journal of Social Science* (1887–), *Bradstreet's* (weekly, financial), *Charities Review* (1891–), *National Geographic Magazine; Economic Journal, Economic Review*, and *Economist* (all English); *Économiste* (weekly, financial); *Annales de l'École des Sciences Politiques; Journal des Économistes; Revue Historique; Finanz-Archiv; Jahrbücher für Nationalökonomie*.

On military and naval questions there are many special journals. The best in America are: *Army and Navy Journal, Army and Navy Register, United Service Magazine, Journal of the United States Military Service Institution, Proceedings of the United States Naval Institute*. The best English journals are *Broad Arrow, United Service Magazine, Nautical Magazine*. The standard German periodical is *Jahrbücher für die Deutsche Armee und Marine. Engineering* and *Engineer* contain much discussion of naval construction and management, and of armaments.

To the newspapers there is no general key: there are annual indexes to the *New York Tribune* and *London Times*. For the periodicals there are the serviceable Poole's *Index to Periodicals*, Jones's *Index to Legal Periodicals*, and the special indexes to the sets of *North American Review, Harper's, Scribner's*, and other periodicals. In the bibliographies enumerated below (§ 12) will be found classified lists of periodical articles and also of books.

More elaborate than periodical articles are the monographs and special treatises. Several universities and publishers have series including political, economic, and social studies. Such are the *Johns Hopkins University Studies;* the *Columbia Studies in History, Economics, and Public Law;* the *Harvard Historical Studies;* the publications of Leland Stanford University and the Universities of Michigan, Wisconsin, and Nebraska. Several publishers have series of related books, as Crowell's *Library of Economics and Politics;* Putnam's *Questions of the Day; English Citizen Series;* Longmans' announced *American Citizen Series;* and Swan and Sonnenschein's *Social Science Series.* To these may be added the publications of special societies, as the American Economic Association, the American Historical Association (*Papers;* and later, *Annual Reports*), and the New York Reform Club (especially on the currency). Many of these sets are analyzed in Fletcher's *A. L. A. Index to General Literature.*

The books relating to debated topics may be found through the printed subject-catalogues of large libraries, especially the Boston Athenæum, the Peabody Library of Baltimore, and the Brooklyn Public Library. Special bibliographies will be enumerated below (§ 12). The most serviceable books are of course the political histories of the modern countries, the special economic, financial, and social histories, and the treatises on constitutional law and government. Of the histories of the United States the most useful are Rhodes, Von Holst, McMaster, Hildreth, Schouler. On the last thirty years there is little exact history written. Woodrow Wilson's *Division and Reunion* is a brief handbook; and Johnston's *American Politics* and Stanford's *Presidential Elections* are helpful outlines. Taussig's *Tariff History of the United States* is the standard brief work on that subject. On constitutional law the great authorities are Joseph Story, *Commentaries on the Constitution* (5 editions, Cooley's or Bigelow's the best); T. M. Cooley, *Constitutional Limitations,* and *Constitutional Law;* John N. Pomeroy, *Constitutional Law;* James Bryce, *American Commonwealth.* On international law the most serviceable treatises are those by Hall, Lawrence, Wheaton

(Lawrence's and Dana's editions), Woolsey, and especially Francis Wharton, *Digest of the International Law of the United States.*

If the special authorities are not available, recourse may be had to the compilations. The late editions of the cyclopædias often have weighty brief articles by experts. The best are *Johnson's, Britannica* (Ninth edition), *Appleton's, Chambers's,* and especially *Appleton's Annual Cyclopædia;* also *Brockhaus,* and *Meyer* (both German).

Manuscript sources are little available for debates, except that letters and written statements may sometimes be secured from men who can contribute something to the argument. Debaters ought to be warned against the practice of writing to busy men for an opinion, so that in the debate they may quote the reply; it is argument and not names that wins debate. A debater's own knowledge of the facts, or that of his friends and connections, may, however, often be made very effective.

5. Use of Materials.

When the debater has found out what has been written upon his subject, his task of actual preparation begins: he must discover what part of it is useful to him, and then must take such notes as will serve him later. Even the preliminary search for references has the joys and disappointments of other hunts. The first step is to use the available bibliographies (among which would be classed for this purpose the Briefs printed below), the library catalogues, the periodical, and other indexes. The best system is to make a memorandum on a card of each title of book or article. Then the books must be examined; and here is necessary skill and practice in the use of tables of contents, book indexes, and catalogues. Of course the debater will always examine his references for himself, and will not take second-hand quotations or extracts if he can find the originals. As soon as a title proves on examination not to be useful, the corresponding card may be thrown out. Debates in Congress may be traced out through the references in previous briefs, and through the indexes to the *Congressional Record*.

The next step, the taking notes on the material, requires much discriminating judgment. Notes ought to be brief, to show the point which they illustrate, and to include such phrases as may well be quoted in the argument. A labor-saving device is to take the notes on separate half-sheets or slips of paper, of uniform size, devoting one slip to each of the separate branches of the argument, which will appear later as divisions of the brief. Notes on that subject, from whatever source, will thus all be assembled at one opening, and may be arranged and re-classified as fast as they come. When the search is completed the slips will then be a kind of inchoate brief.

At the moment when a note is made, a reference to the source should be entered, in a form which cannot afterward be mistaken. Quotations should be exact, so far as they go, and lacunæ should be indicated thus – – – – : and words inserted by the note-taker should appear in brackets [thus] to show that they are no part of the original. This is a protection against any argument that a quotation used is inaccurate or incomplete.

Of course all authorities are not of the same weight. In dealing with facts first-hand authorities are usually the strongest, unless you can find the evidence analyzed and weighed by an expert. A cautious writer is to be preferred to a rash writer. Speeches in legislative bodies are often tinged by party-spirit, and omit essential points. The debater's own deductions from established facts will usually carry more weight than a repetition of a discussion, taken from others at second-hand. And nowhere is discrimination more necessary than in separating the parts which really bear upon the course of the argument, from the merely accidental or trivial.

While the work of search and note-taking is going on the

argument should be shaping itself in the debater's mind, so that he sees what are the main lines, and what is subsidiary. Here the advice of other people becomes valuable; discussion with one's friends will help one to throw overboard weak or dangerous points, and to add force to those which one retains. Nor must a man be contented with the arguments on his own side; he must expect to be taken unawares unless he knows the case of his adversaries almost as well as his own.

6. The Brief System.

This book is intended to assist the debater in acquiring the method of brief-making, for assembling, arranging, and analyzing arguments, as a basis for debate; and it is a method which experience has shown to be very effective. Without it, formal college courses in debate are hard to keep active, and interscholastic and intercollegiate debates have not a sufficient background.

The advantages of carefully prepared briefs are obvious. In the first place, they cannot be made without study, and they thus lay stress on the intellectual training of the whole system. Though an instructor may not always be sure which of two partners had most to do with the drawing of a brief, he knows directly if neither one of them has worked upon it. In the second place, a brief is crystallized logic; it is the plan of campaign for the argument. No brief is possible till the main points have shaped themselves in the debater's mind; and the thought grows more distinct, and the parts of the argument better defined, as the brief grows. In the third place, the brief requires a man—as in legal argument—not to depend on improvisation, nor surprise, but to make up his mind beforehand on what he must base his case. Hence if the brief contain matter which does not find its way into the speech, it is redundant; if the speech soar into arguments not mentioned in the brief, the latter is defective. Whenever—as is commonly the case in debates among friendly rivals—the two sides see each other's briefs before the debate, they have the opportunity to prepare rebuttals. Above all, the brief is a steady training in the most difficult part of reasoning; in putting together things that belong together; in discovering connections and relations; in subordinating the less important matters. The making of a brief is an intellectual exercise like the study of a disease by a physician, of a case by a lawyer, of a sermon by a minister, of a financial report by a president of a corporation. It is a bit of the practical work of life.

Perhaps the system may be best set forth by an account of the manner in which it is carried out in a course in oral debate at one of the large colleges. The thirty men in the course are divided into thirty groups of four "principal disputants," so arranged that in the course of the year no man will be twice associated with anyone else in the course. Each man is therefore a principal disputant four times during the year. Three weeks before their debate the four principal disputants meet an instructor to select a question. If they have a preference for any particular question it is allowed, if it seem interesting, and has not already been debated that year. A question satisfactory to disputants and instructor having been found, the latter makes general suggestions about the material, referring the men to useful bibliographies, to reports of debates, and to periodicals and special works. Sides are also assigned.

The two pairs then go about their work, with the privilege of asking any other instructor for references and suggestions. About a week before the debate, drafts of the two briefs are brought in, and thoroughly discussed by the students and the instructor: the latter notices the thoroughness of the search for material, the value and accuracy of the references, the force of the arguments, their grouping, and the general effect of the work. These criticisms the brief-makers consider, and follow so far as they seem to them justified.

Two days later the revised briefs are handed in, presumably ready for the printer. This is one of the snaggy places in the system: it is almost impossible to get men to abide by that uniformity of paragraphing, lettering, italicizing, and punctuating, which a printer expects. One of the four men is held responsible for taking the briefs, when accepted, to the college daily newspaper, and, as soon as the brief appears, for having the books to which reference is made assembled on a shelf in the library reading-room. By agreement, the briefs appear in the daily at least three days before the debate, so as to allow speakers from the floor to use the references in their preparation.

The characteristics of a good brief need not here be stated in detail: that is a subject which Professor Baker has discussed at large in his *Principles of Argumentation.* The first process is to break the general subject up into a few pertinent and well-distinguished main heads. Such subdivisions are well shown in both the affirmative and negative of Brief No. xlix (p. 129). Sometimes one group of arguments will be historical, another economic, and another constitutional, as in Brief No. ii (p. 4). Again, as in Brief No. lxv (p. 170), the classes or interests affected by the question will be the basis of the division. Each of the main heads, thus selected, is then to be subdivided into pertinent sub-heads; a good example is shown in Brief No. lxx (p. 184). Below these there will usually be another series of ramifications, and there may be still more elaborate sub-classification, as in Brief No. lix (p. 155). Beyond the fourth degree of subdivision—shown in the briefs by (x), (y), (z)—analysis becomes confusing. In all cases the sub-heads ought to be indicated by letters or figures so clearly set in displayed type as to catch the eye. In practice the subdivisions will usually be built up from below, by arranging and concentrating into groups the body of arguments which have been thought out.

Within the briefs the references to authorities ought to be written or printed according to some definite system. Mr. Brookings and Mr. Ringwalt have chosen the very convenient method of setting the names of authors in ordinary Roman, and all titles of books or periodicals in *italics.* Whatever the system, it ought to help the eye, and to be uniform. References should be full enough to explain themselves wherever used, though, of course, a title entered fully at the beginning of the brief may be repeated in shorter form further down. It is a great convenience to insert not only volumes and pages, but dates of publication of articles in newspapers and periodicals, or of the delivery of speeches (see p. 162); since the time when an argument was made often affects its force. So the name of the author of an article should often be inserted (see p. 188).

Debaters from the floor appreciate the block of "General References" which Mr. Brookings and Mr. Ringwalt have prefixed to each of their briefs. References in the body of the brief, to back up single points, are also valuable (see p. 140), but take space and annoy printers. In citing Congressional documents and debates it is convenient to insert the number of the Congress and session, as well as the date; for instance, on page 111 it would be better to read: '*Congressional Record*, 53 Cong. 1 sess. (1893–94) Appendix, p. 1178,' etc. Volume numbers should be Roman numerals, without any prefatory "vol.;" and the abbreviation for page or pages (p., pp.) is only necessary where other figures precede and might cause confusion, as on page 111, *Tariff Hearings Before the Committee on Ways and Means*, 1893, pp. 505, 520, 542.

7. Practice Before Debate.

Like every other art, persuasive debate needs, besides preparation, long and conscientious practice. Corresponding to those preliminary sketches of the painter which he means to train his hand, and not to please the eyes of his friends, are the preliminary rehearsals of the debater. The main rule for good speaking is substantially that set forth in its three branches by the German professor as a guide to learning: "1. Read; 2. Read much; 3. Read very much." It is of course assumed that the debater aims to make the impression of a well-equipped speaker, whose eloquence forms itself as he goes on: hence he never delivers a rigid speech, learned by heart. Orators as late as Charles Sumner used this *memoriter* method: but such orators speak rather to dazzle than to persuade. To convince an audience or a body of judges, the debater must have control of the material, must keep the subdivisions of his subject clearly in mind, and must have gone over it orally many times.

For such practice nothing is better than to stand in one's own room, alone or before a critical friend, and there to talk for the allotted number of minutes; then to begin again and go over the same ground a second and a third and a tenth time. Each attempt must go through from the beginning to the end, without stopping to go back and make a better start. After a few such repetitions the speaker will find that, without ever writing a definite speech or committing it to memory, he has his language well settled, his material organized, his illustrations pat, and knows that he comes within the time limit. By the aid of his faithful mirror or a self-denying friend he must also by this time have noticed and weeded out his most striking faults; and he has the reassuring confidence that comes of speaking without grasping for words or phrases. The language will now take care of itself, and the whole force may go into the effort to send the words home to the minds of the hearers.

The great intercollegiate debates have in many cases been prepared by an extension of the system described above, which closely resembles the training of athletic teams. The debaters are put forward against an '*advocatus diaboli*,' who takes the wrong side in a set argument. The debaters must then follow him and so adjust their points as to meet him on the ground which he has chosen. Sometimes the 'team' which is under preparation, has to debate, man for man, against another team which tries to make the jointed argument which may be expected from the representatives of the rival college. Such practice has the excitement and stimulus of battle, and is a marvellous wit sharpener. Graduates often come in to direct the "coaching," and criticise as though they were following the stroke of a boat crew. When college instructors appear as 'protagonists' in this preliminary training the final debate is likely to be a contest between faculties rather than students, and the zest of personal prowess is taken away.

Such elaborate practice as has just been described not only develops the individual speaker, it also gives thorough training in co-operation and rebuttal. The subject must be somehow divided among the two or three brother-debaters; and each must leave his fellows' fields free for them. The speeches must be arranged so as to lead up to a climax; and each of the later men must stand ready to defend his friends' argument if attacked. The important subject of rebuttal will be considered in another section (§ 9).

During the preliminary practice the debaters must make up their minds as to the probable line of attack of their opponents; and that involves a thorough knowledge of the arguments against them. When either one of two lines of opening is to be feared, there is no easier way than—as was actually done in a recent intercollegiate debate—for the first speaker on the negative to prepare two distinct speeches, and to use that one which fits the case presented to him. To be taken by surprise by an unexpected argument is a disgrace to a good debater.

8. Management of a Debate.

In many debating societies the actual clash of arguments is only a part, and often the less important part, of the exercises. Much attention is given—especially in the South and West—to the practice of parliamentary law. While it is an accomplishment to know how to introduce measures, and follow the twists of legislative procedure, the only part of the system which is of much importance for training in public speaking is the moderator's management. The writer has carried with him a very vivid remembrance of the keen, quick, business-like and yet dignified president of one of the two great debating societies of the University of North Carolina, who felt himself there to expedite business and to keep the debaters to their task. Inasmuch as the first object of a public speaker is to convince, we may leave out of account here all the machinery of debate which relates to measures. The chairman's chief duty is urbanely but sternly to enforce the time limits.

The affirmative has a golden opportunity in opening the debate, by its right to state the case; for, while keeping within the bounds of truth and logic, it may create a presumption which cannot later be shaken out of the minds of the hearers. Hence it is worth while to spend part of the first speaker's time in stating the history of the question, and the economic or social or constitutional principles which underlie it, so as to make his side seem self-evident. The first speaker has also a chance to undermine and break down the negative arguments before they are presented. In this place in the debate, therefore, a speaker should be put who is lucid, agreeable, and prepossessing, who can strike the key-note of the affirmative argument, and put the negative on the defensive. 'The honorablest part of talk is to give the occasion, and again to moderate and pass to somewhat else; for then a man leads the dance.'

The first negative speaker has the same task for his side; but he can begin also to tear down a little of the affirmative fabric. Later speakers must elaborate, and will have increasing chances of rebuttal. In a general debate the leaders should take pains to argue the main points of their brief, and to ask their friends who speak "from the floor" to take up the smaller points, so that the whole ground may be covered.

The closing speakers on each side are always important, because there is an opportunity to sum up the case and to impress on the minds of the hearers the main arguments. Yet skilful closing speeches are uncommon: the usual repetition of a lot of small points carries no conviction; a laborious attempt in a few seconds to reply to a mass of arguments on the other side is confusing. What is needed is to select out a few really telling and essential points, to show that they are established, that they are fundamental, and hence that the proposition is proved. These speeches ought, more than any others, to work up to a climax, and must not be cut in two by the chairman's gavel.

How shall a speaker begin? A quotation, an illustration, a good story—very short—may be a proper start-off, by getting the attention of the audience. Then, within the first sentences, should be clearly made evident what the speaker expects to prove. People like to know where they are in an argument, when the subject is changing, when a new division comes in. In all cases the beginning must be smooth and unhesitating. A speaker who is searching for a phrase has lost his audience at the start.

To state the essential arguments in debate seems too obvious to be suggested, were it not that in most debates the speakers overlook points and especially conditions, which must be taken into account before the question is decided. Thus, in the question of government ownership of railroads (Brief No. xlvii), sooner or later people are bound to notice that lack of good highways in this country is an argument against turning the railroads over to the public, and that the state of the American civil service does not encourage throwing heavier duties upon it. It is the work of real talent to see what is essential and must be argued, and what may safely be neglected.

An effective, though often a misused, practice is for the speaker to enrich his speech with extracts from speeches and documents, and with statistics. The only rules on quotations are that they be to the point, snappy, and very brief. Figures require peculiar tact; people easily get tired of long tables, but a good mouthful of statistics is an argument hard to answer. Still it is always necessary to select—to give only highest and lowest figures, or averages, or totals: and in the same breath one must show how they apply. Sometimes an effect may be produced by opening the book before the audience—as a kind of gesture, to call attention to the matter; but let no man try to read more than a sentence! A battery of quotations or figures may sometimes be used to advantage: 'What does Adam Smith say? What does Ricardo say? What does Mill say? What does Walker say?' But quotations and statistics are not arguments; they are illustrations or confirmations.

For short speeches, five, four, or three minutes, the same general principles apply as to the longer. One must begin smoothly, state his argument, and drive it home: but since there is not time to develop a chain of reasoning, the effort must be to take a single good point; to introduce it, show its bearing on the general question, illustrate it; and then to bring it to a good close within the time limit. For the practical purposes of life the ability to make a good five minutes' speech is rarer and more valuable than the power of speaking well for an hour. Life abounds in brief colloquies, where there is opportunity to make a single distinct point, which hearers can remember; hence ease, readiness, speaking out of one's self, are here especially necessary.

A strict observance of the time limit is another of the speaker's duties. In some societies and larger assemblies a moderator's bell or gavel remorselessly cuts down in the flower of its youth a speech which overruns; but it is humiliating to a speaker so to be bowled out; and a broken speech loses its effect. The chairman on the other hand must remember that fair play requires him to be exact to both sides. In an important intercollegiate debate a few years ago, the amiable chairman permitted a speaker from the college of which he was himself a graduate to run twenty-two minutes beyond the agreed limit of five minutes placed on the closing speech for the affirmative. Doubtless the last speaker from the negative might have had a similar privilege, but he knew better. He laid his watch ostentatiously in sight, spoke about four minutes, and ended with: " I have fifty seconds left: I give them to the gentleman on the affirmative." The negative won the debate.

It is becoming customary in intercollegiate debates to have a formal decision; it adds to the interest of the debate; and compels the speakers to keep constantly before their minds the task of convincing somebody. A small body of judges—say three—is better than a larger number.

9. Rebuttal.

Just so far as debate gets away from the old idea of a mere succession of declamations, first on one side, and then on the other, the refutation of argument comes in as a powerful engine, to be used as it is in actual life. Speakers and hearers alike become interested in a hand-to-hand fight, where one man directly controverts his adversary. In intercollegiate debates rebuttal has come to be recognized as equally important with positive argument.

The 'natural man' has a simple system of refutation: 'The first speaker says that an income tax is just: I assert that it is unjust. The second speaker thinks an income tax easy to collect: I assure you that he is mistaken. The third speaker tells us that an income tax is productive: I deny it.' This is not rebuttal; it is counter assertion. The art of refutation is, not to devote to it a speech or a distinct part of a speech, but to bring it in indirectly as a part of your regular line of argument; to turn the tables unexpectedly. 'An income tax always becomes a hateful inquisition. The gentleman said it was just: is it just to compel a business man to reveal to his rivals the sources and amount of his profits? Experience has shown how an income tax works. Let us take the Swiss income taxes; in Switzerland, if anywhere, they ought to be successful. One gentleman has said that an income tax is easy to collect; he evidently knows nothing of the experience of Switzerland.'

Such an indirect attack is the more effective because it

seems to be a natural part of the general argument. Of course, however, no one can use such argument who does not know both sides of the question. Sometimes it is necessary to raise a distinct issue, to lay down a point as decisive between the two sides, and then to challenge the other party to prove or to disprove: to decline or ignore such a challenge is a confession of weakness. The rebutter must watch for a false step, a dangerous admission, a disinclination to tackle a difficult or dangerous point.

Rebuttal offers one of the best opportunities for that interplay of co-debaters which is so striking a feature in good contests. Success often depends on so arranging the speakers that each may make use of his best powers: the hard-hitter must be put where he will have somebody to attack; the quickest-witted man should be put at the end, where he may gather up the threads of the argument of his side, and unravel his opponents'. In refutation as in the main argument, no two speakers should enter the same ground—except by way of emphasis. Division of labor and 'Team-play' are the two elements of good debating.

The question of formal rebuttal speeches has been settled differently by different societies and conferences. Sometimes there are two brief summing-up speeches: sometimes—and the best practice tends that way—each of the main speakers has a special rebuttal speech. But in any case the rebuttal must not be a mere summary; it must be a coherent, logical speech, leading up to a climax.

10. Persuasive Speaking.

So far nothing has been said about the delivery. Suggestions as to attitude, voice, enunciation, intonation, movement, and gesture, belong to elocution. In this brief treatise the importance of that side of debating is as much taken for granted as grammatical language, a just use of words, and clear expression. Nevertheless there are some essentials of good debate which even an accurate and forcible writer, speaking admirably, may fail to grasp. Of these it remains to speak.

The prime purpose of the debater is not to show that he has a good voice, presence, manner, and power of fluent speech, but that he has something to say which will change or reassure the hearer's mind: in a word, his aim is not oratory but conviction. The world over, and notably in America, speaking 'in the grand manner' has lost its effect; good speaking is looked on as a means to an end: and that end is persuasion.

Hence the very first requisite is self-forgetfulness. The debater must come out of himself, and think only how so to wing his words that they may find lodgment in others' minds. There is only one way of assuring self-forgetfulness: and that is to be so saturated with the subject, so imbued with a sense of the necessity of sending it home to the hearers, that the matter will come into the speaker's mind clear, well arranged, and free; otherwise he will struggle for ideas, his words will elude him, and he will sink back into himself.

One means of success in this 'objective speaking' is to put closely before your mind just what you undertake to prove: to state your thesis early in your speech, to restate it, amplify it, illustrate it, and to keep it so closely before your hearers' minds that they may judge whether you establish it. If your audience is a party to your thought, they will adhere to that and forget the speaker: and that is your object.

Furthermore, the debater must always 'talk to the jury.' That is, he must adapt his line of argument, his method of proof, and his illustrations to those who listen. A speech which would convince a Good Government Club might not find favor in a ward caucus; yet both bodies may be influenced by sincere and well-stated argument. Still more, the debater must get at his hearers, must compel them to listen to him, orally and intellectually. In any room not radically bad, if a proper quality of voice be used, no hearer who is not deaf should lose a single sentence or word. Still less should he be allowed to forfeit the sense of what he hears by drawing off his thoughts, because the speaker does not seem to be addressing him. By voice, gesture, manner, form of statement, as well as by interest and cogency of argument, the audience must be kept within the radius of the speaker's influence.

Since every audience is glad of a decent excuse to leave the speaker out of their minds, great care must be taken to avoid pauses, hitches, substitutions of one word for another, unevenness in passing from one branch of the argument to another. A jerky speaker quickly tires and discontents his hearers, while a smooth, even debater, whether he be slow or rapid, carries people with him from point to point. Still, over-smoothness must also be avoided; for what is said without visible effort or concentration of thought seems too easy to be forcible.

Emphasis is like dynamics in music—one of the means of accenting thought: but emphasis is of many kinds; unusual loudness may be less effective than a sudden dropping of the voice; a quickening of the utterance may be emphatic, and so may unusual deliberation. The good speaker uses all these methods, just as the organist chooses the stops. Only remember that over-emphasis is not emphasis; for it tires, and it destroys the distinction between the less important and the more important. Like italics in print, great emphasis is the more effective because so rare. The famous pulpit orator, Robertson, used to put long dry passages into his sermons, so as to rouse his congregation when he broke out. No speaker can hope to carry an audience with him, either into a generous indignation, or into the essentials of an argument, unless he can, on occasion, use three or four times his ordinary force for a moment.

For a moment only: a Daniel Webster, a Wendell Phillips, a Phillips Brooks, can carry his hearers up with him to a plane above all ordinary experience and then can also hold them there indefinitely; the mortals must expect to return to earth again. Yet he is a poor speaker who cannot at least warm up to an emphatic climax, so as to leave in his final sentence a phrase or thought which will stamp itself on the memory.

One caution is always necessary, especially to those who are obliged to defend a cause in which they have little heart: 'Tell the truth!' As a principle of ethics, to say what you do not know to be true is very close to saying what you know not to be true; as a principle of debating, rash, extravagant, violent, and prejudiced statements damage the hearer's confidence in the speaker, and leave open a joint for the rebutter's dagger. A debater is not called upon to furnish arguments for the other side; nor to call attention to weaknesses on his side: but he is under the ordinary obligation not to deceive anybody by false statements.

He who is by nature furnished with a sense of humor has one of the debater's most effective weapons: story-telling is not argument; but the most renowned American debater of the last forty years, Abraham Lincoln, knew that a good story may make argument unnecessary. 'Some,' says Bacon, 'have in readiness so many tales and stories, as there is nothing they would insinuate, but they can wrap it into a tale; which serveth both to keep themselves more in guard, and to make others carry it with more pleasure.' A telling jest, a quip, a good-natured but arrow-headed allusion to the argument of the other side, puts the speaker into friendly relations with his hearers, and gets their attention for more serious matters. Good brief, pertinent illustrations are the life of debate: and they often cause to be remembered the argument to which they adhere. Sarcasm is a sharp and often a cruel battle-axe: but a jovial twisting of an opponent's argument, a fanciful carrying of his reasonings into preposterous details, may cause his whole structure to crumble. Care must always be taken that the story be pat, and be not blunted by an awkward end. Take for instance the young man who was arguing on the Salvation Army and who destroyed his own argument by an awkward snapper: 'The gentleman says that emotional intoxication is better than other kinds of intoxication: possibly; but emotional intoxication lasts longer; and that is what we want.'

Horace Greeley used to assert with much acumen that in specie payments 'the way to resume is to resume.' So the way to persuade people is to persuade. Constant practice based on hard thought, and a constant effort to improve, make the tyro into a fair speaker, the fair speaker into an adept, sometimes the adept into a champion.

To sum up the question of persuasion: the principles of good speaking are simply those of good business conference or social intercourse. You must know what you are talking about; you must be convinced that it is worth saying; you must say it so that people must listen or lose something; you must convince. Above all you must realize that people will think you a good debater only if you do affect in some degree their mental attitude toward the question which you discuss. An orator may not convince, though he may impress, an audience or judges: a genuine debater, speaking out of knowledge, with a real eagerness to establish his cause, coming as a man to men, is above even the orator, for he can persuade others not only to agree with him but to act with him.

11. Criticism of Debates.

Practice in painting is the foundation of the art, but it can almost never be formed without the criticism of fellows and masters. So it is in debating: older and more experienced minds have the standards of good speaking constantly before them; and they offer also the 'giftie' of seeing ourselves as others see us. Hence, for improvement in debate and for success in contests, there must be expert criticism.

The process is one to which the natural man does not take kindly, least of all from his own fellows and associates. Something may be done by a faithfully incautious friend who will risk a quarrel by telling you in the privacy of his own room how badly you speak : but a far more effective criticism is that delivered in public, at the time of debate. All present get the advantage of the principles of criticism; and a man quickly learns that it saves a mortification if he takes pains.

Three methods of criticism are common. The first is that used in small debating societies, which appoint a member as censor, to report at the end the faults which he has observed. Unless the censor is wiser than all the speakers, he will overlook many faults; and he has not the weight to make a just criticism felt. Another method is to depend upon old members of a society or graduates of the college, in their time distinguished in debating. The third system is to make an instructor the critic; and this fits in well in those schools and colleges in which debates are made a part of the academic work. He should take notes and, at the end of the exercise, in the presence of the class or club, while the speeches are still warm in their memories, he should briefly review each of the speakers in turn. In some cases two instructors criticise, one on the delivery, the other on the effectiveness of argument—one of the two being an expert on the question under discussion. If such a process be repeated every week for a year, especially if there be more than one critic, the debaters will first admit with reluctance that they have serious faults; and then will set to work to eradicate them.

Effective criticism of course includes discriminating praise as well as blame: it is as important to keep up a good habit as to break up a fault. A good speech or good method in a speech is a text for a sermon to the whole class: and judicious praise makes the other kind of accompanying criticism more palatable.

All faults are subjects for criticisms : errors of pronunciation; misuse of words; grammatical slips; or small errors of fact. But the main criticism should go at those defects which spoil matter otherwise fair. Of course the time given to criticism is short at best; and most of it must go to pointing out and enforcing the most characteristic faults. It is a great help to the debater if the criticism upon him end with a statement of his most notable good point and his most serious fault; and a practical hint for breaking up the fault. If he speak indistinctly and hurriedly, tell him to practise in what seems to him too deliberate a manner: if he hesitate and cast about for a word, bid him go over a speech half a dozen times orally, before he presents it. Proper criticism, backed up by honest effort, will blossom in a steady improvement from month to month, an encouragement to the debater, and a relief to his hearers.

12. Bibliography of Debating.

Upon debate as an art, little has been written. The most valuable treatises are Holyoake's *Public Speaking and Debate*, and Professor Baker's *Principles of Argumentation*, which deals with the principles common to written and spoken argument; and Col. Higginson's *Hints*, based on the experience of a successful public speaker. The formal rhetorics all consider the general subject of form in the art of language. Several classified lists of debate subjects are mentioned below.

For a library suitable for a debating society or college, the printed briefs below give many suggestions. The books most useful are: the records of public debates; the standard histories of the United States and other countries; sets of the works of orators and public men, such as Washington, Hamilton, Webster, Lincoln, Burke, Gladstone, Bismarck; sets of the periodicals; a file of at least one New York daily and one local daily newspaper, and of the *Nation;* special works in economic and social history; the best treatises in political economy, finance, sociology, government, and constitutional and international law.

Below are a few titles of books which may be of service to the debater either by suggesting methods, or by leading him to references or to lists of questions: references to newspapers, periodicals, monographs and general works will be found above (§ 4).

Treatises on Debating.

John Quincy Adams. *Lectures on Rhetoric and Oratory.* 2 vols. Cambridge. Hilliard and Metcalfe, 1816.
 The work of a very effective speaker, but formally stated.

George Pierce Baker, *compiler. Specimens of Argumentation. Modern.* New York, Holt, 1893.
 Selected specimens of argument, with a model brief.

George Pierce Baker. *The Principles of Argumentation.* Boston and London, Ginn & Co., 1895.
 Contains careful and thoughtful discussions of argumentation, analysis, brief-drawing, preparatory reading, evidence, and persuasion, with illustrative extracts and model briefs.

[Hugh Blair.] Abraham Mills. *Lectures on Rhetoric and Belles Lettres.* Chiefly from the lectures of Dr. Blair. New York, Lockwood, 1857.
 Lectures xxiii.-xxxii. are on public speaking.

Henry, Lord Brougham. *Rhetorical and Literary Dissertations and Addresses.* London and Glasgow, Griffin, 1856.
 Vol. VII. of his *Works.*

George Campbell. *The Philosophy of Rhetoric.* New York, Harpers, 1851 (another edition, 1873).
 An old book still serviceable. Book I. is devoted to "The Nature and Foundations of Eloquence."

Edward T. Channing. *Lectures read to the Seniors in Harvard College.* Boston, Ticknor, 1856.

Samuel Silas Curry. *The Province of Expression; a search for principles underlying adequate methods of developing dramatic and oratoric delivery.* Boston, School of Expression, 1891.

Henry Noble Day. *The Art of Discourse; a system of rhetoric, adapted for use in colleges and academies and also for private study.* New York, 10th edition, 1889.

Ralph Waldo Emerson. *Eloquence* (included in *Society and Solitude.* Boston, Houghton, 1883).
 A brief essay.

Jefferson Butler Fletcher and George Rice Carpenter. *Introduction to Theme-Writing.* Boston, 1893.
Chapters vi. and vii. on Exposition and Argument.

John Franklin Genung. *The Practical Elements of Rhetoric, with illustrative examples.* Boston, Ginn, 1887.
Chapters vi. and viii. are on Exposition, Argumentation, Persuasion.

Thomas Wentworth Higginson. *Hints on Writing and Speech-making.* New York, Longmans, Green, & Co.
Admirable discussion, by a master of the art of persuasion.

George Jacob Holyoake. *Public Speaking and Debate: a Manual for Advocates and Agitators.* New York, Putnams, 1896.
A systematic treatise on convincing argument, especially on social topics.

William Mathews. *Oratory and Orators.* Chicago, Griggs, 1879.

Austin Phelps. *The Theory of Preaching. Lectures on Homiletics.* New York, Scribners, 1881.
Especially good on exposition and arrangement.

William Callahan Robinson. *Forensic Oratory; a manual for advocates.* Boston, Little, Brown & Co., 1893.
Written especially for law students.

Alfred Sidgwick. *The Process of Argument; a contribution to logic.* London, Black, 1893.
Does not deal especially with spoken argument.

Richard Whately. *Elements of Rhetoric: Comprising an Analysis of the Laws of Moral Evidence and of Persuasion, with Rules for Argumentative Composition and Elocution.* Many editions.
Part IV. is on public speaking.

Compilations for Current Events.

The Annual Register, a Review of Public Events at Home and Abroad. London and New York, Longmans, Green, & Co.
Annual; issued since 1758. Excellent summaries of foreign politics.

Appleton's Annual Cyclopædia and Register of Important Events. New York, Appleton.

Annual; issued 1861–74, as *American Annual Cyclopædia;* contains documents, biographies, and summaries of current events.

Bureau of Statistics. *Statistical Abstract of the United States.* Washington, Government Printing Office.

Annual; issued since 1878; includes banks, taxes, commerce, debts, etc.

Edward McPherson. *A Hand-Book of Politics . . . being a Record of Important Political Action, Legislative and Executive, National and State.* Washington, Beall.

Biennial (even years); issued since 1868.

Michael T. Mulhall. *The Dictionary of Statistics.* London, Routledge, 1892.

Standard compilation of social and economic statistics.

H. V. and H. W. Poor. *Manual of the Railroads of the United States.* New York, Poor.

Annual; issued since 1868; includes also statistics of corporations, and of State, county, and city debts.

Secretary of the Treasury. *Annual Report on the State of the Finances.*

Annual; issued since 1789; includes official statements as to debt, currency, coinage, banks, taxes, etc.

The Statesman's Year-Book, Statistical and Historical Annual of the States of the World. [J. Scott Keltie, editor, assisted by I. P. A. Renwick.] London, Macmillan & Co.

Annual; issued since 1864; contains the latest information about all the governments of the world, with brief lists of books.

The Tribune Almanac and Political Register. [Henry Eckford Rhoades, editor.] New York, The Tribune Association.

Annual; issued since 1856; contains details about the national and State governments, an abstract of important legislation and statements of votes.

Joseph Whitaker. *An Almanack for the Year of Our Lord. . . .* London, Whitaker.

Annual; issued since 1869; contains statistics, etc., on Great Britain and the British colonies.

The World Almanac and Encyclopædia. New York, Press Publishing Co.

Annual; issued since 1873; similar to the Tribune Almanac.

COLLECTIONS OF MODEL SPEECHES.

Charles Kendall Adams, editor. *Representative British Orations: with introductions and explanatory notes.* 3 vols. New York, Putnams, 1885-92.

An excellent collection of English speeches.

William Clarke, editor. *Political Orations, from Wentworth to Macaulay. With an introduction.* London, Scott, 1889. Camelot Series, vol. 40.

C. A. Goodrich. *Select British Eloquence, embracing the best speeches Entire of the most Eminent Orators of Great Britain for the last two centuries.* New York, Harper & Brothers, 1852.

William Hazlitt. *Eloquence of the British Senate, a selection of speeches of Parliamentary speakers from the beginning of the reign of Charles I.* 2 vols. London and Edinburgh, Cradock, 1812.

Frank Moore. *American Eloquence: a collection of speeches and addresses by the most eminent Orators of America.* 2 vols. New York, Appletons, 1857.

Alexander Johnston, editor. *Representative American Orations, to illustrate American Political History.* 3 vols. New York and London, Putnams, 1884; new edition, 1896.

An excellent collection of American speeches—suitable for models.

E. B. Williston, compiler. *Eloquence of the United States.* 5 vols. Middletown, Clark, 1821.

FINDING LISTS.

[1820-91.] John Griffith Ames. *Finding List, showing where in the set of Congressional Documents the individual volumes of certain series of Government publications are found.* Washington, 1893.

Convenient in searching for Government documents.

Richard R. Bowker and George Iles, editors. *The Reader's Guide in Economic, Social, and Political Science.* Economic Tracts, No. 27. New York, Putnams, 1891.

A classified bibliography, American, English, French, and German, with descriptive notes, author, title and subject index, courses of reading, list of college courses, etc. Very convenient on political and economic subjects.

Edward Channing and Albert Bushnell Hart. *Guide to the Study of American History.* Boston, Ginn & Co., 1896.
Classified lists of the important books; and about a hundred and forty topics in American history, with references to secondary books, sources, and bibliographies.

Alonzo W. Church and Henry H. Smith, compilers. *Tables showing the Contents of the several volumes comprising the Annals of Congress, Congressional Debates, Congressional Globe, Supreme Court Reports, etc., arranged by Years and Congresses.* Washington, 1892.
Useful for finding in what volume occurs a particular date or decision.

William I. Fletcher. *The " A. L. A." Index; an index to general literature, biographical, historical, and literary essays and sketches, reports and publications of boards and societies dealing with education, health, labor, charities, corrections, etc.* Issued by the publishing section of the American Library Association. Boston, Houghton, 1892.
This index supplements Poole's by referring to publications not strictly classed as periodicals.

William E. Foster. *References to the Constitution of the United States.* New York, Putnams, 1890.
Admirable on constitutional questions.

William E. Foster. *References to the History of Presidential Administrations, 1789–1885.* New York, Society for Political Education, 1886.
Admirable for American political history.

Albert Bushnell Hart and George Pierce Baker. *Harvard Debating Subjects and Suggestions for Courses in Debate.* Cambridge, Harvard University, 1896.
Includes all the subjects on political, economic, and social topics debated in the Harvard societies and debate courses and also the subjects of the intercollegiate debates.

[George Iles.] *Questions for Debate in Politics and Economics, with Subjects for Essays and Terms for Definition.* New York, Society for Political Education, 1889.
About six hundred classified questions.

J. W. Jenks. *Practical Economic Questions.* Albany, N. Y. University Extension Department, 1892.

An elaborate syllabus, almost in "brief" form, of a course of ten lectures; with lists of debatable questions.

Leonard Augustus Jones. *An Index to Legal Periodical Literature.* Boston, Soule, 1888.

A key to about a hundred and sixty sets of legal periodicals; extremely valuable on constitutional and political subjects.

Henry Matson. *References for Literary Workers: with Introductions to Topics and Questions for Debate.* Chicago, McClurg, 1892.

Refers both to books and periodicals; list of debate questions.

William Frederick Poole. *An Index to Periodical Literature.* Boston, Osgood, 1853. *Third Edition, continued to 1882 with the assistance of W. I. Fletcher.* Boston, Osgood, 1882.

There are two supplements; the *First Supplement*, by Poole and Fletcher, with the assistance of the American Library Association, covers the years 1882-87 (Boston, Houghton, 1888); the *Second Supplement* (without Poole) brings the work to 1892 (Boston, Houghton, 1893). Since then Fletcher and R. R. Bowker, with the co-operation of the American Library Association and of the Library Journal staff, have resumed the work on the same lines in *The Annual Literary Index.* New York, Publishers' Weekly.

Indispensable for collecting information and preparing briefs.

Edwin Erle Sparks. *Topical Reference Lists in American History.* Columbus, Smythe, 1893.

Gives numerous specific references to the standard secondary works.

ALBERT BUSHNELL HART.

HARVARD UNIVERSITY, July 1, 1896.

POLITICS.

SUFFRAGE.

I.

FEDERAL CONTROL OF NATIONAL ELECTIONS.

QUESTION: '*Resolved*, That Congress ought to pass an act establishing federal control over national elections.'

Brief for the Affirmative.

GENERAL REFERENCES: H. C. Lodge in *Congressional Record*, 1889-1890, p. 6538 (June 26, 1890); *North American Review*, Vol. 151, p. 257 (September, 1890), p. 593 (November, 1890); W. E. Chandler in *Forum*, IX., 705 (August, 1890); V., 508 (July, 1888); Report of Select Committee H. of R., *House Reports*, 1889-1890, No. 2493.

I. The welfare of the nation demands the preservation of an honest ballot: *Congressional Record*, 1889-1890, p. 6540. ——(*a*) The fundamental principle of our democratic government is the will of the majority of the people.—(1) The means of expressing that will lies in the ballot.——(*b*) Offences against the ballot which are left unpunished weaken the authority of the Constitution.—(1) Articles in the Constitution expressly call for an honest vote.

II. The present ballot system is corrupt: *Congressional Record*, 1889-1890, p. 6608 (June 27, 1890).——(*a*) The negroes are intimidated and ballots are illegally counted in the South.——(*b*) There are frauds and corruption in northern states.—(1) New York: J. J. Davenport, *The Wig and* the *Jimmy, or a Leaf in the Political History of New York.*—(2) Election of 1889 in Montana: *Public Opinion*, VIII., 55 (October 26, 1889).

III. Federal control offers the best remedy.——(*a*) State governments show no desire to make reform.——(*b*) Federal control would insure uniformity of the laws and would make certain their execution.—(1) Violations of the ballot, instead of being held as offences against one state, would be held as offences against the whole nation.

IV. Congress has the constitutional power to regulate elections.——(*a*) *Constitution of the United States*, Art. I., Sec. 4, § 1.——(*b*) Decisions of the Supreme Court: *Ex parte* Siebold, 100 *U. S.*, 371.——(*c*) Commentators: G. W. McCreary, *Election Laws*, §§ 17, 143, 573; H. von Holst, *Constitutional Law*, p. 72, note; J. I. C. Hare, *Constitutional Law*, I., 527, 528; J. Story, *Commentaries on the Constitution*, §§ 814–827.

Brief for the Negative.

GENERAL REFERENCES: *North American Review*, Vol. 151, p. 266 (September, 1890); *Forum*, V., 134 (April, 1888), 383 (June, 1888); VIII., 365 (December, 1889); *Nation*, XLIX., 185 (September 5, 1889); LI., 104 (August 7, 1890), 161 (August 28, 1890); *Public Opinion*, IX., 237 (June 21, 1890), 261 (June 28, 1890), 285 (July 5, 1890), 309 (July 12, 1890), 383 (August 2, 1890), 427 (August 16, 1890), 471 (August 30, 1890); *Congressional Record*, 1889–1890, pp. 6550, 6560 (June 26, 1890), p. 6702 (June 28, 1890).

I. A federal election bill is contrary to sound public policy.——(*a*) It is unconstitutional: *Congressional Record*, 1889–1890, p. 6560.—(1) It gives to a clause an interpretation not intended when the Constitution was framed.—(2) It deprives the state of the power to determine the qualifications for suffrage.——(*b*) It would violate the custom of our republican institutions.—(1) By breaking down the principle of self-control.—(2) By tending toward too great centralization of popular government.

II. The evils do not warrant national legislation.——(*a*) Fraudulent elections are confined only to a distinct section, while the bill would be general.——(*b*) The present laws would be sufficient if enforced: *Nation*, LI., 104; *Revised Statutes*, 1878, Sec. 2004 *et seq.*

III. National regulation would not benefit conditions in the South: *Nation*, LI., 104.——(*a*) It would aggravate race prejudice: *Congressional Record*, 1889-1890, p. 6705 (June 28, 1890); *Nation*, LI., 104.——(*b*) Interference in southern elections has once been tried and has proved a failure: *Forum*, VII., 246-247 (May, 1889); *Encyclopædia Britannica*, XXIII., 784.

IV. National legislation would be dangerous in effect.——(*a*) It would involve great unnecessary expense: *Congressional Record*, 1889-1890, p. 6550.——(*b*) In the North and West the evils of office-seeking would grow.——(*c*) Corruption would be unnecessarily invited: *North American Review*, Vol. 151, p. 267.——(*d*) It would complicate state elections.——(*e*) Antagonism to the national government would be encouraged: *Congressional Record*, 1889-1890, p. 6772 (June 30, 1890); *Annual Cyclopædia*, *1877*, p. 711; *1879*, p. 561.

II.

FEDERAL PROTECTION OF NEGRO SUFFRAGE.

QUESTION: '*Resolved*, That the United States government ought to interfere to protect the southern negro in the exercise of the suffrage.'

Brief for the Affirmative.

GENERAL REFERENCES: A. W. Tourgée, *An Appeal to Cæsar;* G. W. Cable, *The Silent South ;* H. C. Lodge in

Congressional Record, 1889-1890, pp. 6538-6544 (June 26, 1890); *Forum*, IV., 376-382 (December, 1887); V., 508 (July, 1888); *North American Review*, Vol. 151, p. 257 (September, 1890), pp. 593-600, 604-605 (November, 1890); *Contemporary Review*, LIII., 443 (March, 1888).

I. The negroes are deprived of their rights of suffrage : *An Appeal to Cæsar*, pp. 68-87 ; *Contemporary Review*, LIII., 443 ; *North American Review*, Vol. 151, pp. 593-600, 604, 605.

II. This deprivation is an evil : *Contemporary Review*, LIII., 465 ; *The Silent South*, p. 16.——(*a*) It is harmful to the South.—(1) It causes class friction.—(2) The moral effect of a violation of the Constitution is bad.——(*b*) It is harmful to the negro.—(1) It denies him the educating influence of citizenship.——(*c*) It is opposed to the spirit of American institutions.

III. The evil should be remedied.——(*a*) Individual freedom is a right, not a privilege.——(*b*) The evil is becoming more and more fixed.——(*c*) It will not remedy itself.

IV. The remedy should come from the federal government. ——(*a*) The states cannot be depended upon to guarantee the suffrage to the negroes.——(*b*) The elections are United States elections, and are controlled by federal law.——(*c*) Interference by the United States government would be constitutional : *Constitution of the United States*, Art. I., Sec. 4. § 1 ; Art. IV., Sec. 4 ; *North American Review*, Vol. 128, pp. 458-461 (May, 1879) ; *Congressional Record*, 1878-1879, pp. 997-999 (February 5, 1879).

Brief for the Negative.

GENERAL REFERENCES : James Bryce in *North American Review*, Vol. 153, p. 641 (December, 1891) ; Vol. 154, p. 401 (March, 1892) ; *Nation*, LI., 104 (August 7, 1890) ; LIV., 207 (March 17, 1892) ; Civil Rights Cases, 109

U. S., 3; *Congressional Record*, 1874–1875, pp. 1791–1797 (February 26, 1875), pp. 1861–1870 (February 27, 1875); James Bryce, *The American Commonwealth*, II., Chap. xciii.

I. Interference by the United States government would be unconstitutional: *Congressional Record*, 1874–1875, Appendix, pp. 103, 113, 117, 143, 156.———(*a*) All powers not granted by the Constitution are reserved by the states: *Constitution of the United States*, Amend. X.——— (*b*) The thirteenth, fourteenth, and fifteenth amendments of the Constitution do not interfere with the police powers of the states: Bartemeyer *v.* Iowa, 18 *Wallace*, 138; Slaughter House Cases, 16 *Wallace*, 62.

II. Effective enforcement of such a measure is impracticable.———(*a*) No measure would furnish protection beyond the polls.———(*b*) The present federal law has never been effectively enforced.

III. There are political objections to such a measure.——— (*a*) It would be a partisan measure.———(*b*) It would create a large amount of federal patronage: *North American Review*, Vol. 151, p. 266 (September, 1890).

IV. It would not benefit the negro.———(*a*) His ignorance incapacitates him from voting intelligently or independently. ———(*b*) It would render his position harder than at present: *Nation*, LIV., 207.

V. It would result in serious evils.———(*a*) It would injure the whites.—(1) In several states an ignorant negro vote would hold the balance of power.———(*b*) It would revive sectional animosities.———(*c*) It would arouse antagonism against the national government.———(*d*) It would increase race hatred: *Nation*, LI., 126 (August 14, 1890).

VI. There is a prospect of natural solutions.———(*a*) By a decrease in the proportion of blacks to whites.———(*b*) Through education.

III.

DISFRANCHISEMENT OF THE NEGROES.

QUESTION: '*Resolved*, That the suffrage should be taken from the negroes in the southern states.'

Brief for the Affirmative.

GENERAL REFERENCES: H. W. Grady in *Century*, VII., 909 (April, 1885); James Bryce in *North American Review*, Vol. 153, p. 641 (December, 1891); J. B. Craighead in *Popular Science Monthly*, XXVI., 39 (November, 1884); A. B. Hart in *Nation*, LIV., 207 (March 17, 1892); P. A. Bruce, *The Plantation Negro*, Chap. ii.

I. The suffrage was given to the negroes of the South unwisely.——(*a*) Their training as slaves unfitted them for citizenship: *Forum*, I., 126 (April, 1886).——(*b*) No naturalization process was required.——(*c*) Their enfranchisement was contrary to the expectations of many abolitionists.——(*d*) Their enfranchisement was a partisan measure to perpetuate the Republican party.

II. The negroes are unfitted for the suffrage.——(*a*) Lack of virtue and morality is inherent in the race: *Nation*, LIV., 208; *The Plantation Negro*, Chap. ii.——(*b*) They are easily led by superstition.——(*c*) They are generally incapable of any but the simplest education.——(*d*) When left to themselves they have generally fallen back into barbarism: *Popular Science Monthly*, XXIV., 43.

III. The negroes have proved unworthy of the suffrage.——(*a*) They have not the courage to vote even when they outnumber the whites.——(*b*) They have shown no independent political judgment.—(1) They are easily led by political demagogues.——(*c*) The reconstructive governments controlled by the negroes were marked by reckless expenditure and theft: *Lalor's Cyclopædia*, III., 554–555.

IV. Disfranchisement would result in positive good.——
(*a*) It would remove the intense race antagonism in the South which is caused by the fear of the whites that the negroes will get control of the polls.——(*b*) It would strengthen the authority of the Constitution.—(1) By repealing articles which are inoperative.——(*c*) The negroes for all practical purposes are deprived of the suffrage.

Brief for the Negative.

GENERAL REFERENCES: G. W. Cable, *The Negro Question;* G. W. Cable, *The Silent South;* James Bryce, *The American Commonwealth*, II., Chap. xciii.; A. W. Tourgée, *An Appeal to Cæsar;* James Bryce in *North American Review*, Vol. 153, p. 641 (December, 1891); Vol. 128, p. 225 (March, 1879); *Forum*, I., 562 (August, 1886); X., 335 (November, 1890); *Popular Science Monthly*, XXVIII., 24 (November, 1885); *Nation*, XLVIII., 461 (June 6, 1889); LIII., 208 (September 17, 1891); *Atlantic Monthly*, LIV., 696 (November, 1884).

I. To take away the suffrage from the negroes would be a breach of faith on the part of the government.——(*a*) Suffrage is guaranteed by the Constitution.——(*b*) Disfranchisement would require nullification of the fifteenth amendment.

II. The negro has shown himself worthy of the suffrage.——
(*a*) His improvement, though slow, has been steady: *Popular Science Monthly*, XXVIII., 35.——(*b*) He has always been loyal to the government: *The Negro Question*, p. 39.——
(*c*) His ignorance is no reason for considering him unworthy to vote when the same distinction is not made in the case of ignorant whites.

III. The withdrawal of the suffrage would be disastrous: *North American Review*, Vol. 153, p. 655:——(*a*) It would give the southern whites almost absolute control over the negroes.——(b) It would increase race prejudice by making a distinction on color lines.——(c) The intelligent as well as the ignorant would be deprived of the suffrage.

IV. The remedy for the existing evil lies in education, not in disfranchisement.——(a) The negro is capable of education.——(b) An educational qualification would stimulate his desire for self-improvement.

IV.

WOMAN SUFFRAGE.

QUESTION : ' *Resolved*, That woman suffrage is desirable.'

Brief for the Affirmative.

GENERAL REFERENCES: Dr. M. P. Jacobi, ' *Common Sense*' *Applied to Woman Suffrage;* T. W. Higginson, *Common Sense about Women;* George William Curtis, *Equal Rights for Women;* Julia Ward Howe, T. W. Higginson, Lucy Stone, Elizabeth Cady Stanton, and Wendell Phillips, in *North American Review*, Vol. 129, pp. 413-446 (November, 1879); J. S. Mill, *The Subjection of Women;* J. S. Mill, *Representative Government*, Chap. viii.; Wendell Phillips, *Speeches, Lectures, and Addresses* (First Series), p. 11 ; *Senate Reports*, 1888-1889, No. 2543 ; *Century*, XLVIII., 605 (August, 1894) ; *Forum*, II., 439 (January, 1887) ; III., 131 (April, 1887); XVIII., 406 (December, 1894).

I. Woman suffrage is desirable theoretically.——(a) The best government comes from the consent of the governed.——(1) Women are citizens in all but the right to vote: *U. S. Revised Statutes*, Secs. 1992-1994.——(b) Taxation without representation is unjust.—(1) Women own property as well as men.——(c) The ballot is the only efficient protection to a person's interests.——(1) Women are not represented by men: *Equal Rights for Women*, pp. 8–13.

II. Woman suffrage will raise the position of woman.—— (*a*) Legally.——(1) It will protect her interests.——(*b*) Intellectually.——(1) It will stimulate education.——(*c*) Socially.——(1) It will give her equality in the home.——(*d*) The objection that woman will be taken out of her sphere is unsound: '*Common Sense*' *Applied to Woman Suffrage*, pp. 93–108.——(1) Such a conception is a relic of militarism.——(2) Womanliness is the result of maternal instincts, not of outside influences.——(3) Recent reforms have not made woman unwomanly.

III. Woman suffrage will benefit the government.——(*a*) Politics will be purified.——(1) Women have a higher standard of morality than men.——(*b*) The conservative influence of the home will be brought in.——(*c*) New abilities will be made available.——(*d*) The objection that women are led by impulse is not true.——(1) Women, although given the suffrage by the Populists, overthrew that party in Kansas.

IV. Woman suffrage is demanded by women: *Arena*, XI., 353 (February, 1895).——(*a*) The movement is led by representative women.——(*b*) The movement is growing rapidly: '*Common Sense*' *Applied to Woman Suffrage*, pp. 60–61.—— (*c*) The fact that many women oppose is no objection.——(1) All reforms are met by opposition at first.

V. Woman suffrage is practicable.——(*a*) Woman is man's equal intellectually.——(*b*) In ability to support herself.—— (*c*) In economic importance.——(*d*) The experiment has been successful where it has been tried.——(1) In Wyoming, Colorado, and Kansas: '*Common Sense*' *Applied to Woman Suffrage*, pp. 153–158.

Brief for the Negative.

GENERAL REFERENCES: *New Englander*, XLIII., 193 (March, 1884); *Forum*, IV., 1 (September, 1887); *Nineteenth Century*, XXV., 781 (June, 1889); Catherine E.

Beecher, *Woman's Profession ;* Francis Parkman, *Woman Suffrage ;* Horace Bushnell, *Women's Suffrage, the Reform against Nature ;* J. K. Bluntchli, *Theory of the State,* Bk. II., Chap. xx.; Minority Report on Woman Suffrage, *Senate Reports,* 1888–1889, I., No. 2543; *Forum,* VIII., 515 (January, 1890); *Popular Science Monthly,* V., 427 (August, 1874); *Nation,* XLIV., 310 (April 14, 1887); *Arena,* II., 175 (July, 1890).

I. The suffrage is not a natural right of all citizens.———(*a*) It is a privilege conferred from considerations of expediency : *Lalor's Cyclopædia,* III., 822 ; J. N. Pomeroy, *Constitutional Law,* § 256 h; Minor *v.* Happersett, 21 *Wallace,* 165–178.

II. Woman suffrage is not necessary.———(*a*) Women's interests are already well represented; their interests, though equal to men's, are not identical with them.———(*b*) The majority of women do not want it : *Nineteenth Century,* XXV., 781–785.—(1) Advocated by a few zealots.—(2) Where privilege exists it is little used.

III. Woman suffrage would be prejudicial to state interests. ———(*a*) It would confer the franchise upon persons unfitted for politics : *Nation,* X., 205 (March 31, 1870).—(1) Physically. —(2) By temperament.—(3) By susceptibility to undue influence.———(*b*) It would greatly increase the number of illiterate and unqualified voters : *New Englander,* XLIII., 207.— (1) The women who would use it belong to the lowest classes in our cities.—(2) Competent women would not use it.———(*c*) It would give rise to lax laws and weaken the government.— (1) Laws must be sanctioned by physical strength.—(2) The best governments are supported by a preponderance of physical force.

IV. Woman suffrage would be deleterious to the interests of society.———(*a*) It would take woman from her natural sphere—the home.———(*b*) It would diminish her elevating and refining influence : *Arena,* II., 175 ; H. Bushnell, *Women's Suffrage,* p. 20.

V.

A PROPERTY QUALIFICATION FOR MUNICIPAL SUFFRAGE.

QUESTION: '*Resolved*, That, if it were possible, a reasonable property qualification for the exercise of the municipal franchise in the United States would be desirable.'

Brief for the Affirmative.

GENERAL REFERENCES: *Popular Science Monthly*, XXX., 296 (January, 1887), 520 (February, 1887); *North American Review*, Vol. 137, p. 218 (September, 1883); Andrew D. White in *Forum*, X., 357 (December, 1890); C. W. Eliot in *Forum*, XII., 153 (October, 1891); A. P. Wilder, *The Municipal Problem*, pp. 44–56.

I. The franchise is a privilege to be granted to those most likely to use it for the public welfare: J. N. Pomeroy, *Constitutional Law*, §§ 207–209, 256 h; Minor *v.* Happersett, 21 *Wallace*, 162.

II. A property qualification for the municipal franchise will confer it upon those most likely to use it for the public welfare. ——(*a*) It will make a more intelligent class of voters.—— (*b*) It will exclude those indifferent to the public welfare.— (1) Dependent classes, susceptible to bribery.—(2) Pauper immigrants.

III. Experience shows that those cities which have a property qualification are better governed than those which have an unrestricted suffrage: *Nation*, XXXIV., 245 (March 23, 1882), 267 (March 30, 1882); Albert Shaw, *Municipal Government in Great Britain*, pp. 45, 77; *New Review*, XI., 74 (July, 1894), 499 (November, 1894); *Forum*, XVII., 659 (August, 1894).——(*a*) Municipal government in the

United States is extravagant, inefficient, and corrupt.——(*l*) European cities having property qualification are economically and efficiently governed.

Brief for the Negative.

GENERAL REFERENCES: James Bryce, *The American Commonwealth*, I., Chaps. li., lii.; H. C. Adams, *Public Debts*, pp. 343–375; A. P. Wilder, *The Municipal Problem;* Allinson and Penrose, *Philadelphia, 1681–1887* (Johns Hopkins Studies, extra Vol. II.). Chap. v.; Joseph Chamberlain in *Forum*, XIV., 267 (November, 1892); *Proceedings of National Conference for Good City Government*, 1894; Bibliographies of Municipal Government in preceding, and in *Providence Public Library Bulletin*, Vol. I., No. 2, p. 14 (February, 1895).

I. A broad suffrage in cities is on general principles desirable.——(*a*) All citizens have a stake in the government.——(*b*) It is in keeping with the spirit of democratic institutions.——(*c*) It gives representation to all classes.——(*d*) It gives security to the government.——(*e*) It has great educational value.——(*f*) It has given the best results in practice.

II. Existing municipal evils do not justify a radical change in the suffrage.——(*a*) Improvement is being made on other lines.——(*b*) Existing evils are due chiefly to causes apart from the suffrage.—(1) To the absence of municipal ideals.—(2) To the indifference of the better classes.—(3) To mixing national and state with city politics.—(4) To excessive interference by legislatures in local affairs.—(5) To unsatisfactory charter arrangements.—(6) To corrupt influence of property-owners, corporations, and rich men.——(*c*) Business-like administration and present broad suffrage are not necessarily inconsistent.—(1) Shown by reformed city governments.—(2) Perfection of certain departments, *e.g.*, Fire and Police departments.—(3) Foreign experience, *e.g.*, Birmingham: *Fo-*

rum, XIV., 267.—(4) The judgment of reformers and practical men.——(*d*) Undesirable voters can be excluded in more direct and practicable ways.—(1) The ignorant, by an educational qualification.—(2) The corrupt, by more efficient bribery laws.—(3) Criminals, by disfranchisement.—(4) The 'floaters,' by residence qualifications.

III. A property qualification is especially objectionable.——(*a*) Wealth is not a true index to ability, public virtue, and interest in municipal affairs.——(*b*) It would be accompanied by serious evils.—(1) It would be difficult to determine what is 'reasonable.'—(2) It would be difficult to apply.—(3) It would work crudely and unequally.—(x) By excluding many good voters.—(y) By including many bad voters.—(4) It would remove a strong educational force.—(5) It would lead to agitation and discontent.

PARTIES.

VI.

THE REPUBLICAN PARTY.

QUESTION: '*Resolved*, That the Republican party is entitled to the suffrages of intelligent citizens.'

Brief for the Affirmative.

GENERAL REFERENCES: George S. Boutwell, *Why I am a Republican*; John D. Long, *The Republican Party*; J. H. Patton, *The Democratic Party*; J. G. Blaine, *Twenty Years of Congress*; Edward Stanwood, *History of Presidential Elections*; *Lalor's Cyclopædia*, III., 597; *Forum*, VII., 488 (July, 1889); VIII., 136 (October, 1889); IX., 24 (March, 1890); XIV., 242 (October, 1892); XV., 250 (April, 1893); XVII.,

129 (April, 1894), 268 (May, 1894); *North American Review*, Vol. 146, p. 1 (January, 1888); Vol. 149, p. 616 (November, 1889); Vol. 154, p. 641 (June, 1892); Vol. 155, p. 268 (September, 1892), p. 513 (November, 1892); Vol. 156, p. 54 (January, 1893); Vol. 157, p. 257 (September, 1893).

I. The tariff policy of the Republican party is commendable.――(*a*) American industries protected.――(*b*) Due regard for vested interests.――(*c*) Agricultural, manufacturing, and commercial industries stimulated: *Forum*, III., 550–552.――(*d*) Social and political advancement.――(*e*) Industrial independence.――(*f*) Higher wages for American laborers.――(*g*) Reciprocity.

II. The financial policy of the Republican party is commendable.――(*a*) In favor of sound money.――(*b*) Uncompromisingly opposed to the free coinage of silver.――(*c*) Opposed to the periodic issue of bonds.――(*d*) Advocates a system of national instead of state banks: *Forum*, VII., 495.――(*e*) In favor of a surplus instead of a deficit in the Treasury, and a gold reserve intact.

III. The foreign policy of the Republican party is commendable: *North American Review*, Vol. 154, p. 643.――(*a*) Constantly upholds a strong, dignified, and patriotic course.—(1) Conduct in fishery question: *The Republican Party*, pp. 144–165.—(2) Chilean affair.—(3) New Orleans affair. — (4) Hawaiian controversy. —— (*b*) In favor of a vigorous application of the Monroe Doctrine.――(*c*) Union of American interests.—(1) Pan-American Congress.

IV. The policy of the Republican party regarding the civil service is commendable.――(*a*) Civil service reform begun by the Republican party: *The Republican Party*, p. 296.――(*b*) Excellent make-up of the civil service commission.――(*c*) Mail service placed under civil service rules.――(*d*) Navy-yards.――(*e*) Indian service.

V. The policy of the Republican party regarding other vital

questions is commendable.——(a) Free ballot: *Forum*, III., 544–548.——(b) No soldier with an honorable discharge to go to the almshouse.——(c) Strong coast defences: *The Republican Party*, pp. 182–207.——(d) Strong navy and merchant marine.——(e) Diminished internal revenue taxes.——(f) Exclusion of pauper immigrants.——(g) State and national education.

Brief for the Negative.

GENERAL REFERENCES: Democratic platforms; *Forum*, IV., 117 (October, 1887); V., 79 (March, 1888); VI., 10 (September, 1888); VII., 585 (August, 1889); IX., 243 (May, 1890); XIV., 255 (October, 1892); XV., 242 (April, 1893); *North American Review*, Vol. 145, p. 267 (September, 1887); Vol. 149, p. 539 (November, 1889); Vol. 154, p. 650 (June, 1892); Vol. 155, p. 280 (September, 1892); Vol. 159, p. 385 (October, 1894).

I. The principle of protection upheld by the Republican party is unsound.——(a) Legislation for the benefit of the few.——(b) Discriminating against the poor.——(c) Unconstitutional.——(d) Sectional.——(e) Favors corporations and fosters trusts.——(f) Source of corruption: *Forum*, IV., 125. ——(g) The prosperity of the country has been in spite of, not on account of, the protective system.—(1) We have great natural resources.

II. The foreign policy of the Republican party is bad.—— (a) Blatant jingoism.—(1) Samoan affair: *Nation*, XLVIII., 84.—(2) Fishery question.—(3) Hawaiian affair.——(b) Foreign complications turned to make campaign material.—— (c) Lowers us in the opinion of other nations.——(d) Undignified.

III. The pension policy of the Republican party is vicious. ——(a) Over a hundred and a quarter millions of dollars expended each year.——(b) Pensions given to those who are wholly undeserving.——(c) Changed the entire spirit of the country's volunteer soldiery.——(1) Turned loyal patriotic men into mercenary pension-seekers.———(*d*) Turned the Grand Army of the Republic into a political organization.

IV. The Republican party has lost the confidence of the people in other ways.———(*a*) Bad legislation.——(1) Force bill.—(2) Wasteful and partisan appropriations.———(*b*) Failure to reform the civil service.—(1) Dismissals made for political reasons.—(2) Assessments levied from employees.———(*c*) Corrupt methods used to gain power.—(1) Admission of new states.———(*d*) Corrupt leaders.—(1) Quay, Platt, and Dudley.———(*e*) Attempts to keep up sectional hatred.

V. The Democratic party alone is entitled to the suffrages of intelligent people.———(*a*) It has made a consistent attempt to carry out party pledges.———(*b*) It stands for tariff reform. ———(*c*) It has brought about wise legislation.—(1) Repeal of election laws.—(2) Repeal of the Sherman Act.———(*d*) It stands solidly for reform of the pension system.———(*e*) It has practised economical administrations.———(*f*) It has wrought the only real victories for civil service reform.———(*g*) It upholds a dignified foreign policy.———(*h*) It is opposed to trusts and monopolies.

VII.

THE POPULIST PARTY.

QUESTION: '*Resolved*, That the supporters of the Populist party have substantial grievances which their movement is likely to relieve.'

Brief for the Affirmative.

GENERAL REFERENCES: J. B. Weaver, *A Call to Action;* W. A. Peffer, *The Farmer's Side;* Platform of the People's party, in leading daily papers of July 5, 1892; *Forum,* VIII., 464 (December, 1889); *Arena,* V., 726 (May, 1892); VI.,

201 (July, 1892) ; Secretary Rusk in *North American Review*, Vol. 152, p. 423 (April, 1891); Vol. 153, p. 220 (August, 1891); Vol. 157, p. 665 (December, 1893); Vol. 160, p. 16 (January, 1895); *Century*, XXI., 447 (January, 1892).

I. The existence of substantial grievances behind the Populist movement is proved by——(*a*) The sudden and powerful uprising among the agricultural portion of the community: *Forum*, X., 315-316 (November, 1890); *Arena*, V., 726.——(*b*) Great strength developed by the party in recent elections.

II. Chief among these grievances are the following.——(*a*) Wretched condition of agriculture as compared with other occupations: *The Farmer's Side*, Parts I., II.; *North American Review*, Vol. 152, p. 425; *Forum*, X., 346; *Andover Review*, XIV., 127 (August, 1890).——(*b*) Existence and growth of great monopolies.——(*c*) Inadequacy and unsuitableness of our national currency: *North American Review*, Vol. 153, p. 222; Vol. 157, pp. 665-667.——(*d*) Farmer's lack of influence in politics: *North American Review*, Vol. 153, pp. 9-10 (July, 1891).

III. These grievances are due to causes which can be removed by legislation.——(*a*) Extortions of railroads, middlemen, and banks: *Forum*, VIII., 465; *North American Review*, Vol. 157, pp. 675-678.——(*b*) Exemption of the rich from taxation on their incomes: *Arena*, VI., 202.——(*c*) Contraction of the currency: *The Farmer's Side*, Chap. ix. ——(*d*) Unequal system of tariff taxation: J. G. Carlisle in *Forum*, VIII., 475.

IV. The Populist movement is likely to result in such legislation.——(*a*) It has opened the eyes of the people to the deplorable condition of the farmers: *Andover Review*, XIV., 139.——(*b*) Its strength must inevitably secure concessions from the two great parties.——(*c*) All the questions it raised are vital questions and demand speedy consideration: *Arena*, VI., 204.

Brief for the Negative.

GENERAL REFERENCES: *Nation*, LI., 84 (July 31, 1890); Platform of the People's party, in leading daily papers of July 5, 1892; H. R. Chamberlain, *The Farmer's Alliance*, pp. 13-21, 44-50, 52-64; *Forum*, XIV., 381 (November, 1892).

I. The Populist party seeks to increase rather than to lessen class distinctions: *Public Opinion*, IX., 386 (August 2, 1890), 408 (August 9, 1890).——(*a*) The extravagances of the platform prove this.——(*b*) In its eagerness to fight monopolists the Populist party has adopted ridiculous and inconsistent theories: *Public Opinion*, X., 609 (April 4, 1890); *Nation*, L., 269 (April 3, 1890).

II. The Populist party advocates impossible socialistic and financial schemes.——(*a*) Socialistic.—(1) Sub-treasury and government control of railways: *Public Opinion*, VIII., 532; IX., 167, 168, 241, 408, 475; X., 172, 219, 220, 565, 611, 613.——(*b*) Financial.—(1) Free silver and the abolition of national banks: *Nation*, LII., 104, 229, 230; *Public Opinion*, X., 171, 217, 218.

III. The Populist movement thus far has been only injurious to the public welfare.——(*a*) Valuable statesmen have been driven out of public life.——(*b*) Legislation in the states controlled by Populists has been of the worst kind: *Nation*, L., 480; LI., 390; LII., 188, 310.

IV. The issues raised by the Populist party are not national and therefore cannot prevail: *Forum*, XVI., 240 (October, 1893).——(*a*) The history of the Know-Nothing, Greenback, and Prohibition parties shows this.

VIII.

THE AMERICAN PROTECTIVE ASSOCIATION.

QUESTION: '*Resolved*, That the principles of the American Protective Association deserve the support of American citizens.'

Brief for the Affirmative.

GENERAL REFERENCES: Principles in *Harper's Weekly*, XXXVIII., 1017–1018 (October 27, 1894), and in *The World Almanac, 1895*, p. 115; W. E. Gladstone, *Vatican Decrees and Civil Allegiance*; E. D. Mead, *The Roman Catholic Church and the Public Schools*; Bishop Coxe, *The Jesuit Party in American Politics*; *North American Review*, Vol. 159, p. 67 (July, 1894); Vol. 158, p. 573 (May, 1894); *Forum*, XVII., 427–434 (June, 1894); *Christian Examiner*, LXXVIII., 399 (May, 1865); *Fortnightly Review*, XXV., 385 (March, 1876); *Forum*, XVII., 196 (April, 1894); *Public Opinion*, XVII., 590 (September 20, 1894).

I. The principles of the American Protective Association are in accordance with our Constitution.——(*a*) They do not violate the clause, 'no religious test shall be required,' Art. VI., § 3: Charles Eaton, *A Religious Test*.—(1) 'Required' relates to Congress itself and not to the people.—(2) New Hampshire, Texas, South Carolina, Tennessee have religious qualifications for state officers: Charles Eaton, *A Religious Test*.

II. The American Protective Association tends to strengthen American institutions.——(*a*) Respect for the Constitution.——(*b*) Patriotism and Americanism.

III. The American Protective Association aims at reforms impossible by present parties.——(*a*) No state aid to sectarian institutions.——(*b*) Restriction of immigration.——(*c*) Uniform naturalization laws.——(*d*) Extension of term of probation.

IV. The American Protective Association opposes the unseen yet dangerous power of the Roman Catholic Church.—— (*a*) Enormous influence.—(1) In numbers.—(2) In centralization.—(3) In discipline.—(4) Through ignorance of adherents.——(*b*) Constantly increasing.—(1) Growth by immigration.—(2) Strengthening of discipline.—(x) Case of McGlynn. ——(*c*) Hostile to American institutions.—(1) Makes the Roman Catholics a separate class.—(2) Opposes public schools: E. D. Mead, *The Roman Catholic Church and the Public Schools; North American Review*, Vol. 140, p. 521 (June, 1885).—(3) Controlled by a foreign 'potentate' claiming supremacy over our civil government: Bishop Vincent in *Forum*, XV., 263; Encyclical Letter of Pope Leo XIII. in *American Catholic Quarterly Review*, XIX., 777–789 (October, 1894).—(4) Directly opposed to the advance of civilization.—(x) The United States the Pope's 'one bright hope for the future.'

Brief for the Negative.

GENERAL REFERENCES: *Forum*, XVII., 513 (July, 1894), 524 (July, 1894), 434 (June, 1894), 196 (April, 1894); *North American Review*, Vol. 159, p. 278 (September, 1894); Vol. 158, p. 563 (May, 1894); *Century*, XLVII., 789 (March, 1894); XLVIII., 954 (October, 1894); *Catholic World*, XXXI., 94 (April, 1880); XLIX., 649 (August, 1889); *American Catholic Quarterly Review*, XV., 509 (July, 1890); *Nation*, LIV., 374 (May 19, 1892).

I. The principles of the American Protective Association are found——(*a*) In their professions: *The Citizen* (Boston), November 17, 1894.——(*b*) In their actions: *Century*, XLVII., 789.

II. Taxation of religious, educational, and charitable institutions is inadvisable : *The Citizen*, November 17, 1894 ; *Report of Massachusetts Commission on Taxation and Exemption*, January, 1875, House, No. 15, pp. 150-170, and C. W. Eliot in Appendix, pp. 367-394.——(*a*) These institutions perform necessary public functions.——(*b*) When supported by private benevolence their expense is a saving to the state. ——(*c*) Exemption a better method of encouraging private benevolence than direct grants.

III. Exclusion of Roman Catholics from public office and positions in schools would be an uncalled-for injustice.——(*a*) Membership in Catholic Church not irreconcilable with American citizenship.——(*b*) Alleged machinations of Pope— even if true—would be ineffective.—(1) Decline of Papal power.—(2) Weakness of Catholic Church in United States. —(3) Publicity of action in United States: C. W. Eliot in *Forum*, XVIII., 138 (October, 1894).——(*c*) Establishment of a religious test would be unconstitutional : *Constitution of United States*, Art. VI., § 3 ; *Amendments of the Constitution*, Art. I.——(*d*) A religious test for office-holders would be detrimental to good government.

IV. Secret political organizations are un-American : *Century*, XLVIII., 954.——(*a*) Require votes to be cast as ordered, even contrary to convictions.——(*b*) Unsuitable for public officers whose duties may conflict with pledge.——(*c*) Cloak for underhanded work.——(*d*) Temporary.—(1) History of Know-Nothing Party : Edward Stanwood, *History of Presidential Elections*, p. 93.——(*e*) Dangerous.—(1) Morgan episode in 1826.

V. The proposed boycotts are un-American.——(*a*) Against endorsers of Catholics.—(1) Result in keeping out competent officials : *Century*, XLVII., 789.——(*b*) Against employment of Catholics.—(1) Socially.—(2) Economically.—(x) Delay industry.—(y) Exclude skilled workmen.

VI. The principles of the American Protective Association countenance bad methods.——(*a*) Lies, forgeries, and misrepresentations.——(*b*) Adoption of methods they condemn in

Catholics.———(c) Adoption of other illegal means.—(1) Against the United States and state constitutions.———(d) Retaliation.—(1) Against officials refusing to join.—(2) Against officers performing their duty notwithstanding American Protective Association oath.

IX.

PARTY ALLEGIANCE.

QUESTION : ' *Resolved*, That party allegiance is preferable to independent action in politics.'

Brief for the Affirmative.

GENERAL REFERENCES : J. Macy, *Our Government*, Chap. xxxiv.; H. C. Lodge, ' Party Allegiance,' in *Historical and Political Essays;* Washington Gladden in *Century*, VI., 270 (June, 1884); Roscoe Conkling, *Life and Letters*, p. 538; *Spectator*, LVIII., p. 1367 (October 17, 1885).

I. Parties are inevitable under a republican form of government : *Our Government*, Chap. xxxiv.———(a) The people naturally divide into a liberal and a conservative party : *Historical and Political Essays*, p. 202.———(b) Two great parties are bound to exist, one sufficiently strong to hold the other in check.

II. Parties and party allegiance are highly desirable.——— (a) They unite people of different parts of the country in one common party.———(b) They encourage political activity.——— (c) They keep important issues constantly before the public. ———(d) They make possible a clear insight into all political affairs.———(e) They insure regular and orderly movement. ———(f) They insure stability in legislation, and in its execution.———(*g*) They enable the people to fix the responsibility for bad legislation.

III. Independent voting is harmful: *Historical and Political Essays*, pp. 203, 204.———(*a*) It draws from the great political parties a highly desirable element that can accomplish no good by itself.———(*b*) It obscures legitimate party issues by making an issue of political purity, which is not essential to party policy.———(*c*) It makes prominent the local issues of the country, *e.g.*, sugar, silver, farming.———(*d*) It results in inefficient and irresponsible representation, and gives rise to combinations and corruption in legislative assemblies.

IV. The best means to reform present abuses is by reforming the party.———(*a*) Independent voting is inefficient if cast by itself.———(*b*) It encourages one of the great political parties if cast with one of them.———(*c*) Much has been accomplished by the reform of the civil service and by ballot reforms.

Brief for the Negative.

GENERAL REFERENCES: J. R. Lowell, 'The Independent in Politics,' in *Political Essays; North American Review*, Vol. 144, p. 549 (June, 1887); Vol. 134, p. 431 (May, 1882); *International Review*, XIII., 587 (December, 1882); James Bryce, *The American Commonwealth*, II., Chaps. lxiii., lxv., lxvii.; *Spectator*, XLIX., p. 1027 (July 31, 1886); *Nation*, XLVII., 4 (July 5, 1888); XX., 308 (May 6, 1875).

I. Political parties are not absolutely necessary: A. Stickney, *A True Republic*, Chap. v.; *International Review*, XIII., 588.———(*a*) There are no vital differences between the parties: *The American Commonwealth*, II., 15, 21.———(*b*) The eras of good feeling in American history have been those periods which were free from machine party politics. ———(*c*) The provision made for the veto in the Constitution does away with the necessity for party allegiance.—(1) The President and cabinet are not removable for failure of policy.

II. The present system is bad.———(*a*) It results in government for the machine, instead of for the people: Goldwin Smith in *North American Review*, Vol. 154, p. 583 (May, 1892); *The American Commonwealth*, II., 100, 107, 123.——(*b*) Offices are sought merely for remuneration, resulting in the spoils system: *The American Commonwealth*, II., 58, 59, 132–141; *International Review*, XIII., 587.—(1) Shown by rotation in office.—(2) Geographical appointments.—(3) The appointment of corrupt or unfit officials: T. Roosevelt, *Essays on Practical Politics*, pp. 11–41.——(*c*) It gives undue influence to certain sections.——(*d*) Strict party government results in rule by but little more than one-quarter of the voters.

III. Reform within the parties is impossible: *The American Commonwealth*, II., 87, 113.——(*a*) The better class of citizens will not take an active part in party organization. ——(*b*) The machine controls the primaries.—(1) By fraudulent check-lists.—(2) By force.

IV. Independent action has accomplished reform where party fealty has failed.——(*a*) It gives the independent voters the balance of power.——(*b*) It compels better nominations in the great political parties and thus helps to purify politics. —(1) Cases of Delamater in Pennsylvania, and Maynard in New York: *Nation*, XLIV., 264 (March 31, 1887), 381 (May 5, 1887).——(*c*) It has succeeded in carrying out the pension and the civil service reforms.

X.

PARTY ALLEGIANCE IN MUNICIPAL ELECTIONS.

QUESTION: '*Resolved*, That it is for the interests of good government that the citizen acts with his party in municipal elections.'

Brief for the Affirmative.

GENERAL REFERENCES: James Bryce, *The American Commonwealth*, II., Chaps. lxii.–lxviii.; John Fiske, *Civil Gov-*

ernment, pp. 124, 139; Theodore Roosevelt, *Essays on Practical Politics*, pp. 72, 73; H. H. Darling in *Harvard Monthly*, VIII., 32–34 (March, 1889); S. N. Patten in *Annals of American Academy of Political Science*, I., 26 (July, 1890); J. Macy, *Our Government*, Chap. xxxi.

I. Non-observance of party ties in municipal elections would be contrary to good public policy.——(*a*) Political parties are essential to our form of government: J. Macy, *Our Government*, Chap. xxxiv.—(1) They foster political activity.—(2) They insure publicity of government methods.—(3) They are educators of the people.——(*b*) Non-observance of party ties would weaken political parties.—(1) It would increase the expense of party management by separating municipal from national organizations.—(2) Local politics are a desirable training for national political management.—(3) There would be no substantial basis for encouraging a strong national organization with a fixed policy.

II. Party adhesion is necessary for the welfare of city government.——(*a*) It is favorable to a sense of responsibility.—(1) Officers are more likely to work in harmony; and thus deadlocks are avoided.—(2) Responsibility is thrown on the party as well as on the leaders.—(3) The minority party is quick to criticise.—(4) Abuses are more often due to division of responsibility than to party protection: Seth Low, *Municipal Government*, pp. 15–19.——(*b*) Non-allegiance to party would tend to increase the present abuses.—(1) Factional strife would be more intense.—(2) The numerous factions would encourage corruption and deals.—(3) Bribery would be more frequent.—(4) Conscientious men would not have as much influence as when backed by a strong party.

III. Consistent policy and permanent reform are the result of party rather than of independent action.——(*a*) Individual action is spasmodic and not sustained: *Essays on Practical Politics*, pp. 72, 73.——(*b*) It is seldom thorough.——(*c*)

Whoever bolts his party loses influence in it without gaining influence in another.

Brief for the Negative.

GENERAL REFERENCES: James Bryce, *The American Commonwealth*, Chaps. l.–lxviii.; John Fiske, *Civil Government*, pp. 120–136; *Lalor's Cyclopædia*, I., 463–467; *Nation*, LI., 337 (October 30, 1890); W. C. Ford, *American Citizen's Manual*, Part I., 66–83; *Political Science Quarterly*, II., 291 (June, 1887).

I. Local government ought to engage the first interest of citizens.——(*a*) Municipal affairs more directly affect the individual.—(1) Protection of citizens from fire, riots, unsanitary conditions, etc.—(2) Carrying on public works: street paving, water-works, etc.—(3) Improvement of citizens through schools, libraries, museums, parks, etc.——(*b*) Local taxes are far greater than state and national.——(*c*) Individual influence can be used most effectively for good.

II. Party allegiance subordinates municipal affairs to national issues and defeats the purpose of municipal government: *The American Commonwealth*, I., 639.——(*a*) A city is a business corporation and should be entirely outside of politics: *American Citizen's Manual*, Part I., 73–83.——(*b*) Parties are concerned with national issues and are unfitted for city government.

III. Party allegiance encourages the evils of machine rule. ——(*a*) Professional politicians are enabled to organize rings and deals.——(*b*) Municipal offices are treated as spoils.—— (*c*) Inferior men are elected to fill places requiring technical skill.——(*d*) The state legislature is likely to be drawn into meddling with city affairs: *Encyclopædia Britannica*, XVII., 463; *Lalor's Cyclopædia*, I., 464; *The American Commonwealth*, I., 660.——(*e*) Party rule in New York and in nearly all great cities has resulted in corruption and reckless waste of municipal resources: *The American Commonwealth*, II., Chaps. lxxxviii., lxxxix.

IV. The best governed cities are those conducted on a non-partisan plan.——(*a*) Berlin: Professor Gneist in *Contemporary Review*, XLVI., 769 (December, 1884).——(*b*) Glasgow: *Century*, XXXIX., 721 (March, 1890).

POLITICAL METHODS.

XI.

THE CAUCUS SYSTEM.

QUESTION: '*Resolved*, That the present system of caucus nomination ought to be abandoned.'

Brief for the Affirmative.

GENERAL REFERENCES: *Nineteenth Century*, IV., 695 (October, 1878); *New Englander*, XXXIV., 473 (July, 1875), 734 (October, 1875); *Forum*, XIV., 189 (October, 1892); *Political Science Quarterly*, III., 99 (March, 1888); *Christian Examiner*, LXXXVII., 137 (September, 1869); *North American Review*, Vol. 137, p. 257 (September, 1883); *Penn Monthly*, XII., 177 (March, 1881); *Atlantic Monthly*, LII., 323 (September, 1883); James Bryce, *The American Commonwealth*, Chaps. lvii.–lxxiv.; F. W. Whitridge in *Lalor's Cyclopædia*, I., 360–364; III., 851–856; Theodore Roosevelt, *Essays on Practical Politics*, p. 46; A. Stickney, *A True Republic*, Chap. v.

I. The caucus system has outlived its usefulness.——(*a*) It was first used in the small towns where mass meetings could be held.——(*b*) The only similar conditions to-day are found in the country.———(c) The rapid growth of cities has altered the very foundations of political methods.

II. The system is opposed to democratic principles.———(a) It prevents free thought and action.—(1) Those alone are allowed to take part in caucus meetings who pledge strict allegiance to the party.———(b) It defeats the will of the people.—(1) It restricts the choice of the people to two or three candidates.—(2) Candidates are often nominated in spite of public opposition.———(c) It centralizes power in the hands of a few.

III. The caucus system gives rise to the evils of political machines.———(a) A few political bosses are able to control the caucuses.—(1) By calling the meetings on short notice, at inconvenient places, and at inconvenient hours.—(2) By keeping transactions secret.—(3) By forcibly keeping away those opposed to their wishes, and by packing the meetings with their friends.———(b) The better class of men cannot compete with political bosses who give all their time to political ward heeling.

IV. The party machine is fatal to good government.——— (a) It drives good men out of politics.———(b) It puts the government in the hands of irresponsible parties.———(c) It corrupts the public service.—(1) Offices are regarded as spoils.———(d) It prevents independent action for the public welfare by binding officials to party interests.

V. The caucus system is unnecessary.———(a) Party government has existed without it.———(b) Better systems can be found: *New Englander*, XXXIV., 738-751; *Penn Monthly*, XII., 190; *Forum*, XIV., 192.—(1) Nomination of candidates by citizens at time of registration.—(2) Voting for delegates at general elections.

Brief for the Negative.

GENERAL REFERENCES: W. C. Ford, *American Citizen's Manual*, Part I., pp. 91-97; *Political Science Quarterly*,

III., 106 (March, 1888); *Nation*, VIII., 86 (February 4, 1869); Theodore Roosevelt, *Essays on Practical Politics*; *Fortnightly Review*, XXX., 721 (November, 1878).

1. The caucus is a very old American institution: W. Gordon, *History of American Revolution*, I., 365.——(*a*) It first appeared in New England because of the wide extension of the suffrage.——(*b*) It has spread with the extension of the suffrage.——(*c*) Practically the only change has been the choice of delegates to conventions.——(*d*) This was a natural and necessary development: *American Citizen's Manual*, p. 93.

II. The caucus is the simplest and most practical method of nomination yet devised.——(*a*) It is simply a town meeting of the party voters.——(*b*) The substitutes thus far suggested are impracticable.—(1) The system of self-nominations would not be tolerated.—(2) The system of primary elections involves a needless complication.

III. The evils complained of at present are not due to our present caucus system.——(*a*) These evils are nothing new.——(*b*) The liability of their occurrence is inherent in human nature and in popular government: *Essays on Practical Politics*, pp. 16–20.——(*c*) No system of nomination can make citizens do their duty.

IV. The true remedy for the existing evil of bad nominations is not an abandonment of the caucus system but in reform: *Nation*, VIII., 87.——(*a*) Civil service reform.—(1) The overthrow of the spoils system will remove the chief incentive to machine management of caucuses: R. H. Dana in *Forum*, II., 496 (January, 1887).——(*b*) Introduction of state regulation of caucuses: *Penn Monthly*, XII., 183–185 (March, 1881); *Massachusetts Acts, 1888*, Chap. 441; *1889*, Chap. 413, Sec. 3; *1892*, Chap. 416; *Lalor's Cyclopædia*, I., 363, 364.——(*c*) Education of the voter.

XII.

THE CHOICE OF PRESIDENTIAL ELECTORS.

QUESTION: '*Resolved*, That presidential electors should be chosen by districts instead of on a general ticket.'

Brief for the Affirmative.

GENERAL REFERENCES: *International Review*, V., 198 (March, 1878); C. A. O'Neil, *The American Electoral System*, Chaps. viii., ix., xix., i., ii.; D. A. McKnight, *The Electoral System of the United States;* Edward Stanwood, *History of Presidential Elections*, Chap. i.; A. B. Hart, *Practical Essays on American Government*, pp. 67–71; *Lalor's Cyclopædia*, II., 66–67; Thos. H. Benton, *Thirty Years' View*, II., 628; James Bryce, *The American Commonwealth*, I., 40–45; *Forum*, XII., 702 (February, 1892); *Atlantic Monthly*, XLII., 543 (November, 1878); *Nation*, LII., 421–422 (May 21, 1891).

I. 'At the present day the American people are confronted with the fact that the weakest point in their whole plan of government is the mode of choosing a President.'

II. The present system is contrary to the principles of American institutions.——(*a*) It defeats the purpose of the framers of the Constitution.—(1) The electoral college is not a deliberative body.—(2) The electors do not exercise an independent choice, but simply register the votes of the people for two or three candidates.——(*b*) It gives a preponderating influence to the large states.—(1) The vote of New York is essential to the election of any candidate.——(*c*) It does not represent the will of the majority.—(1) The electoral vote has varied as much as forty per cent. from the popular vote.

—(2) In case the election is thrown into the House a few unimportant states are able to decide the result.

III. The general ticket system gives rise to great evils.——(*a*) It lessens political interest in 'sure' states.—(1) Pennsylvania.—(2) The solid South.——(*b*) The importance of carrying the larger doubtful states gives rise to much fraud and corruption.—(1) Indiana in 1888.

IV. The district system is practicable.——(*a*) It is constitutional.—(1) By decision of the Supreme Court: McPherson *v.* Blacker, 146 *U. S.*, 1.——(*b*) It was advocated by the ablest men in the Constitutional Convention.——(*c*) It has been in use at various times in various states.

V. The district system is desirable.——(*a*) It would decrease sectional feeling.—(1) There could be no solid South. ——(*b*) Local corruption and local issues could influence only one section and not the whole state.——(*c*) It would increase political activity by encouraging parties to exert their whole strength.——(*d*) It would decrease the bitterness of disputed elections by involving but one vote instead of the vote of a whole state.——(*e*) It would do away with gigantic bribery and corruption by withdrawing the necessity for carrying a whole state.——(*f*) It would encourage independent action, and thus by strengthening third parties would approach nearer the intention of the framers of the Constitution.——(*g*) It would represent very nearly the wishes of the majority of the people.

Brief for the Negative.

GENERAL REFERENCES: *International Review*, V., 201–207 (March, 1878); *Century*, VII., 124 (November, 1884); *North American Review*, Vol. 140, pp. 124–128 (February, 1885); J. Story, *Commentaries on the Constitution*, §§ 1453–1460; *American Law Review*, XII., 1 (October, 1877).

I. There are no serious objections to the present system. ——(*a*) It is consistent with the purpose of the framers of the Constitution to avoid too great centralization: *Century*, VII., 124–127.—(1) They wished to guard against popular elections.—(2) The President was to be elected by delegates chosen by states.—(3) A majority vote of the people was not considered essential.——(*b*) Such fraud and corruption as exist are due to the spoils system and are not inherent in general elections.—(1) The evils can be remedied by civil service reform: *International Review*, V., 205–206.

II. The district system is open to grave objections.——(*a*) By encouraging third parties it would make a majority vote difficult and the election would be thrown into the House of Representatives: *Century*, VII., 132.——(*b*) It would result in the uncertainties of popular government by making the President and the House always of the same party.——(*c*) The vote of a state might be lost by being neutralized.—— (*d*) It would result in a greater number of contested elections. ——(*e*) It would encourage fraud and corruption.—(1) By gerrymandering.—(2) Local corruption could carry one district while under the present system it cannot influence the vote of the whole state.——(*f*) The district system has been in use, but has gradually been abandoned for the present system.

XIII.

POPULAR ELECTION OF SENATORS.

QUESTION: '*Resolved*, That a constitutional amendment should be secured by which senators shall be elected by direct vote of the people.'

Brief for the Affirmative.

GENERAL REFERENCES: *Johns Hopkins University Studies*, XI., 547; *Atlantic Monthly*, LXVIII., 227 (August, 1891); *Arena*, X., 453 (September, 1894); *Nation*, LIV., 44 (January 21, 1892); *Congressional Record*, 1891–1892, pp. 76–80 (December 17, 1891); 1891–1892, pp. 1267–1271 (February 18, 1892), 6060–6681 (July 12, 1892); *Public Opinion*, XII., 500 (February 20, 1892), 524 (February 27, 1892); XIV., 391 (January 28, 1893); XV., 46 (April 15, 1893); *House Reports*, 1891–1892, No. 368.

I. The reasons for electing senators by legislatures no longer exist.——(*a*) The distrust of popular elections has been shown to be unwarranted.——(*b*) There is no longer a distrust of the central government.——(*c*) The general movement toward political liberty has produced changed conditions.

II. The people wish the reform: *Public Opinion*, XIV., 392.——(*a*) A resolution in favor of the proposed change has been twice passed by the House.——(*b*) The legislatures of thirteen states have declared for it: *Arena*, X., 457.——(*c*) The people are opposed to indirect elections on principle.— (1) Shown by our experience with presidential electors.— (*d*) The present workings are not in accord with the intentions of the framers.——(*e*) The wishes of the people are ignored.

III. Popular election would improve the character of the Senate.——(*a*) It would remove the present abuses.—(1) Senators would no longer be dependent on political machines. —(2) The Senate would cease to be the field for party manipulation: *Nation*, LIV., 45.—(3) States would be able to reward distinguished men.—(4) The distrust of the Senate would be removed.—(5) Able senators would not be compelled to resort to jobbery to secure re-election.—(6) Bribery would be much more difficult.—(x) The small number of legislators is conducive to bribery.—(7) Senators are now chosen by a majority of the caucus which represents but a small part of the total voters.——(*b*) It would bring to the Senate all the able men now there.—(1) Most of the best men in the Senate have served in offices to which they were elected by popular vote.——(*c*) The conservative character of the Senate would not be lost.—(1) This is due to the long tenure of office and small number of senators: James Bryce, *The American Commonwealth*, I., 112.

IV. Popular election would improve the character of state and local governments: *Nation*, LIV., 45.——(*a*) Local elections are influenced by national issues.—(1) Both the candidates and the people are diverted from vital state issues.—(2) A man may be opposed to the candidate for the legislature and yet be compelled to vote for him on account of his vote for senator.——(*b*) Inferior legislators are chosen.——(*c*) Counties which the dominant party does not control are disfranchised.——(*d*) States are often represented in the Senate by men who do not stand for the abiding convictions of a majority of the people.—(1) The minority may get control of the legislature.—(2) The minority on national issues may be the majority on state issues.

Brief for the Negative.

GENERAL REFERENCES: James Bryce, *The American Commonwealth*, I., Chap. xii.; Senator Hoar in *Forum*, XVIII., 270 (November, 1894); *Congressional Record*, 1891-1892, pp. 3191-3204 (April 12, 1892); 1893. pp. 101-110 (April 7, 1893); *Elliot's Debates*, V., 166-170; J. Story, *Commentaries on the Constitution*, §§ 703-705; *The Federalist*, No. lxii.; *Public Opinion*, XII., 524 (February 27, 1892); XV., 46 (April 15, 1893).

I. The present system of electing senators is wisely conceived.——(*a*) The best legislatures consist of two houses chosen in a different manner.—(1) Both the radical and the conservative tendencies of a nation are most thoroughly represented thus.—(2) Unless the two bodies are chosen in a different way the upper house will not have independent force.——(*b*) The present system gives national representation to the state governments as such.—(1) The legislature is the most fit representative of the state.——(*c*) The present system unites the federal and state governments in mutual support.——(*d*) It checks the tendency toward centralization.

II. The present system has worked well.——(*a*) The Senate has fulfilled the purpose of its founders.—(1) Composed of able men.—(2) Dignified and orderly.—(3) Conservative. ——(*b*) It has proved to be the best upper house in existence.——(*c*) It has more than once checked dangerous political tendencies and arrested vicious legislation on the part of the House of Representatives.——(*d*) It has been widely copied.—(1) By the Southern Confederacy.—(2) By Switzerland.—(3) By Germany.—(4) By the South American republics.

III. The change would be unfavorable to good government. ——(*a*) It would disturb the whole scheme of the national Constitution as designed and adopted by the framers.—(1) This part was adopted unanimously: J. Story, *Commentaries on the Constitution*, § 703.——(*b*) It would transfer the power in the states, now evenly distributed, to the cities and centres of population.——(*c*) It would weaken the union of the state and national governments.——(*d*) It would substitute pluralities for majorities in voting.——(*e*) It would absolve the larger states from the constitutional obligation not to deprive the small states of equal representation in the Senate.— (1) The states never consented to an equality in a differently chosen body.

IV. It would lower the character of the Senate.——(*a*) It would transfer the election of senators to the nominating conventions of the parties which have no personal responsibility, and which do not represent public opinion.——(*b*) It would do away with the probability of re-election which is so desirable.—(1) The people seldom re elect.——(*c*) It would offer more inducement for fraud.—(1) More power given to the machines.—(2) Voting in the legislatures makes voting public and thus prevents bribery and the misrepresentation of constituencies.——(*d*) It would reduce senators to the character of state governors.

XIV.

DISTRICT ELECTION OF CONGRESSMEN.

QUESTION: '*Resolved,* That it would greatly improve public service if members of Congress were elected from any district in their own state.'

Brief for the Affirmative.

GENERAL REFERENCES: James Bryce, *The American Commonwealth*, I., 189; *Journal of Statistical Society*, XLIV., 141 (June, 1881); J. Story, *Commentaries on the Constitution*, I., § 619.

I. The present system is imperfect.——(*a*) Inferior men are elected to Congress.—(1) Country districts and sparsely populated districts are unable to educate men to a high standard of statesmanship: *The American Commonwealth*, I., 193. ——(*b*) Many men of marked ability are unable to follow a political career.—(1) Men of ability are generally collected in the great cities.——(*c*) Continuous political careers are almost impossible.—(1) Seats are lost through sudden fluctuations of opinion or by the scheming of wire-pullers.——(*d*) Good legislation is defeated by making the representative too dependent on his constituents: *The American Commonwealth*, I., 195–196.

II. The change would be beneficial.——(*a*) It would do away with the evils of gerrymandering.——(*b*) It would destroy dependence on party machines and the giving of party patronage.——(*c*) It would encourage independence of thought and improve legislation by returning men of greater ability.

III. The proposed change is constitutional and practical. ——(*a*) The Constitution requires residence only in the state: *Constitution of the United States*, Art. I., Sec. 2, § 2.

——(*b*) The system has been highly successful in England.—— (1) The interests of a district are as carefully watched by a non-resident representative as by a resident representative: *The American Commonwealth*, I., 190.—(2) It insures continuous career to statesmen of marked ability and results in more effective legislation.

Brief for the Negative.

GENERAL REFERENCE: James Bryce, *The American Commonwealth*, I., 190.

I. The proposed system of electing representatives would not be practical.——(*a*) Reasons for the English practice do not exist in this country.——(*b*) The present system of electing representatives is natural to a free country where local government is fully developed: *The American Commonwealth*, I., 192.——(*c*) Non-resident congressmen could not be elected even if nominated.—(1) Local pride would be insulted by the slur implied in the election of a man from outside the district.

II. The present system best represents the interests of the districts.——(*a*) The representative has a more exact knowledge of the needs of his district.——(*b*) He is in closer sympathy with his constituents and is familiar with local sentiment.——(*c*) His statements have more weight in Congress.

XV.

CABINET AND CONGRESSIONAL GOVERNMENTS.

QUESTION: '*Resolved*, That the cabinet system of government is preferable to the congressional system.'

Brief for the Affirmative.

GENERAL REFERENCES: Walter Bagehot, *The English Constitution*, Chaps. i., ii.; James Bryce, *The American Common-*

wealth, I., Chaps. xv., xvi., xxv. ; Woodrow Wilson, *Congressional Government; International Review*, IV., 230 (March, 1877); *Atlantic Monthly*, LVII., 542 (April, 1886); *North American Review*, Vol. 118, p. 1 (January, 1874); *Contemporary Review*, XLVIII., 864 (December, 1885); *Overland Monthly*, III., 17 (January, 1884).

I. The cabinet system of government better insures the fulfilment of party pledges.——(*a*) Members are elected on a definite programme.——(*b*) Responsibility is at once located: H. D. Traill, *Central Government*, pp. 26–27.——(*c*) Tenure of office depends on the will of the people.

II. The cabinet system insures more intelligent legislation. ——(*a*) It makes the whole legislature a great deliberative body.—(1) By subjecting all measures to free discussion.—— (*b*) It intrusts the reins of government to the ablest men.—— (*c*) Through an effective opposition a thorough examination of all measures is assured.——(*d*) Local legislation is avoided.— (1) The government is responsible to the whole nation.—— (*e*) Legislation is open and non-secret.——(*f*) All measures are formulated by skilled hands.

III. The cabinet system insures more systematic legislation. ——(*a*) All important bills come from the government and are the result of a fixed policy.——(*b*) Private bills must receive the sanction of the ministers to pass: *The American Commonwealth*, I., 164.

IV. The cabinet system instructs public opinion.——(*a*) The debates are widely read and carefully considered by the country at large.—(1) The failure or success of the government rests on the vindication of their measures.

V. The cabinet system increases the efficiency of the executive.——(*a*) By giving greater harmony between the legislative and executive branches.——(*b*) By throwing light on the smallest details of administration.——(*c*) By forming legislation with an intimate knowledge of the needs of administration.

Brief for the Negative.

GENERAL REFERENCES: A. Lawrence Lowell, *Essays on Government*, i. ; Henry Sidgwick, *The Elements of Politics*, Chap. xxii. ; Freeman Snow in *American Historical Association Papers*, IV., 109 (July, 1890); *Annals of American Academy of Political Science*, III., 1 (July, 1892), 306 (November, 1892) ; J. I. C. Hare, *American Constitutional Law*, I., Lecture x. ; *The Federalist*, No. li.

I. The cabinet system causes instability of government.——(*a*) Under this system momentary impulses of the people find ready response in legislative enactment.——(*b*) Any breeze of popular disfavor may overturn the government.——(*c*) Socialistic and communistic schemes find insufficient check.——(*d*) The influence of demagogues is effective.

II. The cabinet system causes dangerous concentration of power.——(*a*) The whole authority of government is vested in one house and practically in a few men.—(1) The majority have control of the fundamental as well as the ordinary law of the state.—(2) The authority of the executive is reduced to nothing.—(3) The legislative branch is made omnipotent.—(4) There are no checks or balances.

III. The cabinet system tends toward a superficial administration of affairs.——(*a*) Ministers cannot give adequate attention to both legislative and administrative business.——(*b*) Ministers are likely to be chosen for tact and oratorical ability rather than for especial administrative fitness: H. Sidgwick, *The Elements of Politics*, p. 423.——(*c*) Ministers are compelled to spend, in keeping a working majority together, time which ought to be devoted to transacting business.

IV. The congressional system of government gives great stability.——(*a*) It furnishes pre-eminently a government of law and not one of popular impulse.—(1) By preventing legislation from being the result of temporary opinion, over-excitement, or heated controversy, and by making it the result of mature and lasting opinion, careful consideration, and thorough revision.—(x) There is a complete system of checks and balances.—(y) There is complete separation of the different functions.

V. The congressional system represents the popular will in the best way.——(a) It presents safeguards against demagogism.——(b) It prevents the oppression of the minority by the majority.——(c) It distributes responsibility.——(d) It develops a great number of individual thinkers and trains many men in the functions of government.——(e) It is at once more conservative and more democratic.

XVI.

CABINET MINISTERS IN CONGRESS.

QUESTION: '*Resolved*, That cabinet ministers ought to have seats and the right to speak in Congress.'

Brief for the Affirmative.

GENERAL REFERENCES: Woodrow Wilson, *Congressional Government*, Chap. v.; Walter Bagehot, *The English Constitution*, Chap. i.; Gamaliel Bradford, *The Practical Working of our Government*; H. C. Lockwood, *The Abolition of the Presidency*, Chap. x.; J. Story, *Commentaries on the Constitution*, §§ 869–872; *Annals of American Academy of Political Science*, II., 289 (November, 1891); IV., 404 (November, 1893); *Congressional Globe*, 1864–1865, pp. 419–420 (January 25, 1865), pp. 444–446 (January 26, 1865); *Congressional Record*, 1878–1879, pp. 966–971 (April 28, 1879); *House Reports*, 1863–1864, No. 43; *Senate Reports*, 1880–1881, No. 837; *Atlantic Monthly*, L., 95 (July,

1882); LVII., 542 (April, 1886); LXV., 771–772 (June, 1890); *North American Review*, Vol. 111, p. 330 (October, 1870); *Overland Monthly*, III., 17 (January, 1884); IX., 209 (February, 1887); *International Review*, VII., 146 (August, 1879); *Nation*, XXVIII., 243 (April 10, 1879); XXXII., 107 (February 17, 1881); XLVI., 279 (April 5, 1888).

I. The present system is inadequate.——(*a*) There is want of confidence and co-operation between the cabinet and the government.——(*b*) Legislation is carried on without regard to the necessities of administration.——(*c*) It is impossible to locate responsibility.——(*d*) Congress makes incessant exactions which interfere with departmental business.

II. The proposed change would improve legislation.——(*a*) It would enable Congress to understand better the needs of the country.—(1) Congress would have the constant advice of the secretaries for guidance.——(*b*) It would facilitate the transaction of business.—(1) By removing the necessity of requiring written statements from the heads of departments.—— (*c*) It would insure national instead of sectional legislation. ——(*d*) It would insure a better discussion of measures.—(1) In the House, from an efficient opposition.—(2) Outside, from the fact that a speech by a secretary would be reported and read.——(*e*) It would make legislation continuous.—— (*f*) It would fix responsibility.

III. The change would improve administration.——(*a*) Legislation would be shaped to meet the demands of administration.——(*b*) The personnel of the cabinet would be much improved.—(1) Men would be chosen on the ground of capabilities and past records rather than for political or local considerations.—(x) It would be to the interest of the President to have as able a body as possible to present his views.

IV. The change is practicable.——(*a*) It is constitutional. ——(*b*) It is supported by precedent: *Senate Reports*, 1880–1881, No. 837, pp. 3–4.——(*c*) Favored by our best statesmen: *Senate Reports*, 1880–1881, No. 837.——(*d*) It avoids the evils of European ministries.——(1) The cabinet would not be dependent on Congress for their positions.——(c) It would not establish a 'responsible government.'

Brief for the Negative.

GENERAL REFERENCES: A. Lawrence Lowell, *Essays on Government*, i.; Freeman Snow in *Annals of American Academy of Political Science*, III., 1 (July, 1892); Freeman Snow in *American Historical Association Papers*, IV., 109 (July, 1890); *Congressional Globe*, 1864–1865, pp. 421–424 (January 25, 1865), pp. 437–448 (January 26, 1865); *Congressional Record*, 1878–1879, pp. 971–974 (April 28, 1879); *Atlantic Monthly*, LVII., 180 (February, 1886); *North American Review*, Vol. 124, p. 21 (January, 1877); *Nation*, XVI., 233 (April 3, 1873); J. I. C. Hare, *American Constitutional Law*, I., 176–181.

I. The change is unnecessary.——(a) The Constitution secures as much harmony between the departments as is consistent with their independence.——(b) Congressional legislation has on the whole been effective.——(c) Congress is gradually working out a system much better adapted to our form of government.——(d) The defects in the present system are not inherent.

II. Legislation would not be improved.——(a) The cabinet would not be able to direct legislation.——(b) Responsibility would not be centralized.——(1) Private members could introduce conflicting bills.——(2) The cabinet could introduce unpopular measures through private members.——(c) Responsibility would not be felt.——(1) No penalty for bad measures. ——(d) Uniformity would not be secured.——(1) For uniformity the cabinet officers would have to be united in policy which could only happen if the whole cabinet was responsible for the acts of each member.——(e) The committee system would continue to rule.

III. Information about the affairs of departments would not be more available.——(*a*) Cabinet officers would be under no compulsion to impart their knowledge.——(*b*) They could not be expected to furnish detailed information off-hand.——(*c*) They would not be listened to when advocating measures repugnant to Congress.——(*d*) Written reports furnish better basis for sound legislation.—(1) Poor speakers would fail to give clear expositions, while good speakers could mislead.

IV. Positive harm would result.——(*a*) The business of the departments would suffer.—(1) If the President should appoint men for parliamentary ability the executive work would suffer.—(2) If men were appointed for their administrative power the departments would suffer from weak representation in Congress.—(3) Members of the cabinet have work enough to do as it is.——(*b*) Serious complications would arise.—(1) When the President and either House were of different political parties.—(2) When the conduct of the cabinet became objectionable to Congress, but was sanctioned by the President.——(*c*) Party dissensions would result.—— (*d*) It would lower the dignity of the President and the cabinet.—(1) They would be the objects of badgering, criticism, and personal attacks.——(*e*) It would have a demoralizing influence on members.—(1) Great temptation for the President to use political offices to further his measures.

V. The change is contrary to the spirit of our government. ——(*a*) The executive was not intended to be allied to Congress, but to be a check or balance.——(*b*) The cabinet was intended to furnish advisers to the President and not to become a party machine.——(*c*) It is fundamental in a democracy that the people should move the government and not that any body of men should control legislation.

XVII.

CIVIL SERVICE REFORM.

QUESTION: '*Resolved*, That the Civil Service Act should be extended to all departments of the government service.'

Brief for the Affirmative.

GENERAL REFERENCES: *Report of the United States Civil Service Commission*, 1886-1887, pp. 120-143; *Senate Reports*, 1881-1882, No. 576; *Atlantic Monthly*, LXV., 433 (April, 1890), 671 (May, 1890); James Bryce, *The American Commonwealth*, II., Chap. lxv.; *Lalor's Cyclopædia*, I., 478; III., 895; *Forum*, XIV., 201, 216 (October, 1892); L. G. Tyler, *Parties and Patronage*; G. W. Curtis, 'Party and Patronage,' in *Orations and Addresses*, II., 477; A. B. Hart, *Practical Essays on American Government*, p. 81; H. C. Lodge, 'Why Patronage in Office is Un-American,' in *Historical and Political Essays*, p. 114; *Political Science Quarterly*, III., 247 (June, 1888); *Good Government*, XII., 131 (May 15, 1893); XIV., 75 (December 15, 1894).

I. Rotation in office is the sole cause of the spoils system: *The American Commonwealth*, II., Chap. lxv.; *Lalor's Cyclopædia*, III., 782.——(*a*) Politics are followed simply for the money remuneration which is sure to come with party success.——(*b*) The spoils system has created the professional politician and the local boss, who have been able by the bestowal of political patronage to build up party machines.

II. The spoils system is a menace to our form of government: *Senate Reports*, 1881-1882, No. 576, pp. iii.-iv.—— (*a*) It is able to corrupt legislation: *Report of the United States Civil Service Commission*, 1886-1887, pp. 125-127.—— (1) The President can influence legislation by withholding patronage: *Good Government*, XII., 53 (November 15, 1892). —(2) Members of Congress are hampered by the dictates of machine bosses who have helped to elect them.——(*b*) It consumes valuable time of the President and of congressmen: *Senate Reports*, 1881–1882, No. 576, pp. ii.–iii.——(*c*) The interests of the government and of the people are made subordinate to the success of party.

III. The Civil Service Act has accomplished good results: *Atlantic Monthly*, LXXV., 239 (February, 1895).——(*a*) It has helped to do away with the evil of the spoils system.—(1) Fifty thousand offices have been removed from political patronage: *Report of the United States Civil Service Commission*, 1894, p. 120.—(2) These fifty thousand include the most important offices, and the salaries constitute half the amount, of the whole civil service: *The American Commonwealth*, II., 120.——(*b*) It has raised the standard of the civil service.— (1) Efficient men are chosen.—(2) A continuous career enables men to become more valuable.—(3) It is considered an honor to hold office under the present system.——(*c*) It has been a great saving to the government.

IV. There is no reason why the present system should not be extended.——(*a*) The Civil Service Commission has discharged its duties faithfully: *House Reports*, 1889–1890, No. 2445.—(1) Mistakes and frauds are bound to occur in such an extensive system of examinations.—(2) Complaints are generally attributable to disappointed candidates.—(3) The examinations have been sensible and fair.—(4) There have been few removals, and none for partisan reasons.——(*b*) The commission has had sufficient experience to be able to deal with greater numbers.——(*c*) Many branches of the civil service are proper subjects for classification under the law.—(1) The internal revenue service.—(2) The government printing office.—(3) Employees of navy yards, armories, arsenals.— (4) Light-house service: *Report of the United States Civil Service Commission*, 1874, pp. 26–27.

Brief for the Negative.

GENERAL REFERENCES: *Senate Reports*, 1887-1888, No. 2373, pp. 46-47; *House Reports*, 1885-1886, No. 1001; *North American Review*, Vol. 132, p. 305 (April, 1881).

I. The civil service law is not in accordance with the principles of American institutions.——(*a*) It is unconstitutional: *Constitution of the United States*, Art. II., Sec. 2; *Congressional Record*, 1882-1883, p. 470 (December 20, 1882).—(1) It puts the power of appointment, given to the President, in the hands of a separate board.——(*b*) It tends to destroy the advantages of party government: *House Reports*, 1885-1886, No. 1001.—(1) It removes responsibility from the President and the party and places it on a non-partisan board.—(2) Success of party policy requires that subordinates should be in sympathy with superiors.—(3) Continued and uninterrupted holding of office is sure to result in corruption. ——(*c*) It tends toward a permanent office-holding community.—(1) The present system is borrowed from England, and is consonant with a monarchy.—(2) Public office should not be held as a right by a special class, but should belong to the public.

II. The civil service law is unnecessary for purifying the civil service.——(*a*) If the President and cabinet find that they can better perform the trusts confided to them by the retention of those holding offices in the various departments they have the power to do so without this law.

III. The present law is unjust: *House Reports*, 1885-1886, No. 1001, p. 2.——(*a*) Persons over the age of forty-five are barred from examinations.——(*b*) A great majority of the people are unable to attend the examinations.—(1) Examinations are held in a few cities, at appointed times, and usually last only a day or two.

IV. The law has worked badly.——(*a*) It has not accomplished the promised reforms: *Senate Reports*, 1887-1888, No. 2373. pp. 46-47.—(1) Partisan changes have been made.

—(2) Federal officials have participated in political conventions and have used their official influence.—(3) The system of levying tolls for political purposes has continued.——(*b*) The states are unequally represented: *House Reports*, 1885–1886, No. 1001, p. 2.—(1) Maryland has one person in the service for every thirty-five hundred inhabitants.—(2) Texas has one for every twenty-five thousand.

XVIII.

THE ENGLISH SYSTEM OF PREVENTING ELECTION FRAUDS.

QUESTION: '*Resolved*, That the English system for the prevention of bribery and corruption at elections ought to be adopted in the United States.'

Brief for the Affirmative.

GENERAL REFERENCES: C. K. Cooke, *A Handy Book for Electors*; F. J. Stimson, *The Methods of Bribery and its Prevention at our National Elections*; *Forum*, XV., 129, 148 (April, 1893); *Century*, XLIV., 940 (October, 1892); XLVI., 150 (May, 1893); XLVII., 144, 149 (November, 1893), 781 (March, 1894); *North American Review*, Vol. 146, p. 21 (January, 1888); Vol. 148, p. 82 (January, 1889); *Nineteenth Century*, XV., 123 (January, 1884); *New Englander*, L., 309 (May, 1889); LIII., 505 (December, 1890); *Nation*, XXXIX., 303 (October 9, 1884); XLIII., 386 (November 11, 1886); *Overland Monthly*, (second series), V., 269 (March, 1885); *American Law Review*, XXVII., 345 (May, 1893).

I. There is urgent need for reform of the election abuses of this country.——(*a*) Corruption is the great danger of democracies.—(1) It imperils self-government.—(2) Vitiates the minds of the people.—(3) Raises up demagogues and perpetuates machine rule.——(*b*) Bribery and corruption are common in this country: *The Methods of Bribery and its Prevention at our National Elections,* pp. 7–18; *Century,* XLIV., 942–946.——(*c*) Bribery and corruption are especially potent in our political system.—(1) Certain small localities hold the balance of power.

II. The English system for the prevention of these abuses is the best yet devised.——(*a*) Its provisions are wise.—(1) Prohibits bribery and treating: *A Handy Book for Electors,* p. 8.—(2) Prevents undue influence being used to secure votes.—(3) Prohibits personation.—(4) Prohibits illegal practices.—(x) Hiring conveyances.—(y) Advertising or placarding.—(z) Hiring halls or buildings.—(5) Compels a full account of all election expenses: *A Handy Book for Electors,* p. 41.——(*b*) Its punishments are severe: *Forum,* XV., 136.——(*c*) Its success has been undoubted: *Forum,* XV., 141.—(1) Corrupt practices have almost ceased to exist. —(2) No single member has been unseated for bribery.—(3) An undesirable class has been removed from politics.

III. The English system should be adopted in this country. ——(*a*) No difficulty in applying the act.——(*b*) Corruption would in a great part be stopped.——(*c*) Elections would be purified.——(*d*) Better representatives would be secured.— (1) Poor men of ability would have more chance.—(2) A man's subscription to the campaign fund would not be so influential.——(*e*) The power of bosses would be diminished. ——(*f*) The will of the people would be more likely to be carried out.

Brief for the Negative.

GENERAL REFERENCES: C. K. Cooke, *A Handy Book for Electors;* James Bryce, *The American Commonwealth,* II., Chap. lxiv.: Josiah Quincy in *Forum,* XV., 142 (April, 1893); *Century,* XLIV., 950 (October, 1892); XLVII., 788–789 (March, 1894); *National Review,* II., 189 (October, 1883); *Saturday Review,* LVI., 489 (October 20, 1883).

I. The English system is faulty.——(*a*) It is cumbersome.—(1) Great number of small technical points which have to be observed.——(*b*) Its penalties are too severe.—(1) An election may be invalidated by a slight mistake.—(2) The candidate is made answerable for the wrongs of persons acting without his knowledge and contrary to his wishes.

II. The English system is not adaptable to this country. ——(*a*) The conditions are different.—(1) In England each campaign is separate and not confused with others.—(2) Each campaign is managed by the candidate or his agent, who can easily be held responsible for its conduct.—(3) In this country ten or twenty candidates may run on the same ticket and none of them have anything to do with the conduct of the campaign or its expenses.—(4) In this country elections come so frequently as to make the English system with its complicated mechanism unpracticable.——(*b*) The law would fail in this country if for no other reason than that it is not backed by public opinion.—(1) Public opinion not ready for so stringent an act.

III. Reform of election abuses can be better accomplished by separate measures on the part of the several states.——(*a*) Different localities need different treatment.—(1) Bribery is only sporadic: *The American Commonwealth*, II., 146.— (2) The methods of corruption vary in different parts of the country.——(*b*) A general enactment by Congress would be of doubtful constitutionality.—(1) The method of electing representatives belongs by right to the states: *Constitution of the United States*, Art. I., Sec. 4.

XIX.

THE EXECUTIVE POWER OF THE MAYOR IN CITIES.

QUESTION: '*Resolved*, That all executive duties in American cities should be concentrated in the hands of the mayor, and that his appointments should not require confirmation.'

Brief for the Affirmative.

GENERAL REFERENCES: Seth Low, *The Problem of Municipal Government in the United States*, pp. 13–19; A. P. Wilder, *The Municipal Problem*, Chap. v.; F. J. Parker, *A Study of Municipal Government in Massachusetts*, pp. 16–24; James Bryce, *The American Commonwealth*, I., Chaps. l., li., lii.; *Scribner's Magazine*, II., 485 (October, 1887); *North American Review*, Vol. 153, p. 587 (November, 1891); *Forum*, III., 170 (April, 1887); *Nation*, XIII., 333 (November 23, 1871).

I. Municipal government in the United States has proved a failure: *The American Commonwealth*, I., Chap. li.; *Lalor's Cyclopædia*, I., 463.——(*a*) Shown by the political rings and great corruption in New York, Philadelphia, Chicago, San Francisco.——(*b*) Inefficiency in the administration of city interests.—(1) Poor streets.—(2) Poor sanitary regulation. ——(*c*) Bonded debts of American cities have risen from one hundred millions in 1860 to seven hundred millions in 1890: *Lalor's Cyclopædia*, I., 465.

II. The failure has been due in part to the division of the executive power between the mayor and the council.——(*a*) Speedy action and effective enforcement of the law is impossible through the deliberations of a large council. ——(*b*) Corruption is encouraged, as it is impossible to fix the blame for failure to carry out the law.

III. It has been partly due to the division of the appointing power.——(*a*) Inefficient men are appointed.—(1) Council is obliged to compromise on mediocre men.—(2) Lack of responsibility encourages carelessness in appointments.——(*b*) Corruption is encouraged.—(1) Deals are often made between the mayor and the council: *The Problem of Municipal Government in the United States*, p. 14.—(2) Blame for the appointments of vicious men cannot be fixed.——(*c*) Political machines and rings are built up by allowing too many men to have a part in the act of confirming appointments: *Nation*, XIII., 333.

IV. The remedy lies in placing all executive power and full appointing power in the hands of the mayor: *The American Commonwealth*, I., 654–664.——(*a*) It would fix responsibility for corruption and for slack execution of the laws on the mayor, and the people could readily overthrow the administration.——(*b*) It would call better men to the office of mayor.—(1) The office heretofore has been a mere figurehead.—(2) The increased importance of the office would sober the judgment of mayors.——(*c*) It would cause the people to take a more lively interest in municipal affairs: *The American Commonwealth*, I., 657.—(1) They would exercise more care in the election of such a powerful official.——(*d*) The remedy has been successful.—(1) Case of Brooklyn.

Brief for the Negative.

GENERAL REFERENCES: James Bryce, *The American Commonwealth*, I., Chap. i., 50; C. W. Eliot in *Forum*, XII., 165 (October, 1891); *North American Review*, Vol. 153, p. 580 (November, 1891).

I. The plan suggested would be contrary to American principles of democratic government.——(*a*) The city is a political as well as a business corporation, and political methods should not be sacrificed to the management of the city as a corporation.——(*b*) It has no analogy to our national or state governments.

II. The plan would not accomplish the results hoped for. ——(*a*) Danger of the rejection of good nominations is not greater than that resulting from hasty or ill-advised appointments.——(*b*) The evils which beset city governments would still exist.—(1) State interference.—(2) The spoils system.— (3) The apathy of citizens.——(*c*) It would destroy continuity of policy.—(1) Officials would change with the mayor.

—— (*d*) The chief cause of failure, viz., inefficiency of officials, would not be removed: *Forum*, XII., 165.

III. The plan would give rise to great evils.—— (*a*) Absolute power of appointment and of executive would place too much power in the hands of one man.—— (*b*) The temptation and opportunity for corrupt rings to secure the office would be increased.—— (*c*) The mayor would have every opportunity to work for his re-election.

IV. Remedies have been found which do not expose cities to such great danger.—— (*a*) St. Louis and other cities of Missouri are successfully administered under governments modelled on the national government: *The American Commonwealth*, I., 633.

INSTITUTIONS.

XX.

DANGER TO FREE INSTITUTIONS IN THE UNITED STATES.

QUESTION: '*Resolved*, That free institutions in the United States are now in danger.'

Brief for the Affirmative.

GENERAL REFERENCES: James B. Weaver, *A Call to Action*; Theodore Roosevelt, *Essays on Practical Politics*; E. D. Mead. *The Roman Catholic Church and the Public Schools; Forum*, V., 16 (March, 1888); VII., 235 (May, 1889); XV., 261 (May, 1893); *Century*, XLIV., 940 (October, 1892); *Nation*, LVII., 4 (July 6, 1893); Testimony before Lexow Committee, in *New-York Tribune* (March 9 to April 14, May 22 to June 30, September 10 to November 4, 1894).

I. The rights of the individual are in danger.—— (*a*) Suppression of the vote: A. B. Hart, *Practical Essays on American Government*, p. 32.—— (*b*) Lynchings in the South.——

(c) Oppression by authorities.——(1) Testimony brought out by the Lexow Committee.——(d) Justice tampered with: *Ibid.*——(e) Right to earn one's living abridged.——(1) By the tyranny of labor organizations.

II. There is danger in existing social conditions.——(a) Breach between the social classes widening.——(1) Lower classes living in poverty and filled with a spirit of unrest and discontent.——(2) Upper classes living in extravagant luxury. ——(b) Hostile feeling of labor against capital.——(c) Frequent outbreaks of internecine war.——(1) Homestead.——(2) Chicago.——(3) Haverhill.——(4) Brooklyn.——(d) Increasing power of trusts and monopolies.

III. Our political institutions are in danger.——(a) Tendency toward centralization increasing and the power of the states diminishing.——(b) The best people are indifferent to public affairs.——(c) Ignorant and corrupt municipal administrations allowed to continue.——(d) Legislative bodies inefficient and ridiculous.——(e) Bad men at the head.——(f) Spoils system allowed to go on.——(g) Bribery and corruption permitted in elections.——(h) Excessive representation of ignorance.——(1) From western states.——(2) Negro voters. ——(i) Country being overrun by foreigners.——(j) Everybody absorbed in wealth-getting.

IV. The Roman Catholic Church is dangerous to free institutions.——(a) Teaches that civil laws are binding only when conformable to the rights of the church: *Forum*, XV., 262.——(b) Keeps Catholics apart from other citizens.——(1) Separate schools.——(c) Destroys individual liberty.——(d) Its power is increasing.——(1) By growth.——(2) By centralization of discipline.

Brief for the Negative.

GENERAL REFERENCES: J. R. Lowell, *Democracy and other Addresses*, pp. 1-42; C. W. Eliot, 'The Working of the American Democracy,' *Phi Beta Kappa Oration*, 1888;

James Bryce, *The American Commonwealth*, II., Chaps. lxxxvii., xcix., cxviii., cxix.; James Bryce, 'The Predictions of Hamilton and De Toqueville,' in *Johns Hopkins University Studies*, V., 329; *Forum*, V., 16 (March, 1888); XVIII., 129 (October, 1894).

I. The enormous advantages of our institutions are underrated.——(*a*) Our institutions are second to none.—(1) They unite the advantages of English institutions with greater individual freedom.—(2) Strong constitution.—(3) System of checks and balances.—(4) The Supreme Court an element of great strength.—(5) The function of the state governments will keep social problems from becoming national questions on which the country may split.

II. The danger of our institutions is greatly magnified.—— (*a*) Greater dangers have been met in the past and overcome. —(1) Shay's rebellion.—(2) Whiskey rebellion.—(3) Slavery and the civil war.——(*b*) There is no danger from Roman Catholic Church.—(1) Improbable that an occasion will ever arise in which the church will be opposed to the welfare of the state.—(2) If such an occasion should arise Catholics would be found on the side of the state.——(*c*) There is no real danger in social conditions.

III. The movement toward reform is strong.——(*a*) In national affairs.—(1) Civil service reform making rapid headway.—(2) Ballot reform.——(*b*) In state affairs.—(1) Machines being broken up.——(*c*) In municipal affairs.—(1) Overthrow of rings.—(2) The better class of citizens are awakening to civic duty.——(*d*) Social reforms.—(1) Growing sentiment in favor of restricted emigration.—(2) Scientific charity more common.—(3) Broader educational advantages. —(4) Arbitration and conciliation used in settling labor disputes.—(5) Growing sense of responsibility on the part of the wealthier classes.

XXI.

THE JURY SYSTEM.

QUESTION : '*Resolved*, That the jury system should be abolished.'

Brief for the Affirmative.

GENERAL REFERENCES : *North American Review*, Vol. 134, p. 244 (March, 1882) ; XCII., 304–309 (April, 1861) ; Vol. 139, p. 348 (October, 1884) ; *Century*, III., 124 (November, 1882) ; IV., 302 (June, 1883) ; *Forum*, III., 102 (March, 1887) ; *Atlantic Monthly*, XLVIII., 9 (July, 1881) ; *Popular Science Monthly*, XXVI., 289 (January, 1885) ; *American Law Review*, XX., 661 (September–October, 1886) ; *Lippincott's Magazine*, IX., 334 (March, 1872) ; *Westminster Review*, XCVII., 289 (April, 1872).

I. The jury system makes justice uncertain.——(*a*) Verdicts often rest on chance : *North American Review*, Vol. 134, p. 251.——(*b*) Juries are partial.—(1) Influenced by church interests, secret society bonds, and ties of relationship.—(2) Prejudiced especially against railroad companies : *Westminster Review*, XCVII., 307.——(*c*) Juries are not capable of passing intelligently on technical and scientific points.—(1) They are made up of ignorant and inexperienced men.——(*d*) Juries are moved by sophistry and eloquence rather than by sound argument.——(*e*) Juries are easily deceived by witnesses.

II. The jury system delays justice.——(*a*) Juries very often find it impossible to agree.——(*b*) Appeals to higher courts are common.——(*c*) Mistakes due to the cumbersomeness of system are frequent.——(*d*) The impanelling of juries requires much time.

III. The trial of all cases by judges is desirable.——(*a*) Judges are chosen for their ability, intelligence, and experience.——(*b*) Judges have regard for the honor of their position, while jurors have no professional honor or dignity to sustain.——(c) The sifting of evidence needs the trained mind of judges: *Westminster Review*, XCVII., 304.——(d) If there be any wrong it is much easier to punish a judge than a jury.——(e) The legal profession would be elevated: *American Law Review*, XX., 677.

IV. The innovation would not be a great one.——(a) Many cases are now conducted without juries.—(1) Civil cases in many states: *North American Review*, Vol. 134, p. 256.—(2) Cases in equity.—(3) Cases in appellate courts.

Brief for the Negative.

GENERAL REFERENCES: William Forsyth, *Trial by Jury*, Chap. xviii.; *North American Review*, Vol. 135, p. 447 (November, 1882); Vol. 139, p. 1 (July, 1884); *Century*, IV., 299 (June, 1883); *Popular Science Monthly*, XXIV., 676 (March, 1884); *International Review*, XIV., 158 (March, 1883); *American Law Review*, XXII., 853 (November–December, 1888); *Nation*, XVI., 428 (June 26, 1873).

I. The jury is an indispensable judicial institution.——(a) Law is not a pure science and the jury system is the best means of securing substantial justice: *North American Review*, Vol. 135, p. 457.—(1) A number of ordinary people are better fitted to pass on a question of fact than a judge.—(x) Their experience is more diversified.—(y) They have a better knowledge of common people.—(z) Frequent exercise unfits a judge in this line.—(2) The awards of juries are more generally satisfactory to all concerned than those of arbitrators or referees.—(3) Juries act as checks on judges.—(4) Judges are not infallible.—(x) Their sentences are often very unjust.—(y) Lawyers pick easy judges.—(5) Judges become hardened.—(x) Police court judges.—(6) Disagreements of juries are not many in proportion to the number of cases tried.—(7) Corruption less easy than it would be if there were no juries.

II. The jury is an indispensable social institution.——(*a*) Much of the success of English civilization is due to the jury system: *North American Review*, Vol. 135, p. 448.——(*b*) The jury system prevents the encroachment of one social class on the rights of another.——(*c*) Jury practice increases good sense and sobriety of judgment.——(*d*) It spreads respect for the decisions of the law.——(*e*) It spreads the practice of equitable dealing.——(*f*) It makes men feel that they have a duty to fulfil toward society, and that they take a part in its government.

III. The jury is an indispensable political institution.—— (*a*) Men are fitted for freedom by enjoying the privileges and performing the duties of free men.——(*b*) Men are taught political wisdom and their legal rights.——(*c*) The habit of self-government is greatly encouraged.

XXII.

CAPITAL PUNISHMENT.

QUESTION: '*Resolved*, That capital punishment should be abolished.'

Brief for the Affirmative.

GENERAL REFERENCES: A. J. Palm, *The Death Penalty;* M. H. Bovee, *Reasons for Abolishing Capital Punishment;* Torjiro Mogi, *Capital Punishment;* Wendell Phillips in *North American Review*, Vol. 133, p. 550 (December, 1881); *Forum*, III., 503 (July, 1887); *Fortnightly Review*, LII., 322 (September, 1889); *North American Review*, LXII., 40 (January, 1846); Vol. 116, p. 138 (January, 1873); *Westminster Review*, XCI., 429 (April, 1869).

I. Capital punishment is inexpedient.——(*a*) It is contrary to the tendency of civilization: *The Death Penalty*, pp. 14–24.——(*b*) It fails to protect society.—(1) It does not prevent murder: *The Death Penalty*, pp. 126–129; *North*

American Review, LXII., 50.—(x) New crimes follow hard on executions: *North American Review*, LXII., 61.——(c) It makes punishment uncertain.—(1) Many criminals are acquitted who would be convicted if the penalty were imprisonment.——(d) It is not reformatory.

II. Capital punishment is immoral.——(a) It rests on the old idea of retribution.——(b) It tends to weaken the sacredness of human life.——(c) It endangers the lives of innocent people: *The Death Penalty*, pp. 66–82.——(d) Executions and the sensational newspaper accounts which follow have a corrupting influence.

III. Capital punishment is unjust.——(a) Its mistakes are irremediable.——(b) Many men are criminals from force of circumstances: *Capital Punishment*, pp. 30–32.—(1) From heredity.—(2) From environment.——(c) Inequalities in administration are marked.—(1) In some states men are hung, in others imprisoned for the same crime.—(2) Many jurors have conscientious scruples against condemning a man to death.—(3) Men of wealth and influence are rarely convicted.

IV. The abolition of capital punishment has been followed by satisfactory results: *The Death Penalty*, pp. 130–139.—— (a) In Europe.—(1) Russia.—(2) Switzerland.—(3) Portugal.—(4) Belgium.—(5) Holland.—(6) Finland.——(b) In the United States.—(1) Michigan.—(2) Rhode Island.—(3) Maine.—(4) Wisconsin.

Brief for the Negative.

GENERAL REFERENCES: G. B. Cheever, *Capital Punishment: North American Review*, Vol. 133, pp. 534–550 (December, 1881); *Forum*, III., 381 (June, 1887); *Public Opinion*, XIII., 33 (April 16, 1892); *Nation*, VIII., 166 (March 4, 1869); XVI., 193 (March 20, 1873), 213 (March 27, 1873).

I. Capital punishment is permissible.——(a) It has the sanction of the Bible.—(1) Genesis ix. 2–6: *North Ameri-*

can Review, Vol. 133, pp. 534-538. —— (*b*) It has the sanction of history.—(1) It has been in vogue since the beginning of the world.——(*c*) It has the sanction of reason.—(1) The most fitting punishment is one equal and similar to the injury inflicted.

II. Capital punishment is expedient.——(*a*) It is necessary to protect society from anarchy and private revenge.—(1) Death is the strongest preventative of crime.——(*b*) No sufficient substitute has been offered.—(1) Life imprisonment is a failure.—(x) Few serve the sentence: *Nation*, XVI., 193.——(*c*) Its abolition has not been successful.—(1) In Rhode Island.—(2) In Michigan: *Forum*, III., 388.

III. The objections made to capital punishment are not sound.——(*a*) Prisons are not reformatory: *Forum*, III., 390.——(*b*) The fact that crimes have decreased in some places where executions have stopped is not a valid argument. —(1) All causes which increase the moral well-being of the race decrease crime: *Nation*, VIII., 166.——(*c*) The objection that the innocent sometimes suffer is not strong.— (1) The number of innocent thus suffering is inconsiderable when compared with great number of murders prevented.—— (*d*) The objection that the penalty is uncertain may be overcome by making it certain.

NATIONAL POLICY (FOREIGN).

XXIII.

THE ANNEXATION OF CANADA.

QUESTION: '*Resolved*, That Canada should be annexed to the United States.'

Brief for the Affirmative.

GENERAL REFERENCES: Goldwin Smith, *Canada and the Canadian Question*, pp. 237-301; *North American Review*,

Vol. 136, p. 326 (April, 1883); Vol. 139, pp. 42–50 (July, 1884); Vol. 131, p. 14 (July, 1880); *Forum*, VI., 241 (November, 1888); *Century*, XXXVIII., 236 (June, 1889); *Contemporary Review*, XXXVIII., 821 (November, 1880); XL., 378 (September, 1881); *Public Opinion*, XIV., 349 (January 14, 1893); *Forum*, VII., 361 (June, 1889), 521 (July, 1889).

I. Annexation would be a benefit to Canada.——(a) Economically.—(1) By nature she is a part of the United States.—(2) Country at present almost inaccessible would be brought close to civilization.——(b) Politically.—(1) It would put her under a firm government.—(2) Her present government is weak and unsatisfactory.—(3) Destructive English control would be removed: *Contemporary Review*, XL., 386–398; *Forum*, VI., 249–250.——(c) Commercially.—(1) It would enlarge her market with the United States and Europe.

II. Annexation would be a benefit to the United States.——(a) It would bring to the United States inexhaustible natural resources: *North American Review*, Vol. 139, p. 42; *Handbook of Commercial Union*, pp. 73–99.—(1) Wheat lands.—(2) Forests and mines.——(b) Commercially.—(1) It would give to the United States complete control of transcontinental water routes and railroads.—(x) The mouth of the St. Lawrence River would be in the United States.—(y) The railroads that pass through Ontario would be within the United States.——(c) It would remove danger from a defenceless border.——(d) It would settle long debated quarrels.—(1) Fisheries.—(2) Escaped criminals.—(3) Customs duties.—(4) Smuggling.

III. Annexation would be easily and peacefully accomplished.——(a) No physical features act as a barrier.——(b) Parts of Canada are already tributary.—(1) Manitoba.—(2) Toronto.——(c) People of both nations have long intermingled.—(1) Canadians naturally come to the United States for work.——(d) Great Britain would not oppose the wishes of

Canada.——(c) Sentiment in favor of annexation is strong and increasing.

IV. Reciprocity would be unsuccessful.——(a) Reciprocity was tried in the Treaty of 1854–1866 and failed.

Brief for the Negative.

GENERAL REFERENCES : *Forum*, VI., 451 (January, 1889); VII. (March, 1889); IX., 562 (July, 1890); XVI., 325 (November, 1893); *North American Review*, Vol. 148, p. 665 (June, 1889); Vol. 150, p. 404 (March, 1890); Vol. 152, p. 339 (March, 1891), p. 557 (May, 1891); *Fortnightly Review*, LV., 113 (January, 1891); *Public Opinion*, VI., 214 (December 22, 1888), 323 (January 26, 1889); J. G. Bourinot, *Canada and the United States;* James Douglas, *Canadian Independence, Annexation, and British Imperial Federation,* pp. 46–109.

I. Great Britain would not consent to lose Canada : *Forum*, VI., 642 (February, 1889).——(a) London would lose control of enormous capital invested.——(b) England would lose important military and naval stations at Halifax and Esquimalt, and thereby endanger her possessions in the West Indies.——(c) It might lead to the disintegration of her empire.—(1) Since 1783 Great Britain has constantly gained territory, but given up no land of importance.

II. Canada does not want to be annexed : *Forum*, XVI., 325; *Magazine of American History*, XVI., 180 (August, 1886).——(a) The discussion of 1889–1892 has subsided as in 1849.——(b) Canada is loyal to Great Britain.—(1) Shown in plans for imperial federation.—(2) In national societies.——(c) Canada prefers her own institutions.—(1) Parliamentary rather than congressional government.——(d) Canada objects to many features of our national life : *Forum*, XVI., 325.—(1) To our elective judiciary.—(2) To our varying divorce laws.—(3) To our negro question.—(4) To our large pension list.——(*e*) Annexation would sacrifice millions spent on internal improvements to create national unity.

III. United States does not want Canada.——(*a*) It would involve enormous increase of area.——(*b*) It would crowd the House of Representatives with thirty new members.——(*c*) It would be impossible to assimilate Canadian ideas of government with our own.—(1) Parliamentary legislature and ministerial responsibility.—(2) High property qualifications for voting: *Statesman's Year Book, 1895*, p. 205.——(*d*) It would be difficult to assimilate a compact foreign race of two millions proud of their nationality.—(1) Clannishness shown in the immigrants of Maine and New York.—(2) Quebec is priest ridden: Goldwin Smith, *Canada and the Canadian Question*, pp. 5-12.——(*e*) It would imperil our free institutions.—(1) Stimulate attacks on our unsectarian public schools. —(x) Separate schools for Roman Catholics in Quebec, Ontario, and Northwest Territory.—(y) Manitoba riots.——(*f*) It would sharpen our political wars.—(1) American Protective Association, etc.——(*g*) It would load upon us a great and growing national debt, four times as great as ours per capita.

XXIV.

THE ANNEXATION OF HAWAII.

QUESTION : '*Resolved*, That Hawaii should be speedily annexed to the United States.'

Brief for the Affirmative.

GENERAL REFERENCES: W. D. Alexander, *A Brief History of the Hawaiian People;* Freeman Snow, *American Diplomacy*, pp. 361-397; Francis Wharton, *International Law Digest*, I., § 62; *Congressional Record*, 1893-1894 (see Index, Hawaiian Islands); *Senate Executive Documents*, 1892-1893, Nos. 45, 57, 76, 77; *North American Review*, Vol.

156, p. 265 (March, 1893); Vol. 157, p. 736 (December, 1893); Vol. 160, p. 374 (March, 1895); *Forum*, XV., 1 (March, 1893); *Overland Monthly* (second series), XI., 298 (March, 1888); *Harvard Monthly*, XVI., 45 (April, 1893); *Public Opinion*, XIV., XV., XVI., XVII. (see Indexes).

I. Annexation would benefit Hawaii: *North American Review*, Vol. 156, pp. 271-281.——(*a*) Commercially.—(1) Increased trade.—(2) Restrictions removed.——(*b*) Politically.—(1) More stable government.—(2) The protection of a great power.

II. Annexation would benefit the United States commercially.——(*a*) Hawaii has great material prosperity.—(1) Revenues always in excess of expenditures: *Public Opinion*, XIV., 440.—(2) Large foreign commerce.——(*b*) Hawaii's prosperity would benefit our producers and carriers: *North American Review*, Vol. 156, pp. 271-280.——(*c*) Hawaii's stability would foster our commerce.——(*d*) A good government would develop the resources.

III. Annexation would benefit the United States politically. ——(*a*) A military and naval necessity.—(1) Hawaii is the strategical point for the control of the whole northern Pacific: *North American Review*, Vol. 160, p. 375.—(2) Without Hawaii the United States cannot cope with the military and naval positions which England, France, and Germany have acquired in the Pacific.—(3) Necessary as a coaling station: *North American Review*, Vol. 160, p. 375.—(4) Annexation by the United States would prevent Hawaii ever becoming the base of hostile attack.

IV. Annexation is practicable.——(*a*) It is desired by the Hawaiian government and people.——(*b*) It accords with our policy.—(1) The United States has not refused the acquisition of territory under favorable conditions.—(x) Cases of Louisiana, Florida, Texas, California, and Alaska.—(2) Favored by statesmen.—(x) Marcy, Seward, Fish, and Blaine. ——(*c*) Hawaii is part of the American system: *North Ameri-*

can Review, Vol. 157, p. 741.—(1) In situation.—(2) In customs.——(*d*) There are no administrative difficulties.—(1) No colonial policy required.—(2) The institutions of the country are harmonious.—(3) No large navy required.—(4) The country is handy.——(*e*) No foreign power has protested.

V. There is no other alternative except annexation.——(*a*) The monarchy cannot be re-established.——(*b*) Hawaii cannot govern itself.——(*c*) A protectorate is impracticable.—(1) Treaties subject to abrogation.—(2) At the outbreak of war the country would be seized.—(3) Liability to a change of sentiment.—(x) By England or Japan getting a foothold. ——(*d*) A foreign power cannot be allowed to get control. ——(*e*) The country must not be left to anarchy.

Brief for the Negative.

GENERAL REFERENCES: *North American Review*, Vol. 156, p. 282 (March, 1893), p. 605 (May, 1893); Vol. 157, p. 745 (December, 1893); *Forum*, XV., 389 (June, 1893); XVI., 670 (February, 1894); *Harper's Magazine*, LXXXVII., 737 (October, 1893); *Spectator*, LXX., 153 (February 4, 1893); *Nation*, LVI., 154 (March 2, 1893), 190 (March 16, 1893), 362 (May 18, 1893); LVII., 384, 385 (November 23, 1893); LVIII., 60 (January 25, 1894), 96 (February 8, 1894), 380 (May 24, 1894).

I. Annexation is opposed to the policy of the United States. ——(*a*) Against the construction of the Constitution: *North American Review*, Vol. 156, pp. 282–286.—(1) Efforts to annex Cuba, St. Thomas, and St. Domingo have been defeated.—(2) The annexation of Louisiana, Florida, Texas, and Alaska do not furnish precedents.—(x) Contiguous territories.—(y) Insurmountable reasons for the annexation.—(3) Hawaii is too far away.

II. Annexation is unnecessary.——(*a*) The United States

would gain nothing which it does not now possess: *Nation*, LVI., 154.—(1) The present treaty secures all rights.—(2) Annexation would not alter trade relations: *Public Opinion*, XIV., 416.——(*b*) There is no danger of foreign control.—(1) England does not want Hawaii: *Spectator*, LXX., 153.—(2) Hawaiian sympathies are with the United States.——(*c*) We do not need Hawaii as a stronghold.

III. Annexation is inexpedient.——(*a*) Burdensome.—(1) Protection difficult and expensive.—(x) Island two thousand miles from San Francisco.—(y) A weak spot liable to assault.——(*b*) Bad effect on our social and political institutions.—(1) The people not bound to this country by community of interests or national sentiment: *Spectator*, LXX., 153.——(*c*) Hawaii would always remain a colonial dependency.—(1) Not fit to be incorporated into the Union: *Harper's Magazine*, LXXXVII., 742.——(*d*) The annexation would form a new and dangerous precedent.—(1) No limit to future acquisitions: *North American Review*, Vol. 156, p. 284.

IV. Hawaii does not want annexation.——(*a*) Interferes with self-government.——(*b*) The native population are especially opposed to it.——(*c*) The agitation and clamor comes from speculators.

XXV.

UNITED STATES OWNERSHIP OF THE NICARAGUA CANAL.

QUESTION: '*Resolved*, That the United States ought to construct and operate the Nicaragua Canal.'

Brief for the Affirmative.

GENERAL REFERENCES: *House Reports*, 1888–1889, No. 4167; *Senate Reports*, 1890–1891, No. 1944; *Journal of Franklin Institute*, Vol. 134, p. 1 (July, 1892), p. 109

(August, 1892); J. C. Rodrigues, *The Panama Canal*, Chaps. xiv.–xviii.; *The Nicaragua Canal*, Chaps. i., iv., vi. (published by the Nicaragua Canal Construction Company, 1891); *North American Review*, Vol. 156, p. 195 (February, 1893); Vol. 132, p. 107 (February, 1881); *Forum*, XVI., 690 (February, 1894); XII., 714, 721 (February, 1892); XI., 1 (March, 1891); III., 407 (June, 1887); *Overland Monthly*, XXIII., 489, 497 (May, 1894); (second series) XIX., 247 (March, 1892).

I. The Nicaragua Canal is desirable.———(*a*) Financially.—(1) Its successful completion and operation have been assured by the most competent engineers.—(2) Judging from the returns of the Suez Canal, the Nicaragua Canal would pay at least three per cent on a capital of one hundred millions. ———(*b*) Commercially.—(1) It would shorten interoceanic travel thousands of miles.———(*c*) Economically.—(1) It would develop the Pacific slope.—(2) Unify the United States.

II. Control of the canal by the United States is possible. ———(*a*) Clayton-Bulwer Treaty is ineffective: *The Panama Canal*, pp. 226, 227; W. E. Hall, *International Law*, §§ 107–109; Francis Wharton, *International Law Digest*, II., p. 238, § 150 f.—(1) England has violated it.—(2) Conditions have changed.—(3) England raised no objection to proposed treaty of United States with Nicaragua in 1884.

III. Control of the canal by the United States is desirable. ———(*a*) Neutrality of canal better guaranteed by a single strong nation than by a joint protectorate.———(*b*) The United States is its natural protector.—(1) By its situation.—(2) By the Monroe Doctrine: *The Panama Canal*, Chap. xiv., 174–177.

IV. The best method of United States control is by government ownership: *Public Opinion*, XIV., 298 (December 31, 1892).———(*a*) For public interests.—(1) Complete monopolies should not be run for private profit.———(*b*) For commercial interests.—(1) Early completion.—(2) Economic

construction.—(3) Low tolls.——(c) For national interests.
—(1) Foreign governments cannot meddle under pretext of
protecting capital invested.—(2) The United States will have
undisputed right to canal as a strategic point.

Brief for the Negative.

GENERAL REFERENCES: *The Nicaragua Canal* (published
by the Nicaragua Canal Construction Company, 1891); J.
C. Rodrigues, *The Panama Canal*, pp. 213–220; W. E.
Hall, *International Law*, §§ 107–109; *Nation*, XXXIX.,
516 (December 18, 1884), 538 (December 25, 1884); *Public Opinion*, XVII., 214 (June 7, 1894), 464 (August 16,
1894); *Saturday Review*, LVIII., 784 (December 20,
1884); *Chautauquan*, XIII., 409 (July, 1891); *United
States Foreign Relations*, 1881, pp. 549, 563; 1882, pp.
302–314; President Cleveland's Message, December 8, 1885,
pp. 4–7.

I. If the canal is a great necessity a private company will
construct it.——(a) Such undertakings in past carried out by
private companies: *Public Opinion*, XVII., 214 (June 4,
1894).——(b) Conditions here especially favorable.—(1) No
government obstacles.—(x) Concessions of Nicaragua to Maritime Canal Company, 1887: *Senate Reports*, 1887–1888, No.
221.—(y) Company incorporated by Congress, 1889: *United
States Statutes at Large*, XXV., p. 673.—(2) Scheme demonstrated to be plain and feasible: *The Nicaragua Canal*, pp.
18–59.——(c) The present not a sincere private company attempt.—(1) Company too anxious for government aid and
control: *Senate Reports*, 1887–1888, No. 221, pp. 2–5.

II. Under private management the interests of the United
States are protected.——(a) Equal right to armed protection
of canal.—(1) United States capital will be well represented:
North American Review, Vol. 156, pp. 195–199 (February,
1893). — (x) Government encouragement. —— (b) United
States can land troops more quickly than European powers.

———(c) United States has prior right to protect company from government usurpation.—(1) Monroe Doctrine.

III. Government ownership of canal would be unwise.——(a) As an industrial policy.—(1) Government undertakings are not economically conducted: *Lalor's Cyclopædia*, II., 572.—(x) Our political system.—(2) It would open the door to fraud and corruption.———(b) As a foreign policy.—(1) No single country should control the canal: *Saturday Review*, LVIII., 784; President Cleveland's Message, December 8, 1885, pp. 4–7.—(x) An international affair.—(2) It would seriously complicate our foreign relations: *Nation*, XXXIX., 496.—(x) England and Clayton-Bulwer Treaty.—(y) Other commercial powers interested.—(3) It would lead to acquisition of foreign territory, which is undesirable: *Nation*, XXXIX., 538.—(x) United States has enough to do with present territory.—(y) Absorption of Central America and possibly Mexico with their instable governments and turbulent people.

IV. The Clayton-Bulwer Treaty forbids such action.——(a) Treaty still in force.—(1) Asserted by Great Britain in 1881: *United States Foreign Relations*, 1881, p. 549.—(2) By United States in 1883: *The Panama Canal*, p. 212.—(3) Nothing subsequent to render treaty void: *Nation*, XXXIX., 496; W. E. Hall, *International Law*, §§ 107–109. ———(b) Great Britain will not give up treaty.—(1) Interests vitally at stake: *Saturday Review*, LVIII., 784.

NATIONAL POLICY (DOMESTIC).

XXVI.

RESTRICTION OF IMMIGRATION.

QUESTION: '*Resolved*, That immigration should be further restricted by law.'

Brief for the Affirmative.

GENERAL REFERENCES: *New-York Tribune* (May 17, 1891); *Congressional Record*, 1890–1891, p. 2955 (February

19, 1891); *Political Science Quarterly*, III., 46 (March, 1888), 197 (June, 1888); IV., 480-489 (September, 1889); J. A. Riis, *How the Other Half Lives;* Richmond Mayo-Smith, *Emigration and Immigration; North American Review*, Vol. 152, p. 27 (January, 1891); *Atlantic Monthly*, LXXI., 646 (May, 1893): *Public Opinion*, XVI., 122 (November 9, 1893); F. L. Dingley on European Emigration, *United States Special Consular Reports*, 1890, II., 211.

I. There is no longer any necessity for immigration: *Congressional Record*, 1890-1891, p. 2955.

II. Immigration has led to many bad effects.——(*a*) Political.—(1) Large proportion of adults gives too great voting power: *Emigration and Immigration*, p. 79.—(2) Our degraded municipal administration due to it: *Emigration and Immigration*, p. 87. —— (*b*) Economic. — (1) Immigrants offset what they produce by remittances home.—(2) Nearly half the immigrants are without occupation and this ratio is still increasing: *Congressional Record*, 1890-1891, p. 2955. —(3) There is already a large unemployed class of native laborers: *Emigration and Immigration*, p. 127.—(4) Displacement of American labor: *Congressional Record*, 1890-1891, p. 2955.—(5) By classes used to a lower standard of living.— (6) Introduction of the system: *How the Other Half Lives*, pp. 121-123.——(*c*) Social effects.—(1) Our high rates of mortality, vice, and crime are due to immigration: *Emigration and Immigration*, p. 150.—(2) Immigration the prevailing cause of illiteracy in the United States: *Emigration and Immigration*, p. 161.

III. The present laws are insufficient. —— (*a*) Diseased persons are allowed entrance: *Congressional Record*, 1890-1891, p. 2955.——(*b*) Agents for steamship lines induce men to emigrate.——(*c*) Pauper laws admit immigrants possessing less than the average wealth of residents: *Emigration and Immigration*, p. 101.

Brief for the Negative.

GENERAL REFERENCES: *North American Review*, Vol. 134, p. 347 (April, 1882); Vol. 154, p. 424 (April, 1892); Vol. 158, p. 494 (April, 1894); *Journal of Social Science*, 1870, No. 2; *Forum*, XIII., 360 (May, 1892).

I. The policy of the United States in regard to immigration has been successful and its continuance is necessary to develop the resources of the country: *Lalor's Cyclopædia*, II., 85–94.

II. Immigration is an advantage to the country: *North American Review*, Vol. 134, pp. 364–367. ——(*a*) The prosperity brought by immigrants.——(*b*) The addition to the national power of production.——(*c*) The money value of the immigrants as laborers.

III. The interests of American labor do not suffer by immigration: *Westminster Review*, Vol. 130, p. 474 (October, 1888); J. L. Laughlin in *International Review*, XI., 88 (July, 1881). ——(*a*) Immigrants form 'non-competing groups.'——(*b*) Are ultimately Americanized.

IV. The present immigration laws are satisfactory: *Supplement to the Revised Statutes of the United States*, 1874–1891, I., Chap. 551; *Nation*, XLV., 518 (December 29, 1887).——(*a*) The worst class of immigrants is excluded.——(*b*) The interests of American labor are fully protected.——(*c*) More stringent regulations, even if desirable, could not be enforced.

XXVII.

A TAX ON IMMIGRANTS.

QUESTION: '*Resolved*, That a high tax should be laid on all immigrants to the United States.'

Brief for the Affirmative.

GENERAL REFERENCES: Richmond Mayo-Smith, *Emigration and Immigration;* *Forum*, XI., 635 (August, 1891); XIV.,

110 (September, 1892); *Andover Review*, IX., 251 (March, 1888); *Yale Review*, I., 125 (August, 1892); *Congressional Record*, 1890–1891, p. 2955 (February 19, 1891); *Political Science Quarterly*, III., 46 (March, 1888), 197 (June, 1888); IV., 480–489 (September, 1889); *North American Review*, Vol. 152, p. 27 (January, 1891); J. A. Riis, *How the Other Half Lives;* F. L. Dingley on European Emigration, in *United States Special Consular Reports*, 1890, II., 211; *House Miscellaneous Documents*, 1887–1888, No. 572, part 2, Report on Importation of Contract Labor.

I. Immigration should be further restricted.——(*a*) On social grounds.—(1) The proportion of paupers, diseased, and criminal, is great.——(*b*) On economic grounds.—(1) No longer needed to develop the country: *Popular Science Monthly*, XLI., 762 (October, 1892).—(2) The lower wages and the standard of living: *Forum*, XIV., 113 (September, 1892).—(3) Unskilled occupations are already overcrowded: *Emigration and Immigration*, pp. 117–122.——(*c*) On political grounds.—(1) The immigrants do not understand our institutions.—(2) They become tools of machine politicians: *Emigration and Immigration*, pp. 79–88.—(3) They form communities by themselves.——(*d*) The dangers are increasing.—(1) The immigrants congregate in cities more than formerly: *Emigration and Immigration*, pp. 69–70.—(2) The character of the immigrants is deteriorating: *Yale Review*, I., 132.

II. A high tax would stop undesirable immigration.——(*a*) It would make impossible the sending of undesirable classes.—(1) Paupers.—(2) Convicts.—(3) Contract laborers.—(4) Shiftless and ignorant persons whom agents of steamship companies induce to come: *Yale Review*, I., 132.——(*b*) The Italians and Slavs can barely raise the passage money, and they could not raise the tax.——(*c*) Tax would not keep out the desirable immigrants, such as Germans, Swedes, and Irish. —(1) They bring enough money to pay the tax.

III. A tax is the simplest effective restriction.——(*a*) It cannot be evaded.——(*b*) It is the surest practical guarantee of the qualities desired: *Yale Review*, I., 141.——(*c*) It is a just means.—(1) One immigrant is worth to the country one hundred dollars: *Political Science Quarterly*, III., 204-207 (June, 1888).—(2) Per capita wealth of the United States is one thousand dollars.—(3) The immigrant should pay to be admitted to the wealth and privileges of this country.

Brief for the Negative.

GENERAL REFERENCES: *Westminster Review*, Vol. 130, p. 474 (October, 1888); *North American Review*, Vol. 134, p. 347 (April, 1882); Vol. 154, p. 424 (April, 1892); Vol. 156, p. 220 (February, 1893); *Forum*, XIII., 360 (May, 1892); *Lalor's Cyclopædia*, II., 85; Friedrich Kapp, 'Immigration,' in *Journal of Social Science*, 1870, No. 2, pp. 21-30.

I. A continuance of immigration is desirable: *Forum*, XIV., 601 (January, 1893); *Public Opinion*, III., 251 (July 2, 1887); XIV., 297 (December 31, 1892).——(*a*) There is need of laborers in the South and West: *North American Review*, Vol. 134, p. 350 (April, 1882).——(*b*) Voluntary immigrants are thrifty and active: *Political Science Quarterly*, III., 61 (March, 1888).——(*c*) The troublesome and mischievous immigrants are a small part of the whole: *Nation*, XLV., 519 (December 29, 1887); *Forum*, XIV., 605-606.

II. The present immigration laws are sufficient: *Public Opinion*, III., 249; *Supplement to the Revised Statutes of the United States*, 1874-1891, I., Chap. 551.——(*a*) Laws now exclude paupers, criminals, insane people, and persons liable to become a public charge, as well as imported labor.——(*b*) Immigration is practically self-regulating: *Forum*, XIV., 606.

III. The proposed measure of a high tax is undesirable.—— (*a*) It would literally mean prohibition, which is a complete reversal of American policy.——(*b*) It would be unjust.—(1) It would debar families from emigrating.—(2) It would discriminate against the peasant class, women and the younger men, who are often the most desirable immigrants.——(*c*) It is impracticable: *Political Science Quarterly*, III., 420.—(1) It would be difficult to collect the tax: *Forum*, XIII., 366 (May, 1892).—(2) Our extensive frontiers would make the law perfectly useless.——(*d*) It would create an undesirable class of immigrants.—(1) Those who evaded the laws would be an adventurous, restless element.—(2) Those who paid the tax would be embittered by our narrow policy.

XXVIII.

THE EXCLUSION OF THE CHINESE.

QUESTION: '*Resolved*, That the policy excluding Chinese laborers from the United States should be maintained and rigorously enforced.'

Brief for the Affirmative.

GENERAL REFERENCES: *Forum*, VI., 196 (October, 1888); *North American Review*, Vol. 139, p. 256 (September, 1884); Vol. 157, p. 59 (July, 1893); *Overland Monthly*, VII., 428 (April, 1886); *Scribner's Monthly*, XII., 862 (October, 1876); J. A. Whitney, *The Chinese and the Chinese Question*.

I. The Chinese are a source of danger to American civilization.——(*a*) Morally.—(1) Barbarity of Chinese character: *The Chinese and the Chinese Question*, p. 21.—(2) Inhuman treatment of women.—(3) Practice of gambling.—(4) Degraded religion: *Forum*, VI., 201.—(5) Utter disregard for oaths.—(6) Criminality: *Scribner's Monthly*, XII., 862.——(*b*) Socially.—(1) Unhealthy mode of living.—(2) Impossibility of amalgamation: *Overland Monthly*, VII., 429.—(3) Contamination through opium smoking, leprosy, and small-pox.—(4) Dangers to American youth of both sexes.———(*c*) Politically.—(1) Inability and unwillingness to become citizens: *Senate Reports*, 1876-1877, No. 689.—(2) Refusal to obey our laws.—(3) Secret system of slavery: *Scribner's Monthly*, XII., 860-865.———(*d*) Economically.—(1) Impossibility of competition with Chinese.—(2) Gradual encroachment on all occupations.—(3) Does away with the middle class of artisans and results in the concentration of capital: *Forum*, VI., 198; *North American Review*, Vol. 139, pp. 257, 260-273.

II. Exclusion furnishes the best remedy.———(*a*) It is constitutional under decision of Supreme Court: Fong Yue Ting *v*. U. S., 149 *U. S.*, 698.———(*b*) It will not materially affect our commercial relations with China.———(*c*) It is beneficial to the Chinamen who are legally in the United States.——— (*d*) It is practicable.—(1) Rules are simple and can be readily complied with or enforced.

Brief for the Negative.

GENERAL REFERENCES: *Nation*, LVI., 358 (May 18, 1893); *Forum*, XIV., 85 (September, 1892); XV., 407 (June, 1893); *North American Review*, Vol. 148, p. 476 (April, 1889); Vol. 154, p. 596 (May, 1892); Vol. 157, p. 52 (July, 1893); *Nation*, XXVIII., 145 (February 27, 1879); *Scribner's Monthly*, XIII., 687 (March, 1887); *Nation*, XXXIV., 222 (March 16, 1882); *Overland Monthly*, VII., 414 (April, 1886); XXIII., 518 (May, 1894); Richmond Mayo-Smith, *Emigration and Immigration*, Chap. xi.

I. The exclusion of the Chinese is at variance with fundamental American principles: *Nation*, XXXIV., 222.——— (*a*) It is contrary to the spirit of the Constitution: *Constitution of the United States*, Amend. XV.———(*b*) It is founded on race prejudice.———(*c*) It violates our treaty obligations and good faith between nations: *Forum*, XV., 407; XIV., 85-90.

II. Chinese immigration is no menace to American interests.——(*a*) The Chinese do not immigrate in large numbers. ——(*b*) They do not multiply after their arrival.——(*c*) They take only money—and little of that—out of the country, and leave finished products.——(*d*) They compete with unskilled labor and do not affect the wages of skilled labor.——(*e*) They are honest, industrious, peaceable, and frugal.——(*f*) They form but a small element in political life, and the fact that they are not citizens makes them less dangerous than other immigrants.

III. The policy of exclusion is harmful.——(*a*) It injures good feeling between the two countries.——(*b*) It menaces commerce: *Forum*, XIV., 87-88.—(1) China may retaliate any time.——(*c*) It discourages missionary work.——(*d*) It deprives the United States of effective labor suitable for large enterprises.—(1) Work on transcontinental railroads.—(2) In mines.—(3) Farming.—(4) Construction of irrigation works.

IV. The difficulty in enforcing the legislation makes it impracticable.——(*a*) The penalty for violation has no terrors for the Chinese immigrant: *Popular Science Monthly*, XXXVI., 185 (December, 1889).——(*b*) Many citizens oppose the legislation.——(*c*) It has failed thus far.

XXIX.

THE PENSION POLICY.

QUESTION: '*Resolved*, That the pension policy of the Republican party has been wise.'

Brief for the Affirmative.

GENERAL REFERENCES: Alvin P. Hovey, *Soldiers' Rights; North American Review*, Vol. 153, p. 205 (August, 1891);

Vol. 156, p. 420 (April, 1893), p. 618 (May, 1893); *Century*, XLII., 790 (September, 1891); *Congressional Record*, 1885-1895 (see Indexes, Pensions); *Public Opinion*, I., II., III., VII., IX., XI., XIV., XV. (see Indexes).

I. Many old soldiers are in urgent need of assistance.——
(*a*) Service in the army was disastrous to their health.——(*b*) They were poorly paid and paid in depreciated currency. ——(*c*) The end of the war found the soldiers unfitted for peaceful pursuits.——(*d*) For these reasons they have been unable to provide for their old age.

II. The United States is under moral obligations to pension its old soldiers.——(*a*) The army was made up of our best and most patriotic men.——(*b*) The United States has hitherto always given service pensions to its old soldiers.—— (*c*) Our national honor is involved, for pension legislation is really the fulfilment of a contract.——(*d*) The United States is wealthy enough to afford liberal pensions.

III. Occasional fraud is no argument against pensioning deserving soldiers.——(*a*) Fraud cannot be entirely prevented in transactions so large.——(*b*) Pension frauds have been greatly exaggerated.——(*c*) The Pension Office has on the whole been carefully and methodically administered.

IV. A liberal pension policy strengthens the government. ——(*a*) It intensifies national feeling and patriotism.——(*b*) It acts as a preventive of war by keeping before the public the evils of war.——(*c*) It strengthens the volunteer sentiment of the country.

Brief for the Negative.

GENERAL REFERENCES: D. C. Eaton, *Pensions; Forum*, VI., 540 (January, 1889); XII., 423 (December, 1891), 646 (January, 1892); XV., 377 (May, 1893), 439 (June, 1893), 522-540 (July, 1893); *North American Review*, Vol. 156, p. 416 (April, 1893), pp. 621-630 (May, 1893); *Popular Science Monthly*, XXXV., 722 (October, 1889);

Atlantic Monthly, LXV., 18 (January, 1890); *Century*, XXVIII., 427 (July, 1884); XLII., 179 (June, 1891); XLVI., 135 (May, 1893); *Harper's Magazine*, LXXXVI., 235 (January, 1893); *Nation*, XLIV., 92 (February 3, 1887), 136 (February 17, 1887); XLVIII., 5 (January 3, 1889), 258 (March 28, 1889), 438 (May 30, 1889); LV., 466 (December 22, 1892).

I. The Republican policy has been extravagant.——(*a*) The amount expended for pensions has risen from $13,000,000 in 1866 to $139,000,000 in 1894: *President's Message*, 1894.——(*b*) The present amount is nearly one-third of the total appropriations of Congress.——(*c*) The amount is out of all proportion to what other countries spend.—(1) Our roll is greater than those of England, France, Germany, Russia, and Austria combined: *Forum*, XII., 648.——(*d*) A large part of the appropriations have never reached the pockets of the soldiers.—(1) Large amounts have gone to agents and have been lost through fraud and corruption.——(*e*) Acts have been passed without regard to what the cost would be.

II. The Republican policy has inculcated dangerous principles.——(*a*) It has given pensions to men whose disability is not traceable to service.—(1) Dependent Pension Act.—— (*b*) It keeps up protection by dissipating the surplus.——(*c*) It has hurt national character and purity.—(1) By putting a premium on idleness and stimulating dishonesty, mendacity, and hypocrisy.——(*d*) It tends to a centralized and paternal form of government.

III. The Republican policy has been unfavorable to a military spirit.——(*a*) Pensions given through gratitude have been called a debt.——(*b*) Patriotism is lost sight of in the hope of a money reward.——(*c*) The character of the soldiers has been changed.—(1) Loyal men turned into pension grabbers.——(*d*) Disgust at the mercenary spirit of the veterans has been aroused.

XXX.

INCREASE OF THE NAVY.

QUESTION : ' *Resolved*, That it is for the best interest of the United States to build and maintain a large navy.'

Brief for the Affirmative.

GENERAL REFERENCES: *Congressional Record*, 1894–1895, pp. 2244, 2251, 2258 (February 15, 1895), pp. 2302, 2306 (February 16, 1895), p. 3118 (March 2, 1895); 1892–1893, pp. 1877–1878 (February 20, 1893); Report of Committee on Naval Affairs, in *Congressionl Record*, 1894–1895, p. 2231 (February 15, 1895); Report of the Secretary of the Navy, in *Abridgment of Message and Documents*, 1893–1894, pp. 424–429; *North American Review*, Vol. 149, p. 54 (July, 1889); Vol. 159, p. 137 (August, 1894); *Penn Monthly*, XII., 45 (January, 1881); *Overland Monthly*, XIII., 423 (April, 1889); XXIV., 367 (October, 1894); A. T. Mahan, *The Influence of Sea Power upon History*, pp. 1–89; J. D. J. Kelley, *The Question of Ships*, Chaps. ix., x.

I. A large navy is necessary for the maintenance of national respect: *The Influence of Sea Power upon History*, pp. 1–89. ——(*a*) To protect Americans abroad.—(1) Madagascar.—(2) Bluefields.—(3) Colombia.——(*b*) To add weight to demands.——(*c*) To prevent insults.—(1) Case of Allianca.

II. It is necessary for purposes of defence.——(*a*) Extensive seaboard of 16,000 miles and Alaska.——(*b*) Increasing commerce.——(*c*) Inadequate coast defences.——(*d*) International complications cannot be avoided.—(1) Chile.—(2) Samoa.—(3) Hawaii.—(4) Nicaragua.—(5) Great Britain as to Behring Sea.—(6) Spain as to Cuba.—(7) Venezuela.——(*e*) Monroe Doctrine should be enforced.

III. It is necessary for purposes of offence.———(*a*) Prevention of European interference with America.———(*b*) Necessary in case of war.—(1) Comparison of navies: *Abridgment of Message and Documents*, 1893-1894, pp. 393-400.

IV. Coast defences alone are inadequate: *Congressional Record*, 1894-1895, p. 2307 (February 16, 1895).

V. Cessation of building would be an abrupt break in the policy adhered to since 1886: *Abridgment of Message and Documents*, 1893-1894, p. 424.——— (*a*) Additional ships should be ordered at once.—(1) The usual time for building a battle-ship is five years.—(2) Cramp cannot construct the best in less than two and a half years.———(*b*) Provision for the future is necessary.—(1) Sudden shipwreck, as in the case of Reina Regente.—(2) Ordinary wear and tear.—(3) Older ships made nearly useless by modern improvements.

Brief for the Negative.

GENERAL REFERENCES: *Senate Reports*, 1889-1890, No. 174, Views of the Minority; *Nation*, XLVIII., 319 (April 18, 1889); LIII., 483 (December 24, 1891); LVII., 341 (November 9, 1893); LVIII., 284 (April 19, 1894); LX., 141 (February 21, 1895); *Congressional Record*, 1894-1895, p. 2256 (February 15, 1895), p. 2305 (February 16, 1895); A. B. Hart, 'The Chilean Controversy,' in *Practical Essays on American Government*.

I. The policy of the United States is opposed to a large navy.———(*a*) We are not pugnacious.———(*b*) We have no entangling alliances: *Century*, XXXVII., 951 (April, 1889).

II. An increase is unnecessary.———(*a*) The navy is already large: *Report of the Secretary of the Navy*, 1893-1894, p. 6. ———(*b*) No more ships are needed.———(*c*) No analogy with European navies.—(1) Small commerce.—(2) No colonies. —(3) Isolation.———(*d*) War is not probable.—(1) No strong neighbors.—(2) European nations desire peace with the

United States.—(w) Respect our neutrality.—(x) War with United States would precipitate general European war.—(y) Great foreign investments in the United States.—(z) Arbitration probable.

III. An increase is undesirable.——(a) We already have a deficit.——(b) The navy very expensive.——(c) Promotes jingoism.—(1) Barrundia and Chile: A. B. Hart, 'The Chilean Controversy,' in *Practical Essays on American Government*.

IV. Money may be better spent.——(a) Encouragement of commerce.——(b) Better diplomatic service.——(c) Reserves of ordnance: *Report of the Secretary of the Navy*, 1893–1894, p. 16.——(d) Adequate coast defence: *Congressional Record*, 1894–1895, p. 2306 (February 16, 1895).

XXXI.

AN INTERNATIONAL COPYRIGHT LAW.

QUESTION: '*Resolved*, That an international copyright law is desirable.'

Brief for the Affirmative.

GENERAL REFERENCES: G. H. Putnam, *The Question of Copyright; House Reports*, 1889–1890, No. 2401; R. R. Bowker. *Copyright, Its Law and its Literature; Forum*, XVI., 616 (January, 1894); I., 495 (July, 1886); *Century*, I., 942 (April, 1882); *Literary World*, XX., 24 (January 19, 1889); Henry Van Dyke, *The National Sin of Literary Piracy*, pp. 10–17; Brander Matthews, *Cheap Books and Good Books; International Review*, VIII., 609 (June, 1880).

I. Justice demands an International Copyright Law: *The Question of Copyright*, pp. 121–132, 327–330.——(a) Every author, native or foreign, should be rewarded for his production.—(1) A literary production is the possession of the author.—(2) Literary work requires real expenditure of energy: *Popular Science Monthly*, XIV., 530 (February, 1879).—(3) Literary productions are essential to modern civilization.

II. The present law is highly beneficial.——(*a*) It gives foreign authors their just rights: *Revised Statutes of the United States*, Secs. 4948-4956.—(1) They have control of their publications.—(2) They can receive compensation for their work.——(*b*) It raises the standard of American literature.—(1) American authors are given a fair field.—(2) Legitimate publishers are encouraged to engage in publishing American works.—(3) The withdrawal of the large number of cheap foreign books enables readers to invest more in good American books.——(*c*) It does not make books dearer: *The Question of Copyright*, p. 363.—(1) Americans are accustomed to cheap books and their demands control the book market.—(2) The law makes possible international agreements among publishers and the expense of publication is made less by distribution: *The Question of Copyright*, p. 359.——(*d*) It does not deprive the public of good books.—(1) The best editions of the higher grades of literature are more likely to be published, as publishers are not afraid of unjust competition: *The Question of Copyright*, p. 358.

III. Repeal of the law would be injurious.——(*a*) It would discourage native authors: *The Question of Copyright*, pp. 133-135.—(1) They could not compete with foreign authors who receive no pay for their work from American publishers. ——(*b*) it would degrade public opinion.—(1) The popular demand is for the cheapest and poorest class of foreign books: *The Question of Copyright*, p. 138.

Brief for the Negative.

GENERAL REFERENCES: *Forum*, I., 500 (July, 1886); XVI., 616 (January, 1894); *North American Review*, Vol.

146, pp. 68–76 (January, 1888); Vol. 148, p. 327 (March, 1889); *Nation*, LIX., 168 (September 6, 1894); *Public Opinion*, IX., 161 (May 24, 1890); XV., 608 (September 30, 1893); XVI., 347 (January 11, 1894); H. C. Carey, *Letters on International Copyright;* H. C. Carey, *The International Copyright Question Considered.*

I. Copyright is not a moral right, and the reproduction of literary work is not a crime: *North American Review*, Vol. 148, p. 327.——(*a*) The highest tribunals have decided that copyright is a statutory privilege: *Forum*, I., 500.——(*b*) The monopoly of literary work was given by the Constitution on the principle of public policy, and not of property right: *Constitution of the United States*, Art. I., Sec. 8, § 8; *North American Review*, Vol. 148, p. 330; *Forum*, I., 502.—— (*c*) Literary reproduction is neither criminal *per se*, nor by statute: *North American Review*, Vol. 148, pp. 328–329.

II. The present law has shown the undesirability of an international copyright law.——(*a*) It does not benefit authors.— (1) American authors have not been successful in Europe: *Forum*, XVI., 616.—(2) Foreign authors have been unsuccessful in the United States: *Forum*, XVI., 616; *Nation*, LIX., 169; *Public Opinion*, XV., 608; XVI., 347.——(*b*) It has not improved American literature.—(1) There is no basis for competition between authors.—(2) The disappearance of cheap editions of good foreign authors has removed a powerful stimulus to American writers.——(*c*) It increases the cost of books and lessens educational advantages: *North American Review*, Vol. 146, pp. 68–76.—(1) It makes good foreign books dearer to the public.—(2) It makes American books dearer by removing the incentive given by cheap foreign books to keep down the price.——(*d*) It enriches a few publishers at the expense of the authors and of the readers: *Public Opinion*, IX., 161; *North American Review*, Vol. 146, pp. 68–76.—(1) Foreign writers are obliged to publish their works through American houses.

PARLIAMENTARY PROCEDURE.

XXXII.

CLOSURE IN THE SENATE.

QUESTION: '*Resolved*, That the rules of the Senate ought to be so amended that general debate may be limited.'

Brief for the Affirmative.

GENERAL REFERENCES: Auguste Reynaert, *Histoire de la Dicipline Parlementaire*, II., 355-419; Reginald Dickinson, *Rules and Procedures of Foreign Parliaments*; *Cushing's Manual*, Secs. 220-222, and note to fifth edition; James Bryce, *The American Commonwealth*, I., 130-132; Charles Bradlaugh, *Rules and Procedure of the House of Commons*, pp. 52, 78-79.

I. The adoption of rules limiting debate in the Senate would expedite business.——(*a*) It would enable the wishes of the majority to be carried out more fully and with less delay. —— (*b*) It would prevent dilatory motions and other kinds of filibustering.——(*c*) It would prevent the killing of measures by obstructive proceedings.

II. Such rules would improve the character of legislation. ——(*a*) They would bring about a kind of responsibility for the majority.—(1) There would no longer be valid excuses for accomplishing nothing.——(*b*) They would improve the character of debates.—(1) There would be more life and terseness in the speeches. — (2) Not so much tendency to deliver campaign documents.

III. The freedom of debate and the rights of the minority would not be invaded.——(*a*) There is a difference between freedom of debate and the right to speak indefinitely.——(*b*)

So long as the majority has the conduct of business it ought to have the right to determine the items which shall occupy attention and time which each shall receive.——(c) No danger of abuse.—(1) Fear of the disapproval of the people will keep down high-handedness.—(x) It is so with the House of Representatives: *The American Commonwealth*, I., 130.

IV. Limitation of debate has been found necessary in other parliamentary bodies.——(a) In Europe.—(1) England: *Rules and Procedure of the House of Commons*, pp. 78-79.—(2) France: *Rules and Procedures of Foreign Parliaments*, pp. 229-231.—(3) Austria-Hungary: *Ibid.*, pp. 204, 211.—(4) Denmark: *Ibid.*, p. 224.—(5) Germany: *Ibid.*, p. 243.—(6) Belgium: *Ibid.*, pp. 222-223.—(7) Italy: *Ibid.*, p. 248.—(8) Portugal: *Ibid.*, pp. 258-259.—(9) Netherlands: *Ibid.*, p. 250.—(10) Spain: *Ibid.*, p. 266.—(11) Switzerland: *Ibid.*, p. 276.——(b) In America.—(1) Canada: *Rules of Canadian Senate*, p. 10.

Brief for the Negative.

GENERAL REFERENCES: W. M. Torrens, *Reform of Procedure in Parliament*, Chaps. vi., vii., viii.; *Congressional Globe*, 1841, pp. 183-185 (July 12, 1841), pp. 203-205 (July 15, 1841); 1861-1862, p. 1557 (April 7, 1862); *Congressional Record*, 1873, Special Session of Senate, pp. 114-117 (March 19, 1873); 1890-1891, pp. 1667-1713 (January 22, 1891).

1. There is no valid reason for abridging general debate in the Senate.——(a) The rules of the Senate have always been found ample for the conduct of public business.—(1) The Senate transacts more business than the House which has a rule limiting debate: *Congressional Record*, 1890-1891, p. 1678.——(b) The opposition agree to limit debate on all matters, such as appropriation bills, necessary to the support of the government.——(c) The number of senators is small and the body is dignified and conservative.

II. Such rules would be very dangerous.——(*a*) The Senate is intended to be the deliberative branch of the legislature.—— (*b*) The rights of the minority would be destroyed.—(1) The majority could carry out arbitrary measures.——(*c*) Much of the dignity of the Senate would be taken away.——(*d*) The scheme is opposed to our system of balances.——(*e*) The Senate is the only legislative body in the federal government where absolute freedom of speech is enjoyed: *Congressional Record*, 1890–1891, p. 1669.——(*f*) Free speech is of immense importance in preserving civil liberty: G. F. Hoar in *Congressional Record*, 1890–1891, p. 1670.

III. Such rules are against all traditions.——(*a*) All previous attempts to limit general debate in the Senate have failed.—(1) The Senate has had no such rules since 1806: *Congressional Record*, 1890–1891, p. 1669.—(2) Even in war time when exigencies were greatest no abridgment of debate was permitted.

XXXIII.

THE COUNTING OF A QUORUM.

QUESTION: '*Resolved*, That the principle of a present quorum as laid down in Reed's Rules is sound.'

Brief for the Affirmative.

GENERAL REFERENCES: T. B. Reed, *Parliamentary Rules*, pp. 23–25; G. G. Crocker, *Principles of Procedure*, Chap. v.; *Congressional Record*, 1889–1890, pp. 949–960 (January 29, 1890), pp. 977–994 (January 30, 1890), pp. 1171–1187 (February 10, 1890), pp. 1213–1227 (February 11, 1890), pp. 1234–1266 (February 12, 1890), pp. 1282–1307 (February 13, 1890), pp. 1327–1347 (February 14, 1890); 1893–1894, pp. 3786–3792 (April 17, 1894); *North American Review*, Vol. 149, p. 421 (October, 1889); Vol. 150,

p. 382 (March, 1890), p. 537 (May, 1890); Vol. 151, pp. 229, 237 (August, 1890), p. 367 (September, 1890); *Public Opinion*, VIII., 419 (February 8, 1890), 441 (February 15, 1890), 467 (February 22, 1890); IX., 4 (April 12, 1890); XVII., 71 (April 19, 1894), 90 (April 26, 1894); *Nation*, LVIII., 148 (March 1, 1894).

I. The principle is necessary.——(*a*) Without it business cannot be transacted.—(1) Even though a party has a good majority it is impossible to pass legislation.—(x) On account of illness.—(y) Business duties.——(*b*) The majority are unable to fulfil party pledges.—(1) On account of dilatory motions, filibustering, and obstruction.——(*c*) There is no other alternative.—(1) The House cannot waste its time disciplining members.—(2) The House cannot delegate to the Speaker the power of punishing members.

II. The principle is reasonable.——(*a*) It protects the rights of the majority as well as the minority.——(*b*) It prevents waste of time.——(*c*) It enables business to be taken up and despatched in order of its importance.——(*d*) It does not confer dangerous power on the Speaker.—(1) The power of the Speaker is increased only when the action of the minority renders it necessary.

III. The principle is justified by precedents.——(*a*) By legal decisions: *Congressional Record*, 1889–1890, pp. 1173–1174, 1181–1182: *North American Review*, Vol. 150, pp. 385–387.——(*b*) By the practice of other legislative bodies.—(1) In the United States: *North American Review*, Vol. 150, pp. 387–388.—(2) In Europe: *North American Review*, Vol. 153, pp. 738–749.

Brief for the Negative.

GENERAL REFERENCES: *Congressional Record*, 1879–1880, pp. 575–579 (January 28, 1880): 1889–1890, pp. 1177–1187 (February 10, 1890), pp. 1209–1225 (February 11, 1890), pp. 1234–1266 (February 12, 1890), pp. 1282–1307 (February 13, 1890), pp. 1327–1347 (February 14, 1890); *North American Review*, Vol. 149, p. 665 (December, 1889); Vol. 150, p. 390 (March, 1890); Vol. 151, p. 90 (July, 1890), p. 385 (October, 1890); *Public Opinion*, VIII., 419 (February 8, 1890), 441 (February 15, 1890), 467 (February 22, 1890); XVII., 91 (April 26, 1894); *Nation*, L., 101, 104 (February 6, 1890), 124 (February 13, 1890), 143 (February 20, 1890); LI., 44 (July 17, 1890), 104 (August 7, 1890), 240 (September 25, 1890); LIV., 102 (February 11, 1892); LVIII., 281 (April 19, 1894), 306 (April 26, 1894).

I. The principle is contrary to parliamentary law.——(*a*) Contrary to the principles.—(1) No business can be transacted if attention is called to the fact that a quorum is not present.—(2) The fact of a quorum or no quorum is settled by the record.—(3) The constitutional idea of a quorum implies not the visible presence but the judgment and votes of members.——(*b*) Contrary to precedents: *North American Review*, Vol. 151, p. 91.—(1) Opinion of Mr. Reed: *Nation*, L., 101.—(2) Ruling of Speaker Blaine: *Congressional Record*, 1874–1875, p. 1734 (February 24, 1875).

II. The principle is dangerous.——(*a*) It destroys the deliberative character of the House of Representatives.——(*b*) It violates the rights of the minority.—(1) Rules are intended to protect, not to oppress, minorities.——(*c*) It has a dangerous tendency to centralize party government.——(*d*) It gives the Speaker extraordinary power for sectional and party purposes.

III. The principle is the foundation of legislative fraud.——(*a*) It enables the Speaker to declare a bill passed when the records show the contrary.——(*b*) It will cause anxiety as to the legality of bills passed over a veto.——(*c*) It makes it possible to railroad bills through Congress.——(*d*) It does away with legitimate and necessary checks upon legislation.

ECONOMICS.

CURRENCY.

XXXIV.

AN INTERNATIONAL GOLD STANDARD.

QUESTION: '*Resolved*, That all nations should unite in adopting the same monetary system and that that system should be gold.'

Brief for the Affirmative.

GENERAL REFERENCES: F. W. Taussig, *The Silver Situation in the United States*, Part II.; Robert Giffen, *The Case Against Bimetallism*; J. L. Laughlin in *Quarterly Journal of Economics*, I., 319 (April, 1887).

I. An international monetary system is desirable for the promotion of international commerce: Reports of *International Monetary Conferences*, 1867, 1878, 1881, 1892.

II. Gold would be the best standard: *The Silver Situation in the United States*, p. 124.——(*a*) It is the most convenient: *Fortnightly Review*, XLVI., 480 (October, 1886).——(*b*) It is the most stable: *Journal of Institute of Bankers*, pp. 277–279 (May, 1883).——(*c*) It has the advantage of being universally recognized as a desirable standard.

III. The gold standard could be readily maintained.——(*a*) The output is not declining: F. W. Taussig in *Popular Science Monthly*, XLIII., 582 (September, 1893); *North American Review*, Vol. 160, p. 38 (January, 1895).——(*b*) The use of credit is increasing.——(*c*) The debtor is not burdened.———(d) Money wages are rising though prices are falling: *The Silver Situation in the United States*, pp. 106–108.

IV. The gold standard is the only practical standard.——— (a) The single silver standard is admittedly bad.———(b) The multiple standard is difficult of attainment.———(c) International bimetallism is open to special objections.—(1) An agreement cannot be reached —(2) If made it could not be maintained.—(3) If made and maintained it would be unjust to creditors by raising prices.

Brief for the Negative.

GENERAL REFERENCES: F. A. Walker, *Money*, Chaps. ix.-xiii.; E. Benjamin Andrews in *Political Science Quarterly*, VIII., 197 (June, 1893), 401 (September, 1893); J. S. Nicholson, *Money and Monetary Problems*, Part II.; *Lalor's Cyclopædia*, II., 883.

I. A single gold standard is undesirable.———(a) It lowers prices by decreasing the amount of money: F. A. Walker, *Money*, pp. 268–269.—(1) Lower prices depress industry: *International Monetary Conference*, 1892, pp. 240–245.—(2) They are injurious to the farmers: *The Silver Situation in the United States*, pp. 112–115.—(3) They are unjust to the debtor class: S. M. MacVane, *Political Economy*, p. 123.— (4) Scarcity of money causes dangerous extension of credit. ———(b) It is a fluctuating standard.—(1) Gold has appreciated: *Quarterly Journal of Economics*, III., 153 (January, 1889); *Review of Reviews*, VIII., 406 (October, 1893).—(2) The prices of commodities have fallen at the same rate as silver: *The Silver Situation in the United States*, p. 103.

II. The adoption of a universal gold standard would be impracticable.———(a) Gold is scarce.—(1) The present supply is insufficient.—(2) The annual output is small and is mined largely with silver: F. A. Walker, *Money*, pp. 254, 265.—(3) Much gold is used in the arts: *Money and Mone-*

tary Problems, p. 290.—(4) Some countries have no gold. ——(*b*) It would entail financial loss.

III. Bimetallism is practicable and desirable: *Money and Monetary Problems*, Part II., Chap. iv.——(*a*) The ratio of gold and silver is determined not by relative amounts, but by relative demand: *Money and Monetary Problems*, pp. 214–217.—(1) International legislation can regulate demand.—(2) Single countries can regulate their demand: F. A. Walker, *Money*, p. 266.——(*b*) The over-production of silver is impossible: *Political Science Quarterly*, VIII., 212–215. ——(*c*) Bimetallism would furnish sufficient money.

XXXV.

BIMETALLISM IN THE UNITED STATES.

QUESTION: '*Resolved*, That any further coinage of silver by the United States is undesirable.'

Brief for the Affirmative.

GENERAL REFERENCES: W. S. Jevons, *Investigations in Currency and Finance*, pp. 303–316; F. W. Taussig, *The Silver Situation in the United States;* J. L. Laughlin, *The History of Bimetallism in the United States*, Chaps. xiii., xiv.; *Nation*, LVI., 96 (February 9, 1893), 432 (June 15, 1893), 466 (June 29, 1893), 448 (June 22, 1893); LVII., 22 (July 13, 1893), 61 (July 27, 1893), 94–95 (August 10, 1893), 222 (September 28, 1893); LVIII., 266 (April 12, 1894), 463 (June 21, 1894).

I. International bimetallism is at present impracticable. ——(*a*) Great Britain, the chief commercial nation, would stay out: *Investigations in Currency and Finance*, pp. 307–309.

II. The United States must remain on a gold basis.——(*a*)

Gold is more stable in value than silver: *Investigations in Currency and Finance*, pp. 305, 311–313.——(*b*) A silver standard would injure trade.—(1) Would produce violent fluctuations in foreign exchange: F. A. Walker, *Political Economy*, pp. 409–411.—(2) Would render the value of debts uncertain.——(*c*) The morale of tinkering with the currency is bad: *The Silver Situation in the United States*, pp. 126–127.——(*d*) Change to a silver standard means another financial crisis.——(*e*) A silver standard is dishonest.—(1) Injures creditors.—(2) Does not permanently help debtors.

III. Further coinage of silver would render a gold basis impossible.——(*a*) National bimetallism means silver monometallism.—(1) Only exceptional good fortune has prevented previous issues of silver from driving the United States to a silver basis.—(v) Silver replaced disappearing bank-notes: *The Silver Situation in the United States*, pp. 38–39.—(w) Treasury offered baits to induce use of silver: *Ibid.*, pp. 20, 41.—(x) Banks received treasury notes of 1890 freely: *Ibid.*, p. 59.—(y) Large surplus in 1885, 1886: *Ibid.*, p. 32.—(z) Favorable balance of trade.—(2) Such exceptional good fortune cannot be expected to continue.—(3) Events prove that with an unfavorable balance of trade we cannot maintain gold payments.—(x) The drain of gold falls wholly on the Treasury.—(y) Gold bonds are a temporary expedient.

IV. If a currency supplementary to gold is needed a revised system of national bank-notes is better than silver.

Brief for the Negative.

GENERAL REFERENCES: F. A. Walker, *Money;* J. S. Nicholson, *Money and Monetary Problems;* E. Benjamin Andrews in *Political Science Quarterly*, VIII., 197 (June, 1893); E. Suess, *The Future of Silver;* S. D. Horton, *Silver in Europe;* J. W. Jenks in *Journal of Social Science*, XXXII., 27 (November, 1894).

I. A single gold standard would give rise to great evils.——(*a*) It would depress trade and industry: *Journal of Social*

Science, XXXII., 27.—(1) On a gold basis, the amount of money could not increase with the growth of population and business.—(x) Supply of gold is insufficient: *Report of United States Monetary Commission of 1877*, p. 15; *Political Science Quarterly*, VIII., 211.—(2) Contraction of the amount of money means lower prices: J. S. Mill, *Principles of Political Economy*, II., Bk. III., Chap. viii., 1–36.——(*b*) It would injure the debtor class.—(1) They would have to pay in an appreciated currency: S. M. MacVane, *Political Economy*, p. 123.——(*c*) It would injure the farmers.—(1) Many of them are in debt.—(2) Price of their commodities lowered: *The Silver Situation in the United States*, pp. 112–115.——(*d*) It would place dangerous power in hands of money syndicates to influence the market, prices, etc.——(*e*) Need of more currency would lead to wild schemes for paper currency.——(*f*) Adoption of gold standard injured Germany: Hugh McCulloch, *Addresses, Speeches, and Letters*, pp. 245–259.

II. The use of silver as money is most desirable.——(*a*) Silver and gold are the only suitable money metals: J. S. Mill, *Principles of Political Economy*, II., Bk. III., Chap. viii. ——(*b*) Gold is insufficient: See above I. (*a*). 1 (x).—— (*c*) Silver in relation to other commodities is a more stable standard than gold: *Journal of Social Science*, XXXII., 27; *Congressional Record*, 1893, Appendix, pp. 158–159.——(*d*) Silver and gold together are a non-fluctuating standard: Hugh McCulloch, *Addresses, Speeches, and Letters*, p. 21. ——(*e*) Silver will eventually become the standard money metal of the world.—(1) Exhaustion of the gold-mines.—(2) Increased use of gold in the arts: *The Future of Silver*, pp. 100–101. ——(*f*) Present suspicion of silver unjustifiable.—(1) Silver has not depreciated, but gold has appreciated.—(2) There is no danger of a flood of silver: *The Future of Silver*, p. 51; *Forum*, XV., 67 (March, 1893).

III. The United States alone could safely coin silver at a proper ratio: A. P. Stokes, *Joint-Metallism*; W. C. Oates in *Congressional Record*, 1893, Appendix, pp. 152–155.——(*a*)

The proper ratio would be that which would most nearly coincide with market ratio.——(*b*) This ratio is ascertainable.——(*c*) There would be no tendency for silver to drive out gold.—(1) A silver dollar would contain a gold dollar's worth of silver.——(*d*) Our present silver money could be gradually recoined at a new ratio; meanwhile the government's fiat would maintain it at parity with gold as is now the case.

IV. Such coinage of silver by the United States would be highly beneficial.——(*a*) It would prevent the evils of a single gold standard.——(*b*) It would lead to establishing our whole currency system on a sound basis.—(1) Silver money would be honest.—(2) Greenbacks, which drain the Treasury of gold, might be withdrawn: *Harper's Weekly*, XXXVIII., 1206 (December 22, 1894).—(3) Silver might replace the national bank circulation, which is decreasing and must soon end: *United States Statistical Abstract*, 1893, p. 42.——(*c*) It would be likely to lead to an international bimetallic agreement.

XXXVI.

THE TAX ON STATE BANK-NOTES.

QUESTION: '*Resolved*, That the government tax on state bank-notes should be repealed.'

Brief for the Affirmative.

GENERAL REFERENCES: M. D. Harter in *Forum*, XII., 186 (October, 1891); C. F. Dunbar in *Quarterly Journal of Economics*, VII., 55 (October, 1892); *Commercial and Financial Chronicle*, LVIII., 618 (April 14, 1894); LIV., 781 (May 14, 1892), 868 (May 28, 1892); *Nation*, LV., 193 (September 15, 1892); *Congressional Record*, 1893–1894, pp. 5477–5483 (May 29, 1894), pp. 5604–5608, 5614–5616 (June 1,

1894), pp. 5666–5668 (June 2, 1894), Appendix, pp. 889, 1033.

I. The conditions which brought about the present tax no longer exist.——(*a*) The measure was a temporary war measure to float United States bonds: *Report of the Secretary of the Treasury*, 1862, pp. 1–31.

II. The present currency system is bad and must be changed: C. F. Adams, *Chapters on Erie*, p. 303.——(*a*) The currency is inadequate in volume: *Commercial and Financial Chronicle*, LIV., 781, 868.—(1) Population and trade have grown rapidly.—(2) There is no inducement for national banks to issue notes: *Quarterly Journal of Economics*, I., 414 (July, 1887).——(*b*) It is inelastic.—(1) There is no provision for expansion in financial crises.—(2) No provision is made for small centres: *Quarterly Journal of Economics*, VII., 63.—— (*c*) It is positively dangerous to the country: *Chapters on Erie*, p. 303.—(1) The proportion of gold to certificates, greenbacks, and treasury notes is too small, and is constantly growing smaller: F. W. Taussig, *The Silver Situation in the United States*, p. 54.—(2) Further increase of government issue would make matters worse.——(*d*) The present system cannot last beyond the year 1907.—(1) The public debt on which the present system is founded is liquidated in that year.

III. The repeal of the tax by encouraging a state bank currency would open the way to the best currency obtainable.—— (*a*) The state bank currency would be able to meet the demand for increased currency.——(*b*) It would be elastic: *Forum*, XIII., 726 (August, 1892).——(*c*) It would satisfy the reasonable demands of the South and the West.——(*d*) It is supported by important financial organs: *Commercial and Financial Chronicle*, LIV., 781, 868; LVIII., 618.

IV. The issues of state banks could be made safe.——(*a*) Before the war the majority of state banks issued sound notes: *Nation*, LV., 193.——(*b*) The government could accept for taxes only notes sufficiently secured: *Forum*, XII., 186.——

(*c*) Inflation could be prevented by a tax on circulation above a fixed amount.

Brief for the Negative.

GENERAL REFERENCES: C. F. Dunbar in *Quarterly Journal of Economics*, VII., 55 (October, 1892); *Lalor's Cyclopædia*, I., 204–222; F. A. Walker, *Money*, p. 479; *United States Finance Report*, 1875, pp. 201–207; 1876, pp. 147–152; 1878, pp. 144–168; *Report of Comptroller of Currency*, 1888, I., p. 90; 1889, I., pp. 9–19; *Report of the Secretary of the Treasury*, 1892, pp. 309, 320; W. L. Royall, *Andrew Jackson and the United States Bank*, p. 34; H. W. Richardson, *National Banks* (Harper's Half-Hour Series); President Harrison, Letter of Acceptance, in leading daily papers of September 5, 1892; *Congressional Record*, 1893–1894, pp. 5337–5354 (May 26, 1894), pp. 5483–5492 (May 29, 1894), pp. 5595–5604 (May 31, 1894), Appendix, pp. 1030, 1231.

I. No change in the currency system is necessary.——(*a*) The present national banking system is the best possible.—(1) It is uniform: J. J. Knox in *Forum*, XII., 772 (February, 1892).—(2) History shows it to be absolutely safe: *Chautauquan*, XVI., 32 (October, 1892); *North American Review*, Vol. 154, p. 150 (February, 1892); *United States Finance Report*, 1875, p. 201: *National Banks*, p. 86; *Lalor's Cyclopædia*, I., 217.——(*b*) Ampler currency will not help the South and West: *Quarterly Journal of Economics*, VII., 55. ——(*c*) The currency can be indefinitely extended when it becomes necessary.

II. The repeal of the tax would revive the evils of the old state bank system of currency: *Lalor's Cyclopædia*, I., 211; *Money*, p. 479; *Congressional Record*, 1883–1884, p. 1086 (February 13, 1884).——(*a*) Securities would be insufficient and unequal.—(1) On account of the diversity of laws in the states.—(2) Shown by the present defective banking laws of many states: *United States Finance Report*, 1875, p. 202.—— (*b*) The people cannot be trusted to avoid wild-cat schemes. —(1) Shown by the free-coinage craze.—(2) The silver craze. ——(*c*) Repeal would tend to drive coin from circulation: *Andrew Jackson and the United States Bank*, pp. 55-57, 64. ——(*d*) Discount and exchange would be costly.—(1) Notes would be redeemable only where issued: *Forum*, XII., 186 (October, 1891).——(*e*) There would always be a tendency to increase the issue: *Money*, p. 487.

TARIFF.

XXXVII.

PROTECTION AND FREE TRADE.

QUESTION: '*Resolved*, That the time has now come when the policy of protection should be abandoned by the United States.'

Brief for the Affirmative.

GENERAL REFERENCES: Frédéric Bastiat, *Sophisms of the Protectionists;* W. M. Grosvenor, *Does Protection Protect?;* Henry George, *Protection or Free Trade;* J. S. Mill, *Principles of Political Economy*, II., Bk. V., Chap. x., § 1; article on Protection in *Tariff Reform Series*, IV., No. 12, p. 2 (September 30, 1891); *Lalor's Cyclopædia*, II., 289; *Nation*, XXVIII., 161 (March 6, 1879); XXIX., 338 (November 20, 1879); XXXIV., 288 (April 6, 1882); LXXVI., 118 (February 8, 1883); J. G. Carlisle in *Congressional Record*, 1891–1892, p. 6910 (July 29, 1892); D. A. Wells in *Forum*, XIV., 697 (February, 1893); F. A. Walker in *Quarterly Journal of Economics*, IV., 245 (April, 1890); Edward

Atkinson in *Popular Science Monthly*, XXXVII., 433 (August, 1890); Senator Vest in *North American Review*, Vol. 155, p. 401 (October, 1892); *Harper's Weekly*, XXXVIII., 819 (September 1, 1894).

I. Protection is unsound in theory: J. S. Mill, *Principles of Political Economy*, II., 532.——(*a*) It shuts out what is ours by nature: *Sophisms of the Protectionists*, pp. 73–80. ——(*b*) It raises unnatural obstacles to intercourse: *Sophisms of the Protectionists*, pp. 84–85.——(*c*) It can only raise prices by diminishing the quantity of goods for sale: *Sophisms of the Protectionists*, pp. 7, 17.——(*d*) It endangers the interests it aims to promote: *Nation*, XXXVI., 118.—— (*e*) It may transfer but not increase capital: *Sophisms of the Protectionists*, p. 93. —— (*f*) The doctrine of protection for revenue is inconsistent: J. S. Mill, *Principles of Political Economy*, II., 538.——(*g*) It is anti-social: *Sophisms of the Protectionists*, pp. 15, 127; *Nation*, XXXVI., 118; XXXVIII., 161.

II. Protection is unsound in general practice.——(*a*) It makes capital and labor less efficient: J. S. Mill, *Principles of Political Economy*, II., 532, 539.——(*b*) It hurts our carrying trade: *Nation*, XXXVI., 118. —— (*c*) It closes against us many of the world's best markets: J. S. Mill, *Principles of Political Economy*, II., 537; *Nation*, XXVIII., 161; XXXVI., 118.

III. Protection is not beneficial to any class. —— (*a*) It raises prices to consumers: *Popular Science Monthly*, XXXVII., 433.——(*b*) It does not raise the wages of laborers: *Congressional Record*, 1891–1892, pp. 6910–6917; *Popular Science Monthly*, XXXVII., 433.——(*c*) It hurts farmers: *Nineteenth Century*, XXXII., 733 (November, 1892).——(*d*) It hurts the community by shutting off foreign markets: *North American Review*, Vol. 155, p. 401.——(*e*) It increases the cost of materials.——(*f*) It does not help us against pauper labor: *Popular Science Monthly*, XXXVII.,

433. ——(g) It does not benefit the majority: *Nation*, LV., 299 (October 20, 1892).——(h) Infant industries are not permanently aided: *Quarterly Journal of Economics*, IV., 245.

IV. Protection tends to run to extremes.——(a) It perverts taxation from its proper uses: *Forum*, XIV., 51 (September, 1892). —— (b) It creates dangerous precedents: *Ibid.*——(c) Industries seek permanent protection: *Nation*, LV., 252 (October 6, 1892).——(d) It creates monopolies.

Brief for the Negative.

GENERAL REFERENCES: S. N. Patten, *The Economic Basis of Protection;* H. M. Hoyt, *Protection versus Free Trade ; Congressional Record*, 1889–1890, p. 4248 (May 7, 1890); 1891–1892, p. 6746 (July 26, 1892); J. G. Blaine in *North American Review*, Vol. 150, p. 27 (January, 1890); William McKinley in *North American Review*, Vol. 150, p. 740 (June, 1890); R. E. Thompson, *Social Science and National Economy*, pp. 243–278; *Lalor's Cyclopædia*, III., 413; Van Buren Denslow, *Principles of Economic Philosophy*, Chaps. xiii., xiv., xv., xvi.

I. The policy of protection is sound in principle.——(a) It enables a country to fix the terms of exchange in foreign trade. —(1) Foreign demand for our commodities is necessarily great.—(2) Protection lessens our demand for foreign commodities.——(b) Protection is the best means of increasing the consumer's rent.

II. The policy of protection has proved beneficial in practice.——(a) Without it no country has secured a symmetrical development of its industries: *Social Science and National Economy*, p. 267.——(b) Every period of protection in the United States has been followed by great material prosperity.

III. Protection secures a home market for commodities incapable of transportation abroad: E. E. Hale, *Tom Torrey's*

Tariff Talks.——(*a*) It enhances values, especially the value of land : J. R. Dodge, *How Protection Protects the Farmer.*

IV. A protective tariff does not raise prices.——(*a*) The establishment of a new industry has invariably been followed by lower prices : *Congressional Record*, 1889-1890, p. 4248.—(1) Steel rails.—(2) Glass and earthen ware.—(3) Wool.—(4) Tin-plate.

XXXVIII.

THE TARIFF AND WAGES.

QUESTION : '*Resolved*, That a high protective tariff raises wages.'

Brief for the Affirmative.

GENERAL REFERENCES : S. N. Patten, *The Economic Basis of Protection*, pp. 54-80 ; Lee Meriwether, ' How Workingmen Live in Europe and America,' in *Harper's Magazine*, LXXIV., 780 (April, 1887) ; R. P. Porter, *Bread Winners Abroad* (People's Library), Chaps. xvi., xxviii., xlix., li., liii., lvi., lxvi., lxvii., lxxxiv., civ. ; Van Buren Denslow, *Principles of Economic Philosophy*, pp. 623-627.

I. A high protective tariff raises wages theoretically.——(*a*) It causes more employers to compete for the hire of labor.—(1) By increasing the number of occupations and enterprises that can be carried on : R. E. Thompson, *Social Science and National Economy*, p. 248 ; *Principles of Economic Philosophy*, pp. 623-624.——(*b*) It increases the amount of money available for the compensation of labor.—(1) By increasing the profits of manufacturers : *Principles of Economic Philosophy*, pp. 626-627.——(*c*) It enables laborers to share in the natural resources of the country.—(1) By preventing competition with cheap foreign labor : *The Economic Basis of Protection*, pp. 64-70.

II. A high protective tariff raises wages practically.——(*a*) In the United States, which furnishes the best example of a protective tariff, money wages are higher than in Europe.— (1) This is shown by the opinions of writers: *Principles of Economic Philosophy*, p. 527; *Bread Winners Abroad; Consular Reports of the United States*, No. 40, p. 304 (April, 1884). —(2) It is shown by the opinions of manufacturers: John Roach in *International Review*, XIII., 455 (November, 1882); J. M. Swank, *Our Bessemer Steel Industry*, p. 23; letters from the National Association of Wool Manufacturers and the Titus Sheard Co. in *Congressional Record*, 1891–1892, p. 6751 (July 26, 1892).——(*b*) Wages have risen in other countries under a protective system. — (1) In Germany: *Principles of Economic Philosophy*, pp. 523–524; *Consular Reports of the United States*, No. 42, pp. 12, 13, 15 (June, 1884).—(2) In Canada: *Principles of Economic Philosophy*, pp. 666–668.——(*c*) Real wages are higher in the United States than in Europe.—(1) An American workman can save more than a European: *Consular Reports of the United States*, No. 40, p. 304.—(2) His standard of living is higher: *Harper's Magazine*, LXXIV., 780.

Brief for the Negative.

GENERAL REFERENCES: F. W. Taussig in *Forum*, VI., 167 (October, 1888); W. G. Sumner in *North American Review*, Vol. 136, p. 270 (March, 1883); J. Schoenhof, *The Economy of High Wages*, pp. 175–193; J. Schoenhof, *Wages and Trade;* 'Labor, Wages, and Tariff,' *Tariff Reform Series*, II., No. 21 (January 15, 1890); 'Labor and the Tariff,' *Tariff Reform Series*, I., No. 12, p. 2 (October 10, 1888).

I. Arguments based on comparisons of wages in different countries are untrustworthy.——(*a*) Such comparisons prove too much: D. A. Wells, *Practical Economics*, p. 137.—— (*b*) There is no uniform rate in any country.——(*c*) There are many local causes which must necessarily make wages higher in one country than in another.—(1) Natural advantages: D. A. Wells, *The Relation of the Tariff to Wages*, p. 2. —(2) Standing army service: *Ibid.*—(3) The question of unoccupied land: *North American Review*, Vol. 136, p. 270.

II. Careful use of statistics shows that wages are relatively higher under a low tariff.——(*a*) The high rate of wages in the United States is determined by unprotected industries.— (1) There are more laborers connected with unprotected than with protected industries: J. L. Laughlin's edition of J. S. Mill, *Principles of Political Economy*, p. 619.——(*b*) Wages in certain protected industries in the United States are lower than wages in the same industries in England.——(*c*) In protected industries in which wages are higher than abroad, they were higher before the existence of a protective tariff: *Nation*, XLVII., 327 (October 25, 1888).——(*d*) New South Wales is more prosperous than Victoria: *Fortnightly Review*, XXXVII., 369 (March, 1882).

III. A protective tariff lowers wages by diminishing the amount of capital to be distributed for wages.——(*a*) The general productiveness of industry is less: *Practical Economics*, p. 135.—(1) The effect of limiting the sale of commodities to a domestic market is evil: *Practical Economics*, p. 139.——(*b*) The proportion in which that produced is divided is less favorable to labor.—(1) The producer requires the same ratio of profit, while the number of laborers among whom the smaller wage-fund is divided is as large as before: *North American Review*, Vol. 136, p. 270.

IV. Real wages are less.——(*a*) The tariff increases the price of commodities and puts them out of the reach of the poorer classes: *North American Review*, Vol. 136, p. 270.

XXXIX.

RECIPROCITY WITH CANADA.

QUESTION: '*Resolved*, That it would be to the advantage of the United States to establish complete commercial reciprocity between the United States and Canada.'

Brief for the Affirmative.

GENERAL REFERENCES: Goldwin Smith, *Canada and the Canadian Question*, pp. 281-301; *Handbook of Commercial Union* (Toronto, 1888); *Century*, XVI., 236 (June, 1889); *Forum*, VI., 241 (November, 1888); VII., 361 (June, 1889); *New Englander*, LIII., 1 (July, 1890); *North American Review*, Vol. 148, p. 54 (January, 1889); Vol. 151, p. 212 (August, 1890); Vol. 139, p. 42 (July, 1884); *Harper's Magazine*, LXXVIII., 520 (March, 1889).

I. Greater freedom of trade between the United States and Canada is desirable.——(*a*) It would furnish the United States with much needed raw materials: *Century*, XVI., 236. —(1) Coal, iron, and other mineral products are extensive and easily accessible to the northern and middle states: *Handbook of Commercial Union*, pp. 72-85; *North American Review*, Vol. 139, p. 42.—(2) Agricultural products. ——(*b*) It would open to us a large and convenient market for our manufactures: *Handbook of Commercial Union*, p. 249.——(*c*) Closer commercial relations would remove much of the present ill feeling, and international disputes would be avoided.

II. Reciprocity would be advantageous economically.—— (*a*) It would open up a great field for the investment of American capital: *Handbook of Commercial Union*, p. 247.—— (*b*) It would do away with the enormous expense of maintaining an unnatural customs line four thousand miles long.——(*c*) By the settlement of the fishery question it would give our fishermen valuable privileges.

III. Reciprocity is practical: *Handbook of Commercial Union*, p. 111.——(*a*) Great Britain would not raise serious objections: *Handbook of Commercial Union*, p. 101.—(1) English investments in Canada would be benefited by commercial prosperity.—(2) Greater commercial activity would establish confederation on a firm basis and give assurance that Canada would remain a part of the British domain.——(*b*) The loyalty of Canadians would not be affected.—(1) The common tariff would not discriminate against England.—— (*c*) A common tariff could be agreed upon.—(1) The present policy of the United States is toward a reduction of tariffs, while that of Canada is toward an increase.—(2) Canada would be willing to make concessions, such as the adjustment of internal revenue.——(*d*) The reciprocity treaty of 1854 was a commercial success.—(1) Trade rose from seven millions to twenty: *Encyclopædia Britannica*, IV., 766.—(2) The abrogation of the treaty was due to national animosity caused by acts of the English during the civil war.

Brief for the Negative.

GENERAL REFERENCES: James Douglas, *Canadian Independence, Annexation, and British Imperial Federation; Forum*, VI., 451 (January, 1889); J. N. Larned, Report to the Secretary of the Treasury on the *State of Trade Between the United States and British Possessions in North America*, January 28, 1871; *Penn Monthly*, V., 529 (July, 1874); *Congressional Globe*, 1864–1865, pp. 229–233 (January 12, 1865).

I. Complete commercial reciprocity is impracticable.—— (*a*) The commercial policies of Great Britain and the United States are conflicting.——(*b*) A common tariff could not be decided upon without detriment to one country.——(*c*)

Internal revenue stands in the way.—(1) Excise taxes and internal revenue would have to be made equal; but excise is necessary to Canada, while it is not unlikely that we shall do away with our internal revenue: *Forum*, VI., 451.

II. Complete reciprocity would be contrary to good public policy.——(*a*) It would result in loss of revenue.——(*b*) In case of war with Great Britain the frontier would be in a bad condition, and our whole tariff system would be torn asunder.

III. Complete reciprocity would be economically disastrous. ——(*a*) American and Canadian products are not supplementary, but competitory.——(*b*) Cheaper wages and cheaper raw material would be an inducement for our capital to move to Canada, and would also lower wages in the United States. ——(*c*) We should lose much through emigration to Canada. ——(*d*) It would give Canada the benefit of the market which we have built up for ourselves by protection: *Penn Monthly*, V., 531.

IV. Historically, reciprocity with Canada has proved injurious.——(*a*) The United States tried commercial reciprocity with Canada in 1854, but abrogated the treaty in 1866.

XL.

FREE SHIPS.

QUESTION: '*Resolved*, That foreign-built ships should be admitted to American registry free of duty.'

Brief for the Affirmative.

GENERAL REFERENCES: D. A. Wells, *The Decay of Our Ocean Mercantile Marine*; John Codman, *Free Ships*; J. D. J. Kelly, *The Question of Ships*: *North American Review*, Vol. 142, p. 478 (May, 1886); *House Reports*, 1889–1890, No. 1210, Minority Report; 1882–1883, No. 1827, Views of the Minority; 1891–1892, No. 966; 1887–1888, No. 1874; *Congressional Record*, 1890–1891, p. 1044 (January 8, 1891); *Congressional Globe*, 1871–1872, Part 3, p. 2241 (April 6, 1872).

I. A change in our navigation laws is necessary.—— (*a*) Under their restrictions American shipping has suffered.——(1) Through heavy duties on ships.——(*b*) Though heavily protected, the ship-building industry has not thrived. ——(1) The cost of labor is too great.——(*c*) American capital has been forced abroad.——(*d*) The present provision for the limited admission of foreign ships is inadequate.——(*e*) The development of inventive genius is prevented.

II. Free ships furnish the only practicable remedy: *The Question of Ships*, Chap. v.——(*a*) They enable Americans to compete on equal terms for world's commerce.——(1) Ships can be bought at the lowest price.——(*b*) Carrying trade should not be sacrificed to ship-building.——(1) It employs fifty times as many men: *The Question of Ships*, p. 31.—— (*c*) American ship-building would not be seriously affected.— (1) Only iron ships are concerned.——(*d*) The success of the plan is well illustrated by Germany's policy.

III. Subsidizing schemes are impracticable and inefficient: *The Question of Ships*, Chap. iv.——(*a*) Subsidies large enough to be efficient would be too great a tax on the people.——(1) The cost of building ships is one-third greater than in England: John Codman, *Free Ships*.——(*b*) They must be permanent.——(*c*) They have already been unsuccessfully tried in the United States.——(*d*) They have failed in France.— (1) Ship-building has not been built up in ten years' trial. ——(*e*) England's supremacy is not due to subsidizing: *The Decay of Our Ocean Mercantile Marine*, pp. 29–45.——(1) No payments are made to sailing vessels.——(2) Compensation is given only for carrying mails, and for building according to admiralty requirements.

Brief for the Negative.

GENERAL REFERENCES: W. W. Bates, *American Marine*; C. S. Hill, *History of American Shipping*; H. Hall, *American Navigation*; *North American Review*, Vol. 148, p. 687 (June, 1889); Vol. 154, p. 76 (January, 1892); Vol. 158, p. 433 (April, 1894); *House Reports*, 1891-1892, No. 966. Views of the Minority; 1887-1888, No. 1874, Views of the Minority, p. 10; 1882-1883, No. 1827; 1869-1870, No. 28; Nelson Dingley, Jr., in *Congressional Record*, 1890-1891, p. 997 (January 7, 1891).

I. The lack of free registry was not responsible for the decline in American shipping.——(*a*) Under the present laws our merchant marine reached its height.——(*b*) The decline was due to other causes.—(1) To the destruction of commerce by English-built cruisers: *American Marine*, Chap. ix.—(2) To the commercial depression following war.—(3) To mechanical changes.—(x) From wood to iron.—(y) From sail to steam.

II. Free registry offers no material advantages.——(*a*) American capital now invests in foreign-built ships.—(1) 'Whitewashed' sales: *American Navigation*, p. 75.——(*b*) The advantage of flying American flag would be subject to abuse.

III. Free registry involves grave evils.——(*a*) Economic.—(1) It would annihilate ship-building in the United States.—(2) It would withdraw millions of capital from the country.——(*b*) National.—(1) It would cripple us in time of war.—(x) We should have no trained workmen.—(y) We should have no shipyards to build in an emergency.

IV. There are better alternatives than free registry.——(*a*) The removal of duties on materials.——(*b*) Sufficient mail subsidies to American-built ships: *American Navigation*, p. 77.——(*c*) A change in taxation from the principal invested in ships to net profits.

XLI.

SHIPPING SUBSIDIES.

QUESTION: ' *Resolved,* That the United States should establish a system of shipping subsidies.'

Brief for the Affirmative.

GENERAL REFERENCES: W. W. Bates, *American Marine; House Reports,* 1889–1890, No. 1210; C. S. Hill, *History of American Shipping; House Reports,* 1888–1889, No. 4162, Views of the Minority, p. 5; *Congressional Record,* 1890–1891, p. 997 (January 7, 1891), p. 3355 (February 26, 1891); Statement of Captain W. W. Bates in *House Reports,* 1889–1890, No. 1210, p. 220; *Overland Monthly,* I., 462 (May, 1883); H. Hall, *American Navigation.*

I. The merchant marine of the United States is at present in a deplorable condition and ought to be built up: *House Reports,* 1889–1890, No. 1210, pp. i–vi.——(*a*) A national marine is of the greatest importance to the wealth and the commercial prosperity of a nation: *Lalor's Cyclopædia,* II., 987; J. D. J. Kelly, *The Question of Ships,* p. 108.—(1) It is essential to naval power.—(2) To the development of resources.—(3) To national unity and individualism.——(*b*) The United States has the necessary qualifications for the marine industry: *The Question of Ships,* Chap. i.; *American Navigation,* Chap. ii.—(1) In 1856 the United States merchant marine was the most extensive in the world.—(2) Our extensive sea-coast naturally fosters a maritime spirit.—(3) We have abundant natural resources.—(4) Extensive commerce. —(5) Great ship-building interests.

II. The subsidy system is a desirable means of building up the marine.——(*a*) It is preferable to the policy of free ships.

—(1) Such a policy would destroy our ship-building industry: *American Navigation*, Chap. vii.——(*b*) Subsidies given to vessels for mail service would greatly encourage commerce.—(1) By insuring regular service: *American Navigation*, p. 77; *Congressional Record*, 1885–1886, p. 4009 (April 30. 1886).——(*c*) Vessels subsidized could be put under contract to serve the United States in case of war: *American Navigation*, pp. 83–86.——(*d*) It is an economical system.—(1) The total payments would not exceed $5,000,000 per annum.—(2) The earnings of the foreign mail service, which amount to $10,000,000 per annum, could fittingly be used for subsidies: *Congressional Record*, 1889–1890, p. 6996 (July 7, 1890).

III. Subsidies are necessary.——(*a*) The cost of American ships and their running expenses are greater than those of foreign vessels.——(*b*) The high subsidies given to foreign lines make it impossible for American lines to compete without like subsidies.

IV. Subsidies have proved successful in practice: *American Marine*, pp. 325–327.——(*a*) We have tried such a system and found it effective: W. S. Lindsay, *Merchant Shipping*, IV., 194–228.——(*b*) Nearly all foreign nations maintain shipping subsidies: *Congressional Record*, 1890–1891, pp. 3359–3362 (February 26, 1891).——(*c*) They have been successful in France: *House Reports*, 1889–1890, No. 1210, pp. ix–xv. ——(*d*) Great Britain, the foremost maritime country, has steadily adhered to a system of bounties: *Congressional Record*, 1890–1891, pp. 1001–1003 (January 7, 1891).

Brief for the Negative.

GENERAL REFERENCES: *House Reports*, 1889–1890, No. 1210, Minority Report, p. xxxix.; D. A. Wells, *Our Merchant Marine*; D. A. Wells, *The Decay of Our Ocean Mercantile Marine*; John Codman, *Free Ships*; John Codman, *Shipping Subsidies and Bounties*; *Congressional Record*,

1890–1891, pp. 3348, 3368. 3383 (February 26, 1891); 1889–1890, p. 6959 (July 3. 1890); *House Reports*, 1888–1889, No. 4162; J. D. J. Kelly, *The Question of Ships*.

I. Subsidies are politically objectionable.——(*a*) They have proved and always will prove inducements to corrupt legislation.——(*b*) They create and foster a privileged class at the expense of the whole people: *Our Merchant Marine*, p. 141; *Free Ships*, p. 15.——(*c*) The practice would establish a bad precedent: *House Reports*, 1889–1890, No. 1210, pp. xl., xlii.

II. Subsidies are economically objectionable: *Congressional Record*, 1890–1891, p. 3352.——(*a*) They are merely temporizing measures: *The Decay of Our Ocean Mercantile Marine*, p. 25.——(*b*) They would be a tremendous cost: *House Reports*, 1888–1889, No. 4162, p. 4.——(*c*) They would not contribute to the general prosperity of the country: *House Reports*, 1888–1889, No. 4162, pp. 2–3.—(1) They would not benefit commerce.—(x) Foreign vessels now carry as cheaply as it can be done.—(2) They would benefit one industry at the expense of others.—(3) As profit would come wholly from subsidies, shippers would become uneconomical and the advantages of competition would be lost.

III. There is no truth in the statement that shipping subsidies have built up merchant marines.——(*a*) Great Britain does not subsidize her vessels: *The Decay of Our Ocean Mercantile Marine*, p. 29; *House Reports*, 1889–1890, No. 1210, pp. xlii., l.—(1) British mail subsidies are for actual service rendered as shown by the exacting rules and penalties for non-performance of contracts.——(*b*) The French system has not been successful: *House Reports*, 1888–1889, No. 4162, p. 3; 1889–1890, No. 1210, pp. l–lx.——(*c*) Our own experience has been unfavorable.—(1) The Collins line in 1847: *Congressional Record*, 1890–1891, p. 3386.

IV. The best remedy for American shipping is free ships: *Our Merchant Marine*, pp. 95–128; *North American Review*,

Vol. 142, pp. 481-484 (May, 1886).——(*a*) Free ships would at least allow Americans to compete on equal terms for the commerce of the world.

XLII.

FREE SUGAR.

QUESTION: '*Resolved*, That sugar should be admitted free of duty.'

Brief for the Affirmative.

GENERAL REFERENCES: 'Sugar and the Tariff,' *Tariff Reform Series*, III., No. 12, p. 174 (July 30, 1890); *Harper's Weekly*, XXXVIII., 602 (June 30, 1894), 771 (August 18, 1894), 819 (September 1, 1894); *Nation*, LIX., 74 (August 2, 1894), 112 (August 16, 1894); *Congressional Record*, 1889-1890, p. 10,631 (September 27, 1890).

I. The question of protection does not enter.——(*a*) We produce only ten per cent. of the sugar we use: *Princeton Review*, VI., 322 (November, 1880).——(*b*) The established industry can be more economically protected by bounties.

II. The tariff is a burden on the poor.——(*a*) The poor man must pay more in proportion to his ability than the rich: C. D. Wright in *Seventeenth Annual Report of Massachusetts Bureau of Statistics of Labor*, p. 266; W. O. Atwater in *American Public Health Association*, XV., 208.—(1) Carbohydrates are necessary to life.—(2) Sugar is the most economical carbohydrate.—(3) The laboring man consumes the greatest proportion of this constituent: *American Public Health Association*, XV., 216.

III. The sugar tariff is a check to the country's development.——(*a*) It discourages industries in which sugar is a raw material.—(1) The preserving industry.—(2) The condensed milk industry.—(3) The refining industry.——(*b*) It injures foreign commerce.—(1) With Brazil and Cuba.—(2) Germany has retaliated for our tariff by putting a tax on American beef: *Harper's Weekly*, XXXVIII., 1058 (November 10, 1894).

IV. Sugar taxes are a great source of corruption.——(*a*) They enable importers to defraud the government by manipulating the grades of sugar.——(*b*) They give rise to political corruption such as has disgraced the Senate.—(1) By fostering the sugar trust: *Nation*, LVIII., 440 (June 14, 1894); LIX., 71, 93, 112; *Harper's Weekly*, XXXVIII., 602, 771, 819; *Tariff Reform Series*, VII., No. 2, p. 28 (July 1, 1894).

V. The sugar tax is not necessary for revenue.——(*a*) If the revenues fall short, the deficiency can be made up better by replacing the higher taxes on malt liquors and tobacco.

Brief for the Negative.

GENERAL REFERENCES: *Congressional Record*, 1893–1894, Appendix, p. 1178 (August 13, 1894), p. 634 (January 23, 1894); 1889–1890, Appendix, p. 437 (May 20, 1890); *Harper's Weekly*, XXXVIII., 218 (March 10, 1894); *Tariff Hearings Before the Committee on Ways and Means*, 1893, pp. 505, 520, 542.

I. A tax on sugar is a just way of raising revenue: *Congressional Record*, 1893–1894, Appendix, p. 1182.——(*a*) It is evenly distributed: *Ibid.*—(1) It reaches consumers in proportion to their incomes.—(2) Sugar is to a great extent an article of voluntary consumption.

II. It is a desirable way of raising revenue.——(*a*) It is the only tax which furnishes a steady, reliable revenue, capable of computation beforehand.——(*b*) It is an easy tax to collect. ——(*c*) Precedent has established sugar as a fitting article for taxation: D. A. Wells in *Princeton Review*, VI., 323 (November, 1880); *Congressional Record*, 1893–1894, Appendix, pp. 1180–1186.—(1) It has heretofore furnished one-fourth of the total revenue: D. A. Wells, *The Sugar Industry of the United States and the Tariff*, p. 9.

III. The tax is necessary to encourage the American sugar industry: *Congressional Record*, 1893–1894, Appendix, p. 632.——(*a*) The beet and sugar industries are difficult to establish.—(1) They require a large outlay of capital at the beginning.—(2) The return on the investment is small.—(3) The industries are still experimental.——(*b*) American producers require a special protective tax to offset the large bounties which foreign countries pay to their producers.

IV. The objections to the tax are unsound.——(*a*) The sugar-refining trust would remain even if sugar were admitted free.—(1) As nearly all of the sugar admitted to the United States is raw, it would still have to pass through the refineries. ——(*b*) The frauds against the government, due to the manipulation of grades, are not an inherent result of the tax.

XLIII.

SUGAR BOUNTIES.

QUESTION: '*Resolved*, That a system of sugar bounties is contrary to good public policy.'

Brief for the Affirmative.

GENERAL REFERENCES: D. A. Wells, *Recent Economic Changes*, pp. 295–309; *Lalor's Cyclopedia*, II., 99; *Fortnightly Review*, XLII., 638 (November, 1884); *Nation*, XLV., 164 (September 1, 1887); XLII., 420 (May 20, 1886); *Congressional Record*, 1889–1890, pp. 10,712–10,716 (September 30, 1890), Appendix, p. 391.

I. The bounty system is unconstitutional.——(*a*) It is legislation in favor of a class: *Nation*, XLVII., 24 (July 12,

1888); *Congressional Record*, 1889–1890, pp. 10,712–10,716, Appendix, p. 391; Loan Association *v.* Topeka, 120 *Wallace*, 663–664.

II. The bounty system is burdensome on the people: *Nation*, XLIV., 484 (June 9, 1887).——(*a*) The people are compelled to pay the bounty: *Fortnightly Review*, XLII., 638.——(*b*) They are compelled to pay the highest cost of production for sugar: *Fortnightly Review*, XLII., 638.——(*c*) They are compelled to pay for the expensive system of administration.

III. The bounty system gives rise to fraud.——(*a*) It places a great amount of money and patronage in the hands of political parties: *Congressional Record*, 1889–1890, Appendix, p. 391.——(*b*) The intricate system of bounty payments enables producers to defraud the government: *Recent Economic Changes*, pp. 295–298.

IV. The bounty system is injurious to commerce.——(*a*) It deranges prices.—(1) The producer is led to disregard the law of supply and demand: *Fortnightly Review*, XLII., 638. ——(*b*) It makes foreign exchange uncertain: *Nation*, XLV., 164.—(1) By causing alternate over-production and under-production: *Recent Economic Changes*, pp. 295–309.——(*c*) It enables producers to control the markets.

V. The bounty system is unnecessary for the development of the industry.——(*a*) The United States has as good facilities for raising beets as any other country.——(*b*) The sugar industry is not an infant industry.

VI. The bounty system has proved a failure in Europe: *Nation*, XLVI., 45 (January 19, 1888); *Recent Economic Changes*, pp. 295–309; *Lalor's Cyclopedia*, II., 99.——(*a*) The beet-sugar industry was fostered at the expense of cane sugar: *Nation*, XLV., 164.——(*b*) International complications arose: *Saturday Review*, LXIV., 142 (July 30, 1887), 847 (December 24, 1887).

Brief for the Negative.

GENERAL REFERENCES: Essay on 'Industry and Commerce' in *Works of Alexander Hamilton*, III., 366; *Congressional Record*, 1889-1890, p. 4266 (May 7, 1890); Senators Allison and Sherman in *Congressional Record*, 1888-1889, pp. 888-895 (January 17, 1889).

I. The sugar industry is highly desirable.——(a) The importance of sugar as a food is constantly increasing: *Congressional Record*, 1889-1890, p. 4266.——(b) The industry will be national, not sectional: *Congressional Record*, 1888-1889, p. 892; 1889-1890, p. 4515 (May 10, 1890).——(c) Beets do not exhaust the soil: *Congressional Record*, 1889-1890, p. 4266.

II. The sugar industry would bring general economic advantages.——(a) It would keep at home money now sent abroad in payment for sugar.——(b) Capital greatly exceeding the amount of the bounty would be invested in the industry.——(c) The industry would create a new and a large demand for labor, both agricultural and mechanical.

III. The bounty system is the best means of establishing the sugar industry.——(a) Protective duties are inadequate.—(1) Bounties paid by foreign countries tend to counteract our tariff.—(2) In the past import duties have failed.——(b) Bounties are necessary to tide the industry over the critical time of beginning: *Congressional Record*, 1889-1890, p. 4515.—(1) Establishment is difficult and expensive.—(2) There is small inducement for capital.—(3) Beet and sorghum sugar industries are more or less experimental.——(c) Bounties have been successful in establishing industries abroad.—(1) Beet-sugar industry in Germany: *Congressional Record*, 1889-1890, pp. 4266, 4431 (May 9, 1890).

IV. The bounty system is constitutional. —— (a) The bounty is extended to anyone who is willing to undertake the production of sugar: *American Law Register and Review*, XXXI., 289 (May, 1892).

XLIV.

DUTIES ON WOOL AND WOOLLENS.

QUESTION: '*Resolved*, That a system of duties on wool and woollens is undesirable.'

Brief for the Affirmative.

GENERAL REFERENCES: F. W. Taussig in *Quarterly Journal of Economics*, VIII., 1 (October, 1893); *North American Review*, Vol. 154, p. 133 (February, 1892); 'Wool and Tariff,' *Tariff Reform Series*, III., No. 19, p. 342 (November 15, 1890); 'The Wool Question,' *Tariff Reform Series* (Report of Ways and Means Committee on the Springer Bill), V., No. 1, p. 1 (March 15, 1892).

I. Duties on wool and woollens have failed to bring beneficient results.——(*a*) Wool-growing has not prospered.—(1) The United States cannot raise grades of wool that will compare in quality with the better grades of foreign countries.— (x) Owing to climate: *Quarterly Journal of Economics*, VIII., 18.——(*b*) Woollen manufacturers produce only the cheapest grades of woollens.——(*c*) Under the tariff American producers have succeeded in producing but a small quantity of woollens in comparison with foreign importations: *Quarterly Journal of Economics*, VIII., 28–29; *Tariff Reform Series*, III., No. 19, p. 359.

II. The removal of duties on wool does not hurt wool-growers.——(*a*) The grades of wool raised by American growers are not subject to foreign competition.—(1) In these grades the American producer has an equal advantage with foreign producers: *Quarterly Journal of Economics*, VIII., 5–20.

III. Free woollens are not injurious to manufacturers.—— (*a*) They do not injure the production of cheap grades of woollens for the American market.——(1) The American manufacturer, owing to the greater efficiency of his machinery and the small necessity for hand labor, can compete on equal terms in these grades.

IV. The removal of duties on wool is a benefit to manufacturers.——(*a*) It enables them to engage in the manufacture of finer grades of woollens: *Quarterly Journal of Economics*, VIII., 32–33.—(1) By giving them free raw material of finer grades.——(*b*) It gives them a larger assortment of wools from which to select their grades: *Congressional Record*, 1887–1888, pp. 6519–6530 (July 19, 1888).——(*c*) It enlarges their trade with South America: *Nation*, XLVI., 500 (June 21, 1888).

V. Duties are unjust to consumers.——(*a*) They require them to pay a high price for woollens which are not made in America.—(1) This is shown by the constant increase in the importations of the finer grades of woollens in spite of the high tariff.

Brief for the Negative.

GENERAL REFERENCES: *Bulletin of National Association of Wool Manufacturers*. XVIII., 1888, Nos. 2, 3; XXII., 268 (September, 1892); XXIII., 275 (December, 1893); XXII., 1 (March, 1892); XXI., 333 (December, 1891); XXII., 115 (June, 1892); W. D. Lewis, *Our Sheep and the Tariff* (Publications of the University of Pennsylvania), Chaps. i., vii.: *Congressional Record*, 1893–1894, Appendix, pp. 1064, 1172.

I. Duties on wool are necessary to protect the sheep-raising industry: *Our Sheep and the Tariff*, Chap. vii.——(*a*) Foreign competition is especially active in this industry.—(1) Australia and the Argentine Republic have superior natural advantages.

II. Duties on woollens are necessary to protect manufacturers: *Bulletin of National Association of Wool Manu-*

facturers, XXII., 133.——(*a*) Foreign manufacturers have an advantage in cheap labor.——(*b*) Foreign manufacturers have as good machinery as manufacturers in the United States.—(1) American machinery is used extensively abroad.——(*c*) The return on investments in the United States is less than it is abroad.—(1) A larger capital is required to produce an equivalent amount of woollens: *Bulletin of National Association of Wool Manufacturers*, XXII., 136.

III. The history of the United States shows that duties have been successful in building up the wool and woollen industries: *Bulletin of National Association of Wool Manufacturers*, XVIII., 234.——(*a*) The production of wool has greatly increased since the system was begun.——(*b*) The woollen industry is four times as large as in 1860: *Bulletin of National Association of Wool Manufacturers*, XXII., 3.——(*c*) Under periods of high protection the industries have been most prosperous.

IV. The duties have benefited the consumers: *Bulletin of National Association of Wool Manufacturers*, XXII., 119.——(*a*) They have reduced the price of woollens to less than half what it was thirty years ago.—(1) By causing active competition and rapid improvements in machinery: *Bulletin of National Association of Wool Manufacturers*, XXII., 119.

TAXATION.

XLV.

A NATIONAL INCOME TAX.

Question : '*Resolved*, That an income tax is a desirable part of a scheme of taxation.'

Brief for the Affirmative.

GENERAL REFERENCES: C. F. Bastable, *Public Finance*, Bk. IV., Chap. iv. ; R. T. Ely, *Taxation in American States and Cities*, Part III., Chap. vii.; *Congressional Record*, 1893-1894, pp. 6684-6690 (June 22, 1894); *North American Review*, Vol. 158, p. 1 (January, 1894), p. 150 (February, 1894); *Political Science Quarterly*, IX., 610 (December, 1894); *New Englander*, XXXVII., 543 (July, 1878); *National Review*, II., 771 (February, 1884); *Nation*, IX., 452 (November 25, 1869); *Public Opinion*, XV., XVI., XVII. (see Indexes, Income Tax); *Forum*, XVII., 14 (March, 1894).

I. An income tax is a just tax.——(*a*) It is an assessment on a man's ability to pay.——(*b*) It falls upon those who are best able to pay.—(1) Incomes more than necessary for actual living expenses.——(*c*) It equalizes the burden of taxation.—(1) The poor have to bear most of the taxes on consumption: *Lalor's Cyclopædia*, II., 485.

II. An income tax is an excellent and efficient tax economically considered.——(*a*) The greatest possible amount of the total tax levied gets into the treasury.—(1) Paid directly into the hands of the government.——(*b*) Its operation does not have the deleterious effect of tariff taxes.—(1) It does not affect the normal distribution of capital.—(2) It does not benefit one class over another.——(*c*) Its operation improves the longer it is tried.——(*d*) The incidence of the tax cannot be placed on some other individual or class.

III. The income tax is already well established as a tax in practice and by leading authorities.——(*a*) The great nations of Europe all make it a part of their fiscal system, *e.g.*, Italy, Germany, Austria, France, and Switzerland.—(1) It has been constantly in use in England since 1842: *Public Finance*, pp. 427-428.——(*b*) The income tax is recommended by high economic authority: Ely, Wayland, Thomson, Levi, Cossa: *Congressional Record*, 1893-1894, p. 6685.

IV. An income tax is valuable as permanent part of a tax system.——(*a*) It reaches a great class of wealth which escapes other taxation.—(1) It taps the incomes of great corporations. —(2) It levies on those who escape local taxation.——(*b*) It furnishes a steady source of revenue.——(*c*) It is elastic.—(1) Its rate can be varied from year to year.

Brief for the Negative.

GENERAL REFERENCES: Senator Hill in *Congressional Record*, 1893-1894, pp. 6611-6624 (June 21, 1894); 1894-1895, pp. 840-850 (January 11, 1895); *Lalor's Cyclopædia*, II., 485; D. A. Wells in *Forum*, XVII., 1 (March, 1894); *Annals of American Academy of Political Science*, IV., 557 (January, 1894); *North American Review*, Vol. 130, p. 236 (March, 1880); Vol. 160, p. 601 (May, 1895); *Political Science Quarterly*, IV., 37 (March, 1889); *New Englander*, LIV., 39 (January, 1891); *Nation*, XXVI., 287 (May 2, 1878); LVII., 404 (November 30, 1893); LVIII., 24 (January 11, 1894).

I. An income tax is bad in theory.——(*a*) It is unjust.—(1) It discriminates against personal ability.—(2) Against the well-to-do.—(3) Against temporary incomes.——(*b*) Its effect on morals is bad: *Lalor's Cyclopædia*, III., 880.—(1) It offers every temptation to commit fraud.——(*c*) It tends to stop the accumulation of wealth.——(*d*) It is class legislation. ——(*e*) It secures unjust territorial distribution.——(*f*) The national government should not interfere in the domain of state and municipal taxation: *Public Opinion*, XVI., 477.

II. An income tax is objectionable in administration: J. S. Mill, *Principles of Political Economy*, II., Bk. V., Chap. iii., § 5.——(*a*) It is inquisitorial.——(*b*) It is difficult to collect.—(1) Very hard to ascertain real incomes.—(2) Easily evaded.——(*c*) It has serious inequalities.——(*d*) It is very unpopular.——(*e*) It is completely arbitrary.——(*f*) It leads to great abuses.

III. An income tax is impracticable.——(*a*) Its workings have not proved successful.—(1) In Europe.—(x) Prussia: *Quarterly Journal of Economics*, VI., 219.—(y) In Switzerland.—(z) The English government would be glad to rid themselves of the tax.—(2) In the United States.—(x) The tax levied during the war had to be abolished in 1871 on account of inequalities and irregularities.

XLVI.

A SINGLE TAX.

QUESTION: '*Resolved,* That a single tax on land would be better than the present system of taxation.'

Brief for the Affirmative.

GENERAL REFERENCES: Henry George, *Progress and Poverty;* Henry George, *The Condition of Labor;* Henry George, *Social Problems;* W. H. Dawson, *The Unearned Increment;* S. B. Clarke, *Current Objections to the Exaction of an Economic Rent by Taxation;* R. T. Ely, *Taxation in American States and Cities,* Part II.; David Ricardo, *Political Economy,* Chaps. xxiv., xxxii.; Single Tax Debate in *Journal of Social Science,* No. XXVII., p. 1 (October, 1890); *North American Review,* Vol. 141, p. 1 (July, 1885); Vol. 158, p. 175 (February, 1894); *Forum,* VIII., 40 (September, 1889); *Century,* XL., 394 (July, 1890); *Arena,* X., 52 (June, 1894), 332 (August, 1894); *Public Opinion,* IX., 523 (September 13, 1890).

I. The present system of taxation is bad.——(*a*) Extremely complex.——(*b*) Expensive.——(*c*) Illogical.——(*d*) Clumsy.——(*e*) Demoralizing to taxpayers.——(*f*) Imposes artificial restraints on industry.——(*g*) Discourages improvements.——(*h*) Incidence is concealed.——(*i*) Inequitable.

II. The substitution of a single tax on land would be a decided improvement: Henry George, *Progress and Poverty.*——(*a*) Simple.——(*b*) Economical.——(*c*) Cannot be evaded.——(*d*) Automatic.——(*e*) Less burdensome.——(*f*) Frees industry and commerce.——(*g*) Removes taxes upon labor and capital.——(*h*) Equitable.

III. Land values are the best subject for taxation: David Ricardo, *Political Economy*, Chaps. xxiv., xxxii.——(*a*) Society may justly appropriate land rents.—(1) Rents are due to the development of society, not to the owner's activity. ——(*b*) The taxation of land rents will prevent unjust enrichments from land investments.——(*c*) It will prevent speculation in land.——(*d*) It will lead to the more effective use of land.

Brief for the Negative.

GENERAL REFERENCES: W. H. Mallock, *Property and Progress;* G. B. Stebbins, *Progress from Poverty;* John Rae, *Contemporary Socialism* (second edition), Chap. xii.: F. A. Walker, *Land and Its Rent*, pp. 141–182; Single Tax Debate in *Journal of Social Science*, No. XXVII., p. 1 (October, 1890); *North American Review*, Vol. 137, p. 147 (August, 1883); *Popular Science Monthly*, XXXVI., 481 (February, 1890); *Forum*, III., 15 (March, 1887), 433 (July, 1887); *Political Science Quarterly*, VI., 625 (December, 1891); *Quarterly Journal of Economics*, VII., 433 (July, 1893); *Century*, XL., 384, 403 (July, 1890); XLII., 792 (September, 1891); *Andover Review*, VIII., 592 (December, 1887); *Edinburgh Review*, Vol. 157, p. 263 (January, 1883); *Nineteenth Century*, XV., 537 (April, 1884); *Quarterly Review*, Vol. 155 p. 35 (January, 1883); *Nation*, XXXI., 65 (July 22, 1880), 117 (August 12, 1880); XXXVIII., 237 (March 13, 1884).

I. The single tax is objectionable as a scheme for raising revenue.——(*a*) It is inelastic.——(*b*) It abolishes the entire revenue service.—(1) Thus preventing the assessment of desirable excise taxes.——(*c*) It cannot be perfectly assessed. ——(*d*) It threatens free institutions.—(1) Revenues are raised without legislation: E. Benjamin Andrews in *Journal of Social Science*, No. XXVII., p. 33.———(*c*) It cuts off the possibility of taxing trusts and corporations.

II. The tax is an unjust one.———(*a*) It is not universal.—(1) The whole burden is placed on a small portion of the community.———(*b*) It is not equal.—(1) Professional men would pay practically nothing.—(2) Farmers would overpay.———(*c*) It is not thorough.—(1) The unearned increment on land is taxed.—(2) Other forms of increment escape.

III. The tax would not accomplish the end desired.———(*a*) It would not remove the present hardships.—(1) Does away with only one branch of capitalism.—(x) Trusts, monopolies, and trade combinations would not be affected.—(2) It would not relieve the burdens of the poor.—(x) The country poor would be weighed down by the increased tax.—(y) The city poor would merely be assessed by the state instead of by the individual.———(*b*) It is doubtful whether the tax would yield sufficient revenue.—(1) The practical workings are not understood.—(x) The tax has no basis in history or in practice.—(y) Where it has been tried it has failed.

IV. The tax is revolutionary and socialistic.———(*a*) It would inaugurate government ownership of land.—(1) Confiscates private holdings.———(*b*) It would bring about dangerous centralization of the powers of government.———(*c*) It is aimed at wealth which has grown up under the sanction of the law.

SOCIOLOGY.

GOVERNMENT INTERVENTION.

XLVII.

GOVERNMENT OWNERSHIP OF RAILROADS.

QUESTION: '*Resolved*, That the railroads in the United States should be owned and operated by the federal government.'

Brief for the Affirmative.

GENERAL REFERENCES: R. T. Ely in *Harper's Magazine*, LXXIII., 250 (July, 1886), 450 (August, 1886), 571 (September, 1886); E. J. James in *Publications of American Economic Association*, II., 246 (July, 1887); G. H. Lewis, *National Consolidation of the Railways of the United States;* T. V. Powderly in *Arena*, VII., 58 (December, 1892); *Lalor's Cyclopædia*, III., 493; *Westminster Review*, Vol. 142, p. 1 (July, 1894); *Fortnightly Review*, XLV., 737 (June, 1886); *Forum*, XVIII., 704 (February, 1895).

I. Railroads should be operated for public interests alone. ——(*a*) They are of a public nature.—(1) In their economic relations: *Harper's Magazine*, LXXIII., 250.—(2) In their legal relations.—(3) As public highways.

II. Under private ownership and management public interest is made subservient to private interest.——(*a*) Railroads are now carried on for private ends alone.—(1) Shown by the building of parallel lines: R. T. Ely, *Problems of To-day*, p. 140.—(2) By speculation: A. T. Hadley, *Railroad Trans portation*, Chap. iii.——(*b*) They neglect the welfare of the public.—(1) Shown by the poor service.—(2) The great number of accidents.—(3) The system of rate discriminations: J. F. Hudson, *The Railways and the Republic*, Chaps. ii., iii., iv.—(4) The process known as 'skinning the road.'——(*c*) They are a source of corruption in politics: *Arena*, VII., 58; *The Railways and the Republic*, pp. 450-479.——(*d*) They waste national resources.—(1) By unnecessary competition: *Railroad Transportation*, Chap. v.—(2) By land grants.

III. Only under a system of government ownership and management will the public interest be secure.——(*a*) Government interference is ineffectual.—(1) It has not been satisfactory under the Interstate Commerce Act.——(*b*) Government ownership will result in economy of administration and construction: J. S. Jeans, *Railway Problems*, p. 463.——(*c*) It will result in better service and greater safety.——(*d*) It will do away with labor troubles: *Arena*, VII., 58.

IV. Government ownership is practicable.——(*a*) It has the endorsement of practical railroad men: *National Consolidation of the Railways of the United States*, p. 190.——(*b*) Fair trials in foreign countries have shown its practicability: *Lalor's Cyclopædia*, III., 502.—(1) Seen in the experience of Belgium and Germany: William Larrabee, *The Railroad Question*, p. 409: *Quarterly Journal of Economics*, I., 453 (July, 1887).——(*c*) The extension of the civil service would hasten the necessary reform.

Brief for the Negative.

GENERAL REFERENCES: A. T. Hadley, *Railroad Transportation*; W. S. Jevons, *Methods of Social Reform*, pp. 353-383; J. F. Hudson, *The Railways and the Republic*; *Political Science Quarterly*, III., 572 (December, 1888); *Nation*, XLV., 346 (November 3, 1887); LI., 205 (September 11, 1890); J. M. Bonham, *Railway Secrecy and Trusts*, Chaps. ii., iv.; *Forum*, XI., 79 (March, 1891); W. M. Acworth, *The Railways and the Traders*.

I. Private ownership of railroads in the United States has been successful.——(*a*) The efficiency of the roads is equal to that of any in the world.—(1) In cheapness of rates.—(2) In speed.—(3) In safety of service.——(*b*) Discriminations, unstable rate schedules, and rate wars have been remedied by the Interstate Commerce Act: *Quarterly Journal of Economics*, II., 162 (January, 1888).——(*c*) The country has been developed by the building of new lines to meet all needs. ——(*d*) The railroads do not earn more than a fair return on the capital invested: *North American Review*, Vol. 156, p. 556 (May, 1893).

II. The fact that government ownership of telegraph and postal systems has been successful is no indication that government ownership of railroads will be successful.——(*a*) The telegraph and postal systems are simply routine work.——(*b*) The amount of capital in railroads is exceedingly large.—— (*c*) The financial arrangement is too elaborate and complex to be understood by the average citizen: *Railroad Transportation*, pp. 57–60.

III. Government ownership, by destroying competition, would be contrary to good commercial policy.——(*a*) It would weaken the efficiency of the railroads.—(1) By discouraging the development of improved methods of equipment.——(*b*) It would raise the price of transportation.—— (*c*) It would encourage careless and useless expenditure of public wealth.

IV. Government ownership would be contrary to good public policy: *Railroad Transportation*, Chap. xiii.——(*a*) In our republican form of government the railroad would be a source of political corruption.—(1) It would afford great opportunities for political patronage.—(2) The complex financial arrangements would make frauds easy.——(*b*) Government intervention in commerce is undesirable.

V. Government ownership has been unsuccessful abroad. ——(*a*) In Australia: *Economic Journal*, II., 636 (December, 1892).——(*b*) In Italy and France: *Railroad Transportation*,

Chaps. x., xiii.; *Nation*, XXXV., 150 (August 24, 1892); *The Railways and the Republic*, p. 326.

XLVIII.

GOVERNMENT OWNERSHIP OF THE TELEGRAPH.

QUESTION: '*Resolved*, That all telegraph lines in the United States should be owned and controlled by the government.'

Brief for the Affirmative.

GENERAL REFERENCES: *Forum*, IV., 561 (February, 1888); IX., 450 (June, 1890); *North American Review*, Vol. 142, p. 227 (March, 1886); Vol. 143, p. 35 (July, 1886); Vol. 149, p. 44 (July, 1889); *Nation*, XXXVII., 90 (August 2, 1883); XXXVIII., 136 (February 14, 1884); *Popular Science Monthly*, XIX., 400 (July, 1881); *Quarterly Journal of Economics*, II., 353 (April, 1888); *Atlantic Monthly*, XXXI., 230 (February, 1873); *International Review*, I., 383–384 (May, 1874); A. T. Hadley, *Railroad Transportation*, pp. 251–258; W. S. Jevons, *Methods of Social Reform*, p. 277; Report of the Postmaster-General, *House Executive Documents*, 1871–1872, IV., pp. xxv.–xxx.; *Senate Reports*, 1883–1884, No. 577, pp. 1–20, 51–118; Pensacola Telegraph Co. *v.* Western Union Telegraph Co., 6 *Otto*, 1.

I. The progress of commerce and civilization in the United States demands better and cheaper facilities for the rapid transmission of intelligence.

II. The present method of controlling telegraph lines is inadequate for the purposes.——(*a*) The lines are practically controlled by a monopoly.——(*b*) Tariffs are exorbitant, unequal, and complex.——(*c*) There is discrimination in service.——(*d*) Great and irresponsible influence is exercised over the press, commerce, and legislation.——(*e*) The free-message system is a tax on the public.——(*f*) Alliances are made with railroads to the detriment of the public.——(*g*) It is possible to misuse wires for private ends.

III. The most efficient and cheapest service can be obtained by government ownership and control: *North American Review*, Vol. 132, p. 369 (April, 1881).——(*a*) Lines would be managed in the interest of the public.——(*b*) Rates could be greatly reduced and the general use of the telegraph increased.—(1) The reduction of rates in Paris was followed by a tenfold increase in the number of users: *Methods of Social Reform*, p. 283.—(2) There would be no unnecessary outlay for parallel lines.—(3) The telegraph is naturally a department of the post-office and use could be made of local post-office facilities: *Forum*, IV., 561.—(4) There would be freedom from taxation.——(*c*) Service would be better.—(1) Lines would be made more efficient and would be extended to suburbs and outlying districts.—(2) Offices would be more centrally situated.—(3) Strikes would be impossible.

IV. Government ownership is practicable.——(*a*) It is constitutional: H. von Holst, *Constitutional Law of the United States*, p. 147, note; Pensacola Telegraph Co. *v.* Western Union Telegraph Co., 6 *Otto*, 1.——(*b*) By act of 1886 the government has the right to purchase lines at an appraised value: *Constitutional Law of the United States*, p. 145, note 2.——(*c*) There is no argument for the postal service which does not apply to the telegraph: *Methods of Social Reform*, pp. 279-281; *Senate Reports*, 1883-1884, No. 577, p. 66; *Nation*, XXXVII., 90.—(1) The capital invested is comparatively small.—(2) The work is routine.—(3) Strict public supervision is possible from the character of the work. ——(*d*) The objection as to the civil service is not valid: *North American Review*, Vol. 132, p. 382.—(1) Telegraph employees are skilled operators who cannot safely be removed. ——(*e*) Government ownership of telegraph systems has been successful in Europe: *Popular Science Monthly*, XIX., 400; *North American Review*, Vol. 143, p. 35.

Brief for the Negative.

GENERAL REFERENCES: *Political Science Quarterly*, III., 572 (December, 1888); D. A. Wells in *House Miscellaneous Documents*, 1872-1873, No. 73, p. 39; A. T. Hadley, *Railroad Transportation*, p. 272; *Public Opinion*, IV., 399 (February 4. 1888); *Senate Reports*, 1883-1884, V., No. 577, pp. 13-50; *North American Review*, Vol. 139, p. 51 (July, 1884); *Nation*, XLIX., 85 (August 1, 1889).

I. Government ownership is contrary to wise public policy. ——(*a*) It would be unconstitutional: Pensacola Telegraph Co. *v.* Western Union Telegraph Co., 6 *Otto*, 14.——(*b*) It would be a step toward the centralization of private interests in the hands of the government.——(*c*) Government interference in commercial relations is foreign to the spirit of our institutions: *House Miscellaneous Documents*, 1872-1873, No. 73, pp. 55, 58, 61.

II. The present system is satisfactory: *Railroad Transportation*, p. 255; *House Miscellaneous Documents*, 1872-1873, No. 73, pp. 42-46.——(*a*) It is as good as any foreign system.——(*b*) There has been a steady reduction in rates.—— (*c*) New lines are constantly being built.——(*d*) In most states consolidation and abuses can be prevented by state laws.

III. Government ownership would lead to great evils: *House Miscellaneous Documents*, 1872-1873, No. 73, pp. 48-62.——(*a*) By destroying competition it would give rise to economic evils.—(1) The removal of the necessity to pay interest on investments would result in waste and careless expenditure.—(2) Rates would be arbitrarily raised to show a profit.—(3) There would be no special incentive to meet the needs of the country.——(*b*) It would offer opportunity for political corruption.—(1) Since all political telegrams would pass through the hands of the government, political secrets would be exposed to the party in power.—(2) It would greatly increase the opportunity for political patronage: *House Miscellaneous Documents*, 1872–1873, No. 73, p. 56; *Railroad Transportation*, p. 256.

XLIX.

STATE OWNERSHIP OF MANUFACTORIES.

QUESTION: '*Resolved*, That the state ought to organize and conduct manufactories and commerce.'

Brief for the Affirmative.

GENERAL REFERENCES: *The Social Horizon*; *Andover Review*, II., 455 (November, 1884); *Forum*, X., 174 (October, 1890); XVII., 699 (August, 1894); *Harper's Magazine*, LXXIII., 250 (July, 1886), 450 (August, 1886), 571 (September, 1886); *Fortnightly Review*, XX., 557 (November, 1873); *Nineteenth Century*, V., 1114 (June, 1879); *Nation*, XXXVII., 90 (August 2, 1883); XXXVIII., 136 (February 14, 1884); *Public Opinion*, IV., 103 (November 12, 1887), 222 (December 17, 1887); X., 31 (October 18, 1890); XIV., 446 (February 11, 1893).

I. The system of private ownership is unsatisfactory.—— (*a*) Socially.—(1) It causes great inequality in social conditions.—(x) A class living in extreme poverty.—(y) A class living in great luxury.——(*b*) Economically.—(1) It causes financial crises and the frequent recurrence of periods of business stagnation.—(x) Supply is not regulated by demand.—— (*c*) Politically.—(1) It is dangerous for the state.—(x) Trusts and corporations influence legislation and place the welfare of the community in the hands of a few men.

II. State ownership is desirable socially.——(*a*) It would put an end to the friction between social classes.—(1) By reducing large fortunes and elevating the condition of working people.——(b) It would cause a better distribution of labor. ——(c) It would do away with strikes and lockouts.——(d) It would introduce into the industrial world more humane relations.

III. State ownership is desirable economically.——(a) The state has especial advantages as an employer.—(1) Unlimited capital.—(2) Great stability.——(b) Production would be cheapened.—(1) Business would be united under one management.—(2) Goods would be bought and sold in the largest quantities.—(3) There would be fewer people for whom a profit would have to be made.——(c) There would be none of the extravagances of private ownership.—(1) No competition.—(2) No advertising necessary.—(3) No display necessary.—(4) No credit or bad debts.—(5) No waste of resources.

IV. State ownership is desirable politically.——(a) It is a wise application of the doctrine of increasing the functions of the state.——(b) It would do away with the power of corporations which shakes the stability of our government.——(c) It would give the control of business interests to the masses. ——(d) It would increase the intelligence and promote the welfare of the state.—(1) By bettering the condition of the people.

V. State ownership is practicable.——(a) The change from the present system would not be great.—(1) The whole growth of industry is toward centralization.——(b) State ownership has been successful where it has been tried.—(1) In Germany: W. W. Dawson, *Bismarck and State Socialism.*—(2) In England.—(x) In the post-office and in the postal telegraph service.—(3) In the United States.—(x) In the post-office and in the government dock-yards.

Brief for the Negative.

GENERAL REFERENCES: John Rae, *Contemporary Socialism* (second edition), Chap. xi.; H. C. Adams in *Publica-*

tions of American Economic Association, I., No. 6, p. 471 (January, 1887); J. S. Mill, *Principles of Political Economy*, II., Bk. V., Chap. xi.; *North American Review*, Vol. 137, p. 422 (November, 1883); Vol. 139, p. 51 (July, 1884); *Century*, IX., 737 (March, 1886); *Forum*, XVII., 394 (June, 1884); *Atlantic Monthly*, XXXVII., 360 (March, 1876); *Public Opinion*, VII., 230 (June 22, 1889).

I. State ownership would be extravagant.——(*a*) Joint-stock companies do not produce as much or pay as high wages as private companies: *Contemporary Socialism*, p. 417.——(*b*) There would be great danger of jobbery and corruption.——(1) A large amount of capital invested.——(2) No direct responsibility.——(3) The check of public opinion would be distant and ineffectual.——(*c*) Idleness would be common.

II. State ownership would be inefficient.——(*a*) The service would not get the best men.——(1) Offices would be given for political services.——(*b*) The business policy would change with each new administration.——(*c*) There would be no incentive for men to do good work.——(*d*) The only reason that the post-office is successful is because of the routine character of the work.

III. State ownership would be unprogressive.——(*a*) There would be great delay in meeting existing conditions.——(*b*) Little opportunity would be given for originality or inventiveness.——(*c*) There would be no competition to brighten the talents of officials.——(*d*) Government work is proverbially sluggish.

IV. State ownership would be dangerous.——(*a*) It would create thousands of officials whose influence in politics would be harmful.——(*b*) It would bring the government and the government employees into the daily lives of the people in a distasteful way.——(*c*) It would destroy liberty of action. ——(*d*) It would retard progress.

V. The system of private ownership is the best.——(*a*) It has brought the world where it is to-day.——(*b*) It has cheapened manufactures.——(*c*) It develops to the utmost the talents of employees and employers alike.——(*d*) It would be unwise for the state to undertake new functions when it performs so ill those already allotted to it.

L.

MUNICIPAL OWNERSHIP OF NATURAL MONOPOLIES.

QUESTION: '*Resolved*, That municipalities in the United States should own and operate plants for supplying light, water, and surface transportation.'

Brief for the Affirmative.

GENERAL REFERENCES: R. T. Ely, *Problems of To-day*, pp. 120–146, 260–273; A. H. Sinclair, *Municipal Monopolies and their Management;* C. W. Baker, *Monopolies and the People*, Chap. v.; J. S. Mill, *Principles of Political Economy*, II., Bk. V., Chap. xi., § 11; *Publications of American Economic Association*, I., Nos. 2 and 3. p. 53 (May and July, 1886); II., No. 6, p. 507 (January, 1888); VI., Nos. 4 and 5. p. 295 (July and September, 1891); *Harper's Magazine*, LXXXI., 99 (June, 1890); *Century*, XXXIX., 721 (March, 1890); *Forum*, VIII., 286 (November, 1889); *North American Review*, Vol. 158, p. 294 (March, 1894).

I. The ownership of light, water, and transportation plants is a proper function for city government.——(*a*) The *laissez faire* doctrine is fallacious: Arnold Toynbee, *The Industrial Revolution in England*, pp. 1–27.——(*b*) The ends of government embrace all the benefits and all the immunities from evil which government can confer: *Publications of American Economic Association*, I., Nos. 2 and 3, p. 82.——(*c*) It is not socialism.

II. Private ownership gives rise to great evils.——(*a*)

There is great waste of forces.——(1) Business is not regulated by competition.——(b) The public is plundered.——(1) Enormous dividends are secured from franchises which belong to the public: *Municipal Monopolies and their Management*, p. 32.——(c) The public is dependent on those who own the monopolies.——(d) The public is victimized by bribery and corruption.——(1) The companies spend large sums controlling boards of aldermen: R. T. Ely, *Taxation in American States and Cities*, p. 276.

III. Municipal ownership is followed by great advantages. ——(a) Plants are run for the benefit of the public.——(b) Rates for service are lowered: *Municipal Monopolies and their Management*, pp. 27–37.——(c) Whatever profits are made lessen taxation.——(d) Needless investment and speculation is checked.——(e) Regularity and economy of administration is insured.——(1) Strict watch is kept by every taxpayer who is a stockholder.

IV. Municipal ownership is more successful in practice than private ownership.——(a) In operating water plants: *Municipal Monopolies and their Management*, pp. 27–29; *Problems of To-day*, pp. 134–137.——(b) In operating gas plants: *Publications of American Economic Association*, I., Nos. 2 and 3; *Forum*, VIII., 286–296.——(c) In operating plants for surface transportation: *Century*, XXXIX., 733.

Brief for the Negative.

GENERAL REFERENCES: A. R. Foote, *Municipal Ownership of Quasi-Public Works*; T. H. Farrer, *The State in its Relation to Trade*, Chap. x.; A. T. Hadley in *Political Science Quarterly*, III., 572 (December, 1888); V., 411 (September, 1890); *Nation*, LVI., 449 (June 22, 1893); VIII., 285 (April 19, 1894); *Public Opinion*, XVI., 576 (March 22, 1894).

I. Municipal ownership of light, water, and transportation plants is unwise in theory.——(a) It is not a proper function of government.—(1) It is not necessary for the promotion of intelligence, the care of the unfortunate, or to establish justice: *Municipal Ownership of Quasi-Public Works,* p. 9.——(b) It increases government interference in the field of private action. ——(c) It deprives industry of the moral and economic advantage of self-interest.

II. Municipal ownership is financially disastrous. —— (a) Waste and extravagance result.—(1) Those who have the direction have little skill or experience.—(2) They have little interest in an economic administration.——(b) There is a constant tendency to rely on the city's ability to tax to make up deficiencies.——(c) There is little chance of any extra revenue.—(1) The clamor for low rates does away with the revenue.

III. Municipal ownership is inefficient.——(a) It is not alive to new inventions.——(b) The service does not secure the best men.—(1) Not enough salary is paid.—(2) There is too little opportunity for advancement.——(c) The service is subject to the change of political parties.

IV. The present status of American city governments alone precludes further consideration of the question.——(a) Most American cities do abominably what little they have to do.—(1) Jobbery and corruption are common.—(2) The police service is poor.—(3) Laws are unenforced.—(4) The streets are ill-kept.——(b) To add to municipal functions is simply to aggravate present conditions and to delay reforms indefinitely.

LI.

THE PROHIBITION OF TRUSTS.

QUESTION : ' *Resolved,* That all trusts and combinations intended to monopolize industries should be prohibited.'

Brief for the Affirmative.

GENERAL REFERENCES : H. D. Lloyd, *Wealth against Commonwealth;* J. F. Hudson in *North American Review,* Vol.

144, p. 277 (March, 1887); A. W. Tourgée in *North American Review*, Vol. 157, p. 30 (July, 1893); *Quarterly Journal of Economics*, III., 136 (January, 1889); *Nation*, XLVII., 125 (August 16, 1888); XLIV., 380 (May 5, 1887); XLV., 68 (July 28, 1887); XLVIII., 108 (February 7, 1889); XLIX., 186 (September 5, 1889); *Unitarian Review*, XXVI., 522–529 (December, 1886); *Congressional Record*, 1889–1890, p. 2456 (March 21, 1890); *Lalor's Cyclopædia*, I., 539–547; J. S. Jeans, *Trusts, Pools, and Corners*.

I. Trusts are unnecessary.——(*a*) The concentration of capital is possible without them.—(1) Trades are sufficiently large to admit several great competitors.——(*b*) Monopoly is not necessary to resist labor organizations.—(1) Labor unions do not have a complete monopoly of labor.—(x) Strikes are often a failure.—(2) Union to resist labor is possible without trusts.

II. Trusts are an economic evil.——(*a*) They limit natural production: *Nation*, XLIX., 186.——(*b*) They destroy competition.—(1) By absorbing all large producers.—(2) By crushing smaller rivals: *Popular Science Monthly*, XXXIV.. 619 (March, 1889); *Nation*, XLVIII., 108.——(*c*) They raise prices: *North American Review*, Vol. 144, p. 277.

III. Trusts are a social evil.——(*a*) They put wealth in the hands of a few: *Nation*, XLVIII., 108.——(*b*) Individual enterprise is discouraged: *Nation*, XLV., 68.—(1) Small capitalists are driven out.—(2) Independent producers are made dependents.—(3) The tyranny over dependents is great. ——(*c*) Trusts are irresponsible.——(*d*) They use power unscrupulously.—(1) The Standard Oil Co.——(*e*) They encourage gambling and speculation.——(*f*) They interfere in politics.

IV. The prohibition of trusts is practicable.——(*a*) It is constitutional.—(1) Congress has power over interstate commerce: *Constitution of the United States*, Art. I., Sec. 8, § 3.

—(2) The jurisdiction of United States courts is sufficiently extensive: *Constitution of the United States*, Art. I., Sec. 8, § 9; Art. III., Sec. 2, §§ 1, 2, 3.—(3) The states have jurisdiction within their limits.———(*b*) It can be accomplished.—(1) Laws can be made sufficiently stringent to reach trusts effectually.

V. Prohibition is desirable.———(*a*) Other methods are insufficient.—(1) Mere government regulation is inadequate.

Brief for the Negative.

GENERAL REFERENCES: *Political Science Quarterly*, III., 385 (September, 1888), 592 (December, 1888); IX., 486 (September, 1894); *Popular Science Monthly*, XLIV., 740 (April, 1894); XLV., 289 (July, 1894); *Forum*, V., 584 (July, 1888); VIII., 61 (September, 1889); S. C. T. Dodd, *Combinations, their Uses and Abuses;* E. von Halle, *Trusts or Industrial Combinations in the United States*, Chap. viii.; *House Reports*, 1888-1889, No. 4165, Part 2; *Congressional Record*, 1889-1890, p. 1765 (February 27, 1890).

I. Trusts are not in themselves illegal: *Political Science Quarterly*, III., 592.———(*a*) They are contrivances of every-day occurrence in common law.———(*b*) The right of stockholders to place stock in hands of trustees is undeniable.———(*c*) The abuses of trusts can be made amenable to law: *New Englander*, LII., 360 (April, 1890).———(*d*) States are able to provide against all non-observances of the law.

II. Trusts are the natural result of industrial conditions. ———(*a*) They are the result of lower prices caused by overproduction and the opposition of labor to corresponding reductions in wages.———(*b*) They were organized for self-protection as an offset to trade unions: *Forum*, VIII., 66.———(*c*) The trend of all industry is toward combination: Washington Gladden, *Tools and the Man*, Chap. vi.

III. Trusts are not harmful: *Popular Science Monthly*,

XLIV., 740.——(*a*) They can never maintain abnormal prices.—(1) Competition, latent or active, is always a check.—(2) Too great increase in prices lessens demand.——(*b*) Profits are increased by cheapening the cost of production, not by raising prices.——(*c*) A *régime* of combination is less harmful than one of free competition: *Forum*, VIII., 67.——(*d*) Trusts differ from corporate and individualistic forms of industry only in size and complexity.——(*e*) The popular prejudice against trusts is illogical.—(1) The classes most injured by competition are the loudest in denouncing trusts.

IV. Trusts are of positive economic advantage.——(*a*) They decrease the cost of production.—(1) Competition is wasteful.—(2) Improved methods are introduced: *North American Review*, Vol. 136, p. 188 (February, 1883).——(*b*) They prevent over-production: *Quarterly Journal of Economics*, III., 136 (January, 1889).—(1) By regulating supply and demand.——(*c*) They steady the labor market.——(*d*) They prevent ruinous competition.——(*e*) They increase consumption.—(1) By increasing facilities for transportation.—(2) By lowering prices.—(x) Prices may rise temporarily, but they fall steadily afterward.

LII.

THE PROHIBITION OF RAILROAD POOLING.

QUESTION: '*Resolved*, That the Interstate Commerce Act should be so amended as to allow pooling.'

Brief for the Affirmative.

GENERAL REFERENCES: *Quarterly Journal of Economics*, III., 184–185 (January, 1889); IV., 158 (January, 1890); *Political Science Quarterly*, II., 369 (September, 1887); *Forum*, V., 652 (August, 1888); *Reports of Interstate Commerce Commission*, I., 307–312; II., 436 *et seq.*;

IV., 351–358 ; Report of Senate Committee on Interstate Commerce, *Senate Reports*, 1885–1886, III., Part 2, pp. 71–77, 114–117, 119–120, 123–126, 170–173, 194, 202, 203.

I. The prohibition of pooling was the result of popular misapprehension: *Quarterly Journal of Economics*, II., 164 (January, 1888).

II. The prohibition of pooling is injurious to railroads. ——(*a*) It results in ruinous competition.—(1) By causing rate wars: *Quarterly Journal of Economics*, III., 182–183.—(2) By causing the construction of unnecessary parallel lines: *Quarterly Journal of Economics*, III., 182–183.

III. The prohibition is injurious to commerce : A. T. Hadley, *Railroad Transportation*, Chap. iv.——(*a*) It makes rates unstable : *Quarterly Journal of Economics*, IV., 159–160.—(1) There is no incentive to adhere to a systematic schedule.——(*b*) It compels the railroads to manipulate secretly the rates and to discriminate through rebates.

IV. Pooling is a desirable form of railroad combination. ——(*a*) Combination of some kind is a necessity and cannot be prevented: *Political Science Quarterly*, II., 374 (September, 1887).——(*b*) Pooling insures unvarying rates to shippers.—(1) Each railroad being in a pool, and feeling sure of a fair profit, has no incentive to cut rates.——(*c*) Pooling does away with discriminations and rebates.—(1) The forces which give competitive points cheaper rates than non-competitive points are removed.——(*d*) Pooling has worked well in this country and in Europe: *Political Science Quarterly*, II., 378, 385 (September, 1887).

Brief for the Negative.

GENERAL REFERENCES: J. F. Hudson, *The Railways and the Republic*, pp. 194–250 ; *Report of the Senate Select Committee on Interstate Commerce*, 1886, pp. 660, 880, 1204 ; William Larrabee, *The Railway Question*, pp. 194–204.

I. There is no necessity for pooling.——(*a*) Serious rate wars have ceased since the passage of the Interstate Commerce Act.——(*b*) The discriminations and fluctuations in rates which pooling is supposed to prevent are prohibited by the Interstate Commerce Act.

II. Pooling is an evil.——(*a*) It destroys healthful competition.—(1) It withdraws the incentive for individual effort.——(*b*) It deteriorates railroad service.——(*c*) It puts arbitrary power over the commerce of the country into the hands of a few men: A. T. Hadley, *Railroad Transportation*, p. 76.——(*d*) It raises rates by destroying competition: *The Railways and the Republic*, p. 217; *Report of the Senate Select Committee on Interstate Commerce*, 1886, p. 363.——(*e*) It leads to the maintenance of unnecessary roads at public expense: *The Railways and the Republic*, pp. 230, 418.——(*f*) It results in frequent rate wars and uncertain rates.—(1) Through the efforts of one road in the pool to force the other roads to terms dictated by it: *The Railways and the Republic*, p. 232.

III. Pooling under the control of the Interstate Commerce Commission would not be practicable: *Congressional Record*, 1892–1893, pp. 709–715 (January 19, 1893), p. 712, report of minority against pooling.——(*a*) Owing to the great number of railroads.——(*b*) It would put too much power in the hands of the commission.

LIII.

STATE CONTROL OF EDUCATION.

QUESTION: '*Resolved*, That it is the right and duty of the state to supervise and control primary and secondary education.'

Brief for the Affirmative.

GENERAL REFERENCES: *Lalor's Cyclopædia*, II., 29; *Popular Science Monthly*, XIX., 635 (September, 1881); *Forum*,

XI., 59 (March, 1891); XII., 208 (October, 1891); *Contemporary Review*, XXVII., 70 (December, 1875); *Educational Review*, I., 26, 52 (January, 1891); V., 424 (May, 1893); *Barnard's American Journal of Education*, III., 81 (March, 1857); *Education*, XII., 293 (January, 1892); *Social Economist*, II., 152 (January, 1892).

I. The welfare of the state depends on the intelligence and virtue of its people.——(*a*) The people make the state.——(*b*) If the people are ignorant and vicious the laws and institutions which they adopt will be unwise and injurious.——(*c*) In a republic where the people rule through universal suffrage the dependence of the state on the character of its people is especially marked.

II. Intelligence and virtue can only be assured by the existence of schools.——(*a*) It is only thus that intellectual and moral training can be given.——(*b*) It is only thus that obedience to law and regard for the rights of one's fellow-creatures can be inculcated.——(*c*) It is only thus that proper attention can be given to health and physical development.

III. The control and supervision of schools should be in the hands of the state.——(*a*) Unless the state assumes this function there is no assurance that citizens will have proper training.—(1) Without state supervision, studies calculated to foster patriotism and promote good citizenship may be wholly neglected.—(2) Compulsory attendance is necessary.—(3) Fixed qualifications for teachers are desirable.——(*b*) Private and sectarian schools have a deleterious influence.—(1) In many such schools allegiance to church before allegiance to state is taught.—(x) Catholic schools.—(2) The English language and literature are neglected for the study of a foreign language and literature.—(3) Un-American ideas are promulgated, and American citizenship is thus degraded.

Brief for the Negative.

GENERAL REFERENCES: Paul Leroy Beaulieu, *The Modern State*, pp. 63-91, 155-162; *Popular Science Monthly*, XVII., 664 (March, 1881); XXX., 699 (March, 1887); XXXI., 124 (May, 1887); *North American Review*, Vol. 133, p. 215 (September, 1881); Vol. 153, p. 193 (August, 1891); *Forum*, XII., 196 (October, 1891); *Fortnightly Review*, XXXIV., 42 (July, 1880); *Nation*, XLII., 51 (January 21, 1886).

I. State supervision and control is unwise in theory.——(*a*) It is a direct step toward state centralization and the destruction of local autonomy.——(*b*) It is a recognized theory of Anglo-Saxon nations that local self-government is the essence of freedom.——(*c*) The modern state is unable to perform well its present functions.

II. State control is detrimental to education.——(*a*) Education is most successful when adapted to the especial needs of the community and the individual.——(*b*) State control reduces all education to a uniform and dead level.——(*c*) State control brings education into politics with unfavorable results.—(1) The publishers of text-books secure their adoption by state legislatures through measures which are highly questionable.——(*d*) State control tends to destroy the self-reliance and the interest of parents and communities in educational matters.——(*e*) State control causes unequal burdens on the well-to-do classes.——(*f*) State control discourages private benevolence.

III. Education can best be carried on by private enterprise. ——(*a*) Greater variety of education is possible.——(*b*) Education suitable to special needs can be obtained.——(*c*) The liberty of the individual is not encroached upon.——(*d*) Better teachers can be secured.——(*e*) More immediate and individual attention is possible.——(*f*) Race and class prejudices are not excited.——(*g*) More thorough and general education is the result.

LIV.

FEDERAL CONTROL OF DIVORCE.

QUESTION: '*Resolved*, That a constitutional amendment should be secured giving to the federal government exclusive control over divorces.'

Brief for the Affirmative.

GENERAL REFERENCES: *Forum*, II., 429 (January, 1887); *Popular Science Monthly*, XXIII., 224 (June, 1883); D. Convers, *Marriage and Divorce*, pp. 220–230; *Journal of Social Science*, No. XIV., p. 152 (November, 1881); *Princeton Review*, IX., 90–92 (January, 1882); T. D. Woolsey, *Divorce and Divorce Legislation*, Chap. v.; *New Englander*, XLIII., 48 (January, 1884); *Forum*, VIII., 349–356 (December, 1889); *Arena*, II., 399 (September, 1890).

I. Reform of our divorce laws is necessary.——(*a*) The present lax system affects the stability of American institutions: *Journal of Social Science*, No. XIV., pp. 155–163. —(1) It has a bad effect on the individual.—(2) On the family: *New Englander*, XLIII., 61.—(3) On the nation at large: *Princeton Review*, IX., 92.——(*b*) Divorces are increasing rapidly: *Tribune Almanac*, 1893, pp. 212–213.

II. The lack of uniformity is the worst evil: *Popular Science Monthly*, XXIII., 224.——(*a*) It gives rise to endless confusion: *Century*, I., 419 (January, 1882); *Marriage and Divorce*, pp. 220–230; *Princeton Review*, IX., 90–92.— (1) As to the status of the parties in different states.—(2) The grounds for divorce.—(3) Legal proceedings.—(4) Subsequent status of parties: *Forum*, II., 434.—(5) Property rights.— (6) Legitimacy of children.——(*b*) It is largely responsible for the increase in number of divorces: *Lalor's Cyclopædia*,

III., 808.——(*c*) It lessens respect for law in general: *Forum*, II., 429.

III. Federal control offers the best solution: *New Englander*, XLIII., 65.——(*a*) A uniform remedy should be applied to a uniform evil: *Forum*, II., 429.——(*b*) Federal control would prevent fraud: *New Englander*, XLIII., 57.—(1) By preventing change of residence.—(2) By discouraging divorce lawyers.—(3) By abolishing lax laws and loose procedure: *Journal of Social Science*, No. XIV., pp. 152–155. ——(*c*) There is no hope of uniform state laws: *Public Opinion*, VIII., 103 (November 9, 1889).——(*d*) It would not be difficult to secure an amendment to the Constitution: *Forum*, II., 437.

Brief for the Negative.

GENERAL REFERENCES: J. P. Bishop, *Marriage and Divorce*, II., §§ 143–199; *Forum*, VIII., 357 (December, 1889); *Public Opinion*, VIII., 104–107 (November 9, 1889); *North American Review*, Vol. 144, pp. 429–431 (April, 1887); Vol. 149, pp. 513–516 (November, 1889); *Journal of Social Science*, No. XIV., p. 136 (November, 1881); *Political Science Quarterly*, IV., 592 (December, 1891).

I. A national divorce law would be contrary to the theory of our political system: *Public Opinion*, VIII., 104.——(*a*) It would tend to impair local self-government.——(*b*) It would be a radical step toward further interference by the general government: *North American Review*, Vol. 144, p. 429.

II. It would be impracticable.——(*a*) Diversified laws are necessary for diversity of sentiment: *Public Opinion*, VIII., 105.——(*b*) The subject is too complex for general legislation: *North American Review*, Vol. 149, p. 516.—(1) The elements are too little understood.—(2) The people are not ready for so great a change.—(3) The evil consequences of any mistake would be difficult to remedy.

III. **It is unnecessary.**——(*a*) The abuses of the laws are not due to any lack of uniformity: *Journal of Social Science*, No. XIV., p. 136.—(1) Many states require actual residence for a considerable time as well as other uniform regulations. —(2) In four-fifths of the cases divorce occurs in the same state as the marriage: *North American Review*, Vol. 149, p. 516.

IV. **The best remedy lies in state regulation:** *Forum*, VIII., 359.——(*a*) The roots of the evil can better be attacked.——(*b*) Laws can best be framed to meet special conditions.

LV.

GOVERNMENT CONSTRUCTION OF IRRIGATION WORKS.

QUESTION: '*Resolved*, That the government ought to construct an extensive system of irrigation works.'

Brief for the Affirmative.

GENERAL REFERENCES: A. M. Wilson, 'Irrigation in India,' in *House Executive Documents*, 1891–1892, XVIII., 390; 1890–1891. XV., pp. xi.–xiv.; *Nation*, XLVII., 390 (November 15, 1888); *Forum*, XII., 740 (January, 1892); *North American Review*. Vol. 150, p. 370 (March, 1890); *Popular Science Monthly*. XXXVI., 364 (January, 1890); XLIII., 145, 162 (June, 1893).

I. **Irrigation is of the greatest value to this country.**——(*a*) Large areas are now worthless without it.——(*b*) One hundred and twenty million acres are reclaimable.——(*c*) The government no longer has any good agricultural land left.——(*d*) Irrigated land is better for agriculture than common land.—— (*e*) Irrigation has developed countries immensely.—(1) India:

House Executive Documents, 1891-1892, XVIII., 418-420.—(2) Southern California and New Mexico.

II. Irrigation is perfectly possible in this country.——(*a*) There is plenty of water if it be properly managed.——(*b*) The nature of the soil is favorable.——(*c*) The conditions in India, where it has succeeded, are similar: *House Executive Documents*, 1891-1892, XVIII., 391.

III. The control of irrigation otherwise than by the government would be unwise.——(*a*) The states should not control it.—(1) River systems extend over several states.—(2) The one nearest the head could take all the water.——(*b*) Individual farmers should not control it.—(1) It would be on too small a scale to be effective except in a few places.——(*c*) Corporations should not control it.—(1) It would leave a large number of farmers at the mercy of water companies.—(2) It would lead to the creation of large estates and the crushing out of small holders.—(3) It would lead to popular hatred as in the case of the railroads in the West.

IV. Irrigation to be successful must be carried on by the government.——(*a*) It must be on a very large scale.——(*b*) The return on the investment, although sure, is very slow at first: *House Executive Documents*, 1891-1892, XVIII., 416-418.——(*c*) It is necessary to wait for immigration to fill up the irrigated land: *Ibid.*, p. 391.

Brief for the Negative.

GENERAL REFERENCES: J. D. Whitney, *The United States*, Supplement I.; *House Reports*, 1890-1891, IV., No. 3767, p. 6; *Senate Reports*, 1889-1890, V., No. 928, Part 1, pp. 7-8, 167, Sec. xxxix.; *Review of Reviews*, VIII., 403-406 (October, 1893); *Forum*, XII., 740 (January, 1892).

I. The proposed system is inexpedient.——(*a*) It would be very expensive.——(*b*) It would increase unwisely the civil service.——(*c*) It would divert public attention from more pressing questions.—(1) Finance.—(2) The tariff.—(3) Labor.——(*d*) Irrigation might be introduced for political motives.——(*e*) Government construction is usually wasteful: *Forum*, XII., 747-750.——(*f*) Government control is not economical: *Ibid.*——(*g*) The example of India is not applicable: *The United States*, Supplement I., p. 34.

II. The constitutionality of such a system is questionable.——(*a*) The power is not specifically granted in the Constitution.——(*b*) Such power is not easily inferred.

III. Whatever is necessary can be done without government intervention.——(*a*) Private enterprise is the most economical: *Forum*, XII., 747-750.——(*b*) Private capital is able to create and manage such a system.—(1) Private capitalists have undertaken such works in the West.—(x) In New Mexico.—(2) Private capitalists have undertaken equally large operations.—(x) The Niagara Falls Water Power Co.—(y) Great railway systems.

IV. Possible abuses can be prevented by state and government oversight: *Forum*, XII., 740; *Nation*, XLVII., 390 (November 15, 1888).

V. There are many obstacles to irrigation on a large scale.——(*a*) Insufficiency of water supply.——(*b*) Danger from large reservoirs.——(*c*) Destructive alkaline deposits.

LVI.

FEDERAL CONTROL OF QUARANTINE.

QUESTION: '*Resolved*, That a national quarantine act is desirable.'

Brief for the Affirmative.

GENERAL REFERENCES: *Forum*, XIV., 133 (October, 1892), 579 (January, 1893); *American Law Review*, XXV., 45 (January, 1891); *Congressional Record*, 1878-1879, pp.

1002–1011 (May 1, 1879), pp. 1024–1028 (May 2, 1879), pp. 1507–1520 (May 22, 1879); 1892–1893, pp. 750–765 (January 21, 1893), pp. 793–804 (January 23, 1893); *Nation*, LVI., 78 (February 2, 1893); *Science*, VI., 23 (July 10, 1885); X., 315 (December 30, 1887); *Public Opinion*, XIV., 295 (December 31, 1892), 323 (January 7, 1893), 393 (January 28, 1893), 470 (February 18, 1893); XV., 554 (September 16, 1893).

I. State quarantine laws are inadequate.——(*a*) The lives of citizens and the whole commerce of the country are put at the mercy of local ignorance and negligence.——(*b*) The handling of foreigners in the United States is not a fit matter for state legislation.—(1) The central authority is responsible for all wrongs done to foreign subjects.——(*c*) States can only control vessels and goods within their own limits.——(*d*) Local boards are controlled by local politicians.—(1) The case of New York during the cholera epidemic of 1892.

II. State quarantine laws are needlessly burdensome.—— (*a*) There is no uniformity.——(*b*) Commerce is impeded. —(1) Needless rules and regulations are enacted.—(2) Shipmasters are unable to know the regulations at every port when all are different.—(3) Local authorities get scared.——(*c*) State regulation is costly.

III. Complete national control is preferable.——(*a*) It would be just.—(1) The danger is national, and the inland states ought to contribute to the expense.——(*b*) It would diminish the restrictions on travel and commerce.—(1) It would do away with embarrassments arising from lack of facilities and the maladministration of local affairs.——(*c*) It would prevent panic, allay anxiety, and afford a reasonable sense of security.——(*d*) It would avoid the enforcement of unnecessary measures.

IV. National control would be more efficient.——(*a*) The service would be in the charge of men of training and experience.——(*b*) No misunderstandings in regard to authority would arise.——(*c*) Concentration of force, money, and attention, would be practicable when necessary.——(*d*) Officers would be free from local politics and from the commercial influence of rival ports.——(*e*) The objects of the quarantine could be furthered by reliable consular reports and by the sanitary inspection of emigrants at ports of embarkation.

V. National control would be constitutional.——(*a*) As a regulation of commerce: S. F. Miller, *Lectures on the Constitution of the United States*, p. 480; T. M. Cooley, *Principles of Constitutional Law*, p. 75; *Nation*, LVI., 78; *Forum*, XIV., 579.

Brief for the Negative.

GENERAL REFERENCES: J. Story, *Commentaries on the Constitution*, §§ 1017, 1070, 1075; *Congressional Record*, 1879, pp. 987–993 (April 30, 1879), pp. 1002–1011 (May 1, 1879); *Annals of Congress*, 1795–1796, pp. 1349–1359 (May 12, 1796); *National Board of Health Bulletin*, II., 613 (December 4, 1880); *Public Opinion*, XIV., 323 (January 7, 1893); *Nation*, LV., 178 (September 8, 1892).

I. A national quarantine act would be unconstitutional.——(*a*) Congress has no powers except those granted to it.——(*b*) The power over commerce does not include the quarantine power: *Commentaries on the Constitution*, § 1017.—(1) Quarantine regulations are regulations of health.——(*c*) The power over quarantine is not granted by any other clause in the Constitution.

II. A national quarantine act would be impracticable.——(*a*) The different sanitary conditions of each port render uniform action impossible.——(*b*) Mismanagement at one port is less harmful than mismanagement at all.——(*c*) The differences between local and national authorities would lead to jealousies and conflicts.——(*d*) The system would be unnecessarily expensive.—(1) Organization would have to be maintained during periods when there was little or no need.

III. A national quarantine act would be inelastic.——(*a*) Epidemics require instantaneous treatment.——(*b*) The service under national regulation could not be increased speedily or diminished readily when the danger had passed.—(1) All orders for supplies and additional equipment would have to come from a headquarters.—(2) Any unusual epidemic would require special appropriations from Congress.

IV. A national quarantine act would be inefficient.——(*a*) No national board would be so careful in keeping out diseases as local authorities are.——(*b*) Local authorities are better equipped by experience to meet local dangers than a national board would be.—(1) No national board would have the ability to cope with a yellow-fever epidemic as has the Louisiana Board of Health.

V. A national quarantine act is unnecessary.——(*a*) Local quarantines have been highly satisfactory in the past : *Nation*, LV., 178.—(1) New York regulations are perfect.—(2) So also in Boston.——(*b*) Local equipments are ample.—(1) At New York.—(2) Boston.—(3) Norfolk.—(4) New Orleans.

LVII.

THE RIGHT TO PROHIBIT THE SALE OF OLEOMARGARINE.

QUESTION : '*Resolved*, That each state has the right to prohibit the sale of oleomargarine within its limits.'

Brief for the Affirmative.

GENERAL REFERENCES : Powell *v*. Pennsylvania, 127 *U. S.*, 678 ; Mugler *v*. Kansas, 123 *U. S.*, 623 : *Congressional Record*, 1885–1886, pp. 4869–4870 (May 24, 1886), p. 4900 (May 25, 1886) ; T. M. Cooley, *Constitutional Limitations*, pp. 720, 721, 741.

I. The states have the right to exercise the police power. ——(a) The Constitution gives to the states all powers not granted to Congress: *Constitution of the United States*, Amend. X.——(b) The police power is not granted to Congress: *Constitutional Limitations*, p. 11, note 2.

II. The police power includes the power to regulate health: J. N. Pomeroy, *Constitutional Law*, § 329; T. M. Cooley, *Principles of Constitutional Law*, p. 75.——(a) Each state has the constitutional right to prohibit the sale of any article which it considers harmful to the public: *Constitutional Limitations*, p. 741.——(b) Nothing in the Fourteenth Amendment interferes with the power of the state to regulate health: Powell *v.* Pennsylvania, 127 *U. S.*, 678; J. N. Pomeroy, *Constitutional Law*, § 329.

III. To prohibit the sale of oleomargarine is a lawful exercise of the power to regulate health.——(a) The manufacture and sale of any oleaginous substance designed to take the place of butter may be forbidden though it is healthful and marked 'oleomargarine butter': *Constitutional Limitations*, p. 741.——(b) The question as to whether oleomargarine is injurious is a question of fact and public policy which is for the legislature to determine: Powell *v.* Pennsylvania, 127 *U. S.*, 685.

Brief for the Negative.

GENERAL REFERENCES: Powell *v.* Pennsylvania, 127 *U. S.*, 687; In re Jacobs, 98 *N. Y.*, 98; The People *v.* Marx, 99 *N. Y.*, 377; *Political Science Quarterly*, II., 545 (December, 1887); Massachusetts State Board of Health, *Nineteenth Annual Report*, 1888, pp. 199–289; *Nation*, XLIII., 90 (July 29, 1889); *Foods and Food Adulterants*, United States Department of Agriculture, Division of Chemistry, Bulletin 13, Part First.

I. Oleomargarine is a pure article of food: Massachusetts State Board of Health, *Nineteenth Annual Report*, p. 272;

Political Science Quarterly, II., 548.——(*a*) Not an adulteration of dairy products.——(*b*) Wholesome and nutritious.——(*c*) Resists rancidity longer than butter.

II. No legislature has the right to prohibit the sale of a pure article of food.——(*a*) Such an act violates that clause in the Fourteenth Amendment which provides that no one shall be deprived of 'life, liberty, or property, without due process of law.'—(1) 'Liberty' here means the freedom to do such acts as a man judges best for his interests and not inconsistent with the rights of others: Powell *v.* Pennsylvania, 127 *U. S.*, 692.—(x) This includes the inalienable right to procure healthful and nutritious food.—(y) Otherwise the state might proscribe the different articles of healthful food that are manufactured and sold within its limits.

III. Such legislation is not justified under the police power.——(*a*) It does not forbid what is injurious to the health and morals of the people.——(*b*) It does not provide for the peace or promote the safety of the state.——(*c*) Under the mere guise of police regulations personal rights and private property cannot be invaded.——(*d*) The determination of the legislature is not final or conclusive.

LABOR.

LVIII.

LABOR ORGANIZATIONS.

QUESTION: '*Resolved,* That labor organizations promote the best interests of workingmen.'

Brief for the Affirmative.

GENERAL REFERENCES: William Trant, *Trade Unions;* George Howell, *The Conflicts of Capital and Labor;* George

Howell, *Trade Unionism, New and Old;* Sidney and Beatrice Webb, *The History of Trade Unionism;* G. von Schulze-Gaevernitz, *Social Peace;* Edward Cummings in *Quarterly Journal of Economics,* III., 403 (July, 1889); *Fortnightly Review,* XIV., 517 (November, 1870).

I. Labor organizations are necessary to enable workingmen to deal with employers on terms of equality.——(*a*) In dealing individually with employers workingmen are at great disadvantage.—(1) Employers are combined.—(2) Employers, through the control of capital and machinery, have control of industry.—(3) Capital can wait for an opening, while labor, if not used, is lost.——(*b*) Through labor organizations much of this disadvantage is overcome.—(1) In union there is strength.—(2) Business can be carried on through intelligent and competent representatives.

II. Labor organizations have been of great advantage to workingmen economically.——(*a*) They have raised wages: *Trade Unions,* pp. 68-85.——(*b*) They have shortened the hours of labor: *Trade Unions,* pp. 86-90.——(*c*) They have secured factory regulations.——(*d*) They have secured legislation affecting the employment of women and children.——(*e*) They have discouraged piece-work and overtime work.

III. Labor organizations have been of great advantage morally.——(*a*) They have diminished the number of strikes: *Trade Unions,* pp. 102-105.——(*b*) They have encouraged frugality and economy.—(1) By their system of benefits.——(*c*) They have brought about the arbitration of labor disputes whenever possible.——(*d*) They have established better relations between employers and employees.——(*e*) They have elevated the character of workingmen.—(1) By rules which stigmatize and punish the idle, the vicious, and the unfit.——(*f*) They have inculcated the spirit of mutual assistance and support.

IV. Labor organizations have been of great educational advantage.——(*a*) By collecting and disseminating knowledge regarding the state of trade.———(*b*) By obtaining for the working classes more leisure for recreation and study.———(*c*) By teaching laborers the necessity of submitting to the unchangeable laws of political economy.———(*d*) By providing lectures and other means for making members better workmen.

Brief for the Negative.

GENERAL REFERENCES: *Fortnightly Review*, IX., 77 (January, 1868), 437 (April, 1868); *Edinburgh Review*, Vol. 130, p. 390 (October, 1869); *Blackwood's Magazine*, Vol. 102, p. 487 (October, 1867); Vol. 107, p. 554 (May, 1870), p. 744 (June, 1870); *Popular Science Monthly*, VIII., 586 (March, 1876); XXXIII., 361 (July, 1888); *Forum*, XI., 205 (April, 1891); *Nation*, XXXVII., 428 (November 22, 1883); XLVI., 190 (March 8, 1888), 227 (March 22, 1888); XLII., 418 (May 20, 1886), 440 (May 27, 1886); LIX., 5 (July 5, 1894).

I. Labor organizations cannot permanently raise wages.———(*a*) They cannot increase the fund from which wages are paid or diminish the number among whom this fund is distributed.———(*b*) If wages rise at a given time it is due to improvements which increase profits.

II. Labor organizations are disastrous to industry.———(*a*) They turn capital from trade.—(1) By harassing employers.—(2) By decreasing profits and increasing risks.———(*b*) They foster dissensions between employers and employees.———(*c*) They cause stagnation in business and great loss of wealth.—(1) By stopping industry through strikes and lock-outs.

III. Labor organizations are injurious to members.———(*a*) They have despotic powers which destroy the independence of the individual and make him subject to ignorant and dangerous labor agitators.———(*b*) They deny to men the right to dispose of their labor when and where they choose.———(*c*) They insist on certain rules and standards which reduce all workingmen to a level and which prevent individuals from bettering their condition.——(*d*) They sanction strikes. violence, outrage, and even murder.——(*e*) They teach wrong views of political economy.——(*f*) They order strikes when there is no grievance.—(1) Sympathetic strikes.——(*g*) They lead men to be dissatisfied with their station in life, to hate capitalists, and to attempt by violence to bring about a change in the present social order.

LIX.

A LABOR PARTY.

QUESTION: '*Resolved,* That the best interests of the laboring classes would be advanced by the formation of a separate labor party.'

Brief for the Affirmative.

GENERAL REFERENCES: R. T. Ely, *The Labor Movement in America;* Edward Everett, *Lecture on the Working Men's Party;* R. T. Ely, 'Recent American Socialism,' in *Johns Hopkins University Studies,* III., No. IV., pp. 276–283; *National Review,* XXIII., 637 (July, 1894); *Nineteenth Century,* XXXII., 864–898 (December, 1892); XXXVII., 1 (January, 1895); *Public Opinion,* XII., 317 (January 9, 1892); XV., 567 (September 16, 1893); XVI., 313 (January 4, 1894), 338 (January 11, 1894).

I. The laboring classes have interests which can only be advanced by political associations.——(*a*) Matters requiring state and national legislation.—(1) The limiting of the hours of the working day.—(2) The restriction of foreign immigration. —(3) The restriction of the power of trusts and corporations. —(4) The abolition of overtime, piece-work, and child labor, in factories.—(5) Securing a tax on the unearned increment and a graduated income tax.—(6) Relief for the unemployed.

II. None of the great political parties advance the interests of the laboring classes.——(*a*) The legislators of the great parties represent the capitalistic class.—(1) They are subsidized with passes on railroads and in other ways.——(*b*) The old parties have pet theories of their own to work for. ——(*c*) They have little real sympathy with the labor movement.—(1) Their seeming interest is only to secure the labor vote.

III. A separate labor party would advance the interests of laborers.——(*a*) It would give accurate and definite expression to the needs of the laboring classes.——(*b*) It would unite and bring into solid organization men interested in securing a common end.——(*c*) It would have great educational advantage.—(1) In bringing principles before the people.—(2) Through agitation.——(*d*) It would force the old parties to action.—(1) Even if the labor party did not have a majority its numbers would secure more regard for the interests of laborers.——(*e*) The ballot is the best possible evidence of strength, and the growth which it registers would encourage and stimulate adherents.——(*f*) A labor party has been very successful in England.

Brief for the Negative.

GENERAL REFERENCES: *Westminster Review*, Vol. 132, p. 581 (December, 1889); *Public Opinion*, II., 279 (January 15, 1887); XI., 352 (July 18, 1891); *Spectator*, LXX., 39 (January 14, 1893); LXXIII., 330 (September 15, 1894), 879 (December 22, 1894).

I. A labor party is impracticable.——(*a*) A union of all the laboring classes in one organization is impossible.—(1) Workingmen differ widely as to what their best interests are and as to the best means of advancing them.—(x) Some workingmen favor the eight-hour movement and some do not.—(y) Some join trade unions and some do not.—(z) Some favor state aid and some do not.—(2) A union of all the working classes is not more possible than a union of the intellectual classes.—(x) There is no real community of interest.—(y) There are great differences between skilled and unskilled laborers.—(z) There are great differences between different trades.

II. A separate labor party is unnecessary.——(a) Laborers have no real interests apart from the rest of the community.—(1) Capital and labor are both necessary to carry on industry, and one cannot succeed at the expense of the other.—(2) Any temporary advantages which a labor party might secure would ultimately result in harm to the class as a whole.——(b) All just demands on the part of laborers for legislation are carried out by the existing parties.—(1) Most states have enacted laws providing for factory regulations, protecting female and child labor, limiting the hours of labor, and securing other beneficient changes.

III. A labor party is undesirable.——(a) Such a party would have a most baneful effect upon society.—(1) If it were successful everything goes to show that it would try to bring about rampant socialism.—(2) Even if it were not successful it would divide the country into two classes.—(x) It would array capital and labor against each other in fierce and uncompromising strife.—(3) It would increase the tendency toward disorder, lawlessness, and social revolution.

LX.

THE EIGHT-HOUR DAY.

QUESTION: '*Resolved*, That an eight-hour working day should be adopted within the United States by law.'

Brief for the Affirmative.

GENERAL REFERENCES: Sidney Webb and Harold Cox, *The Eight Hours Day;* George Gunton, *Wealth and Progress,* pp. 240-382; John Rae, *Eight Hours for Work*; R. A. Hadfield and H. de B. Gibbins, *A Shorter Working Day*; *Eighth Annual Report of New York Bureau of Statistics of Labor*, 1890, Part I.; *North American Review*, Vol. 150, p. 464 (April, 1890); *Forum*, I., 136 (April, 1886); *Nineteenth Century*, XXVI., 21 (July, 1889), 509 (September, 1889); XXVII., 553 (April, 1890); *Contemporary Review*, LVI., 859 (December, 1889); *Westminster Review*, Vol. 134, p. 642 (December, 1890); *Public Opinion*, I., 69 (May 8, 1886); IX., 55 (April 26, 1890), 79 (May 3, 1890), 104 (May 10, 1890).

I. An eight-hour day would not be economically disadvantageous.——(*a*) Production would not be diminished.—(1) The successive reductions of the hours of labor in this century have been followed by an increase rather than a diminution of production: *A Shorter Working Day*, p. 88.—(2) The amount of production depends largely on the intellectual and moral status of the producers.—(3) More laborers would be absorbed.—(4) Invention and the use of new machinery would be stimulated.——(*b*) Wages generally would more likely be raised than lowered: *The Eight Hours Day*, pp. 94-102, 110-114.——(*c*) The total export trade would not be diminished.—(1) Similar reductions of hours in former times have not diminished the export trade.—(2) Competition is keenest now where hours are shortest.—(3) Other countries are increasing their factory legislation.——(*d*) Demand and supply in the aggregate would not be diminished.——(*e*) Prices generally would not be affected: *The Eight Hours Day*, pp. 114-115.

II. An eight-hour day would be beneficial socially.——(*a*) It would take away much of the poverty of the masses.—(1) By giving work to many of the unemployed: *Wealth and Progress*, pp. 251-256.——(*b*) It would improve the health of working people.—(1) They would not have to spend so much time under unhealthy conditions.——(*c*) It would add to intelligence and culture.——(1) More time could be given to reading, to lectures, and to evening schools.——(d) It would raise the standard of living.——(1) Workingmen would have more varied wants and the means to gratify them.——(e) It would promote better citizenship: *Wealth and Progress*, pp. 373-377.

III. An eight-hour day has been successful wherever introduced.——(a) In Australia: C. W. Dilke, *Problems of Greater Britain*, II., 285-286.——(b) In England: *The Eight Hours Day*, pp. 254-264; *A Shorter Working Day*, Chap. vii. and Appendix I.——(c) In the United States.——(1) The experience of the United States government.

IV. An eight-hour day should be adopted by law.——(a) The voluntary adoption by employers is improbable.——(b) Intelligent legislation is better than violent agitation and strikes by labor organizations.——(c) Legal enactment is necessary to secure uniformity and enforcement.

Brief for the Negative.

GENERAL REFERENCES: J. M. Robertson, *The Eight Hours Question*; F. A. Walker in *Atlantic Monthly*, LXV., 800 (June, 1890); *National Review*, XVI., 496 (December, 1890); *Fortnightly Review*, LIII., 440 (March, 1890); *Contemporary Review*, LVII., 240 (February, 1890); *Westminster Review*, Vol. 139, p. 526 (May, 1893); *Lippincott's Magazine*, II., 527 (November, 1868); *Spectator*, LXII., 392 (March 23, 1889); *Nation*, I., 517 (October 26, 1865), 615 (November 16, 1865); III., 412 (November 22, 1866); VII., 6 (July 2, 1868); X., 399 (June 23, 1870).

I. An eight-hour law would be harmful to industry.——(a) It would decrease wages: *Atlantic Monthly*, LXV., 808; *Nation*, III., 413.——(b) It would decrease production: *The Eight Hours Question*, pp. 62-69.—(1) A man cannot do as much work in eight hours as he can in ten.—(2) Much work is done by machinery which could not be increased in speed.——(*c*) It would depress domestic trade.—(1) By raising prices: *The Eight Hours Question,* pp. 69-75.——(*d*) It would give an impetus to foreign trade.—(1) Goods manufactured under an eight-hour system could not compete with those manufactured under a system of longer hours.——(*e*) It is no argument to say that since hours have been reduced with good results from twelve to ten they ought further to be reduced from ten to eight.

II. An eight-hour law is unnecessary.——(*a*) More than eight hours work does not overtax either mental or manual laborers.——(*b*) Not all workmen desire the change.——(*c*) Great industrial success and prosperity has been obtained without such legislation.

III. An eight-hour law would be unjust.——(*a*) In some industries men can reasonably work longer than in others. ——(*b*) In some trades work is carried on more months in the year than in others.——(*c*) Job work would be discriminated against.

IV. An eight-hour law would be inexpedient.——(*a*) The state should interfere only when necessary to protect life and limb.——(*b*) This legislation would be destructive to the self-reliance of the community.——(*c*) No man has the moral right to tell another how long he shall work.——(*d*) The measure would not help the problem of the unemployed: *Atlantic Monthly,* LXV., 809.—(1) The majority of the unemployed are not fitted for skilled work.——(*e*) The law would increase the sweating system.——(*f*) It is not certain that the time gained would be well spent.——(*g*) There are forces at work which will bring about the result whenever it is really desirable.

LXI.

GENERAL BOOTH'S EMPLOYMENT SYSTEM.

QUESTION: '*Resolved,* That General Booth's employment system as outlined in 'Darkest England' should be adopted in this country.'

Brief for the Affirmative.

GENERAL REFERENCES: General Booth, *In Darkest England and the Way Out; Review of Reviews* (English edition), II., 492 (November. 1890); *New Review*, III., 489 (December, 1890); VII., 493 (October, 1892); *National Review*, XVI., 781 (February. 1891); *Westminster Review*, Vol. 135, p. 429 (April, 1891); *Contemporary Review*, LVIII., 796 (December, 1890); *Quarterly Journal of Economics*, V., 1 (October, 1890); *Forum*, XII., 751, 762 (February, 1892); XVII., 52 (March, 1894).

I. Conditions in this country demand an extensive scheme for the relief of the unemployed.

II. This demand can best be met by applying the scheme of General Booth, which is for a system of colonization, consisting of—(1) Home shelters.—(2) Farm colonies.—(3) Emigration colonies: *In Darkest England and the Way Out*, pp. 90–93.

III. The scheme of General Booth is scientific.——(*a*) It rebuilds character.——(*b*) Takes away temptation.——(*c*) Protects the community by isolating the unfit.——(*d*) Decreases vagrancy: *Quarterly Journal of Economics*, V., 14. ——(*e*) Reverses the tide from cities.——(*f*) Discriminates between the deserving and undeserving.——(*g*) Diminishes promiscuous charity.

IV. General Booth's scheme is practical.——(*a*) It has been successful as far as applied in England: *Forum*, XII.,

762-771.——(b) Its principles have long been in use in Germany: *Quarterly Journal of Economics*, V., 6-22.——(c) It is the cheapest method of caring for vagrants.

V. General Booth's scheme is adaptable to this country. ——(a) The conditions in this country and England are similar.——(b) The plan has already had some application here. —(1) Home shelters have been established.—(2) An industrial farm was operated 1874-1888 at Plainfield, New Jersey: *Forum*, XVII., 58.—(3) The principle of deportation has had the best results in the work of the Children's Aid Society of New York City.

Brief for the Negative.

GENERAL REFERENCES: General Booth, *In Darkest England and the Way Out;* W. J. Ashley in *Political Science Quarterly*, VI., 537 (September, 1891); *Church Quarterly Review*, XXXII., 223 (April, 1891); *Contemporary Review*, LXII., 59 (July, 1892); *National Review*, XVI., 697 (January, 1891); *Forum*, XV., 753 (August, 1893).

I. The whole scheme is adapted to but a small portion of the needy, viz.: the homeless. —— (a) It is applicable to unencumbered individuals and not to families: *Contemporary Review*, LXII., 64.——(b) The class of homeless unemployed does not require so great a scheme: *Ibid.*

II. The scheme is objectionable even for the homeless.—— (a) The city colony is objectionable.—(1) The shelters encourage vagrancy and dissolution of family ties by wife desertion: *Contemporary Review*, LXII., 65-66.—(2) The 'Elevators' attract but a few.—(3) The occupants become dependent on charity.—(4) The labor bureaus have but slight advantage.—(x) Employers distrust applicants.—(y) Salvation Army sympathizers discriminate against other workmen.— (5) The 'Salvage Brigade' is unnecessary.

III. The farm colony is objectionable.——(a) Few patronize the farm any length of time: *Forum*, XII., 757.—(1)

Because of dislike for farm work.—(2) Because of lack of city allurements.—(3) On account of the stigma of being known as an object of charity.——(b) The farm colony is objectionable for colonists.—(1) It makes them willingly dependent: *Contemporary Review*, LXII., 76.—(2) Colonists are discriminated against by employers on leaving.——(c) Farm colonies lower wages in their neighborhood.——(d) Farm colonies are exceedingly hard to manage.

IV. The over-sea colony is objectionable.——(a) It is very difficult to procure suitable land.——(b) Few farm graduates are willing to return to ordinary life.——(c) Those who do return have doubtful successes.

LXII.

A NATIONAL BOARD OF ARBITRATION FOR RAILROAD DISPUTES.

QUESTION: '*Resolved*, That there should be a national board of arbitration for matters in dispute between employers and employees on inter-state railroads, and that this board should be given compulsory powers.'

Brief for the Affirmative.

GENERAL REFERENCES: C. D. Wright, *Industrial Conciliation and Arbitration*; J. S. Lowell, *Industrial Arbitration and Conciliation*; United States Strike Commission, *Report on the Chicago Strike*; abstract in *Public Opinion*, XVII., 809 (November 22, 1894); C. D. Wright in *Forum*, XVIII., 425 (December, 1894); Lyman Abbott in *Arena*, VII., 30 (December, 1892); *Atlantic Monthly*, LXVII., 34 (January, 1891); *Journal of Social Science*, No. XXVIII., p. 86 (October, 1891); No. XXXI., p. lxiii (January, 1894); *Arena*, VII., 306 (February, 1893); *Century*, XXXI., 946 (April, 1886).

I. Labor disputes on inter-state railroads demand prompt and decisive action.——(a) A large number of employees are concerned.——(b) Public interests are affected.—(1) Railroads have great economic importance.——(c) The public have a legal right to continued operation.—(1) Railroads are common carriers.——(d) Congress has power over inter-state commerce.

II. All other methods for the prevention of strikes and for the peaceful settlement of disputes are ineffectual.——(a) Voluntary arbitration is not binding.——(b) Conciliation does not bring about the wished-for results.——(c) State interference in inter-state traffic is impossible.

III. A national board would give the most efficient and satisfactory solution.——(a) It would be composed of men experienced in railroad matters and personally disinterested.—— (b) Efficiency and promptness would be secured by the compulsory power.——(c) The board would have the respect of all parties concerned.

IV. Experience in the past demands such a board for the future.——(a) Where fairly tried compulsory arbitration has been effectual.—(1) The *Conseils des Prud'hommes* in France: *Century*, IX., 947.——(b) Public interference is necessary where business is of public importance.—(1) The coal strike in England: *Spectator*, LXXII., 705.—(2) The London cab strike: *The Times* (London), June 7-9, 1894.— (3) The strike in Chicago in 1894.

Brief for the Negative.

GENERAL REFERENCES: T. M. Cooley in *Forum*, I., 307 (June, 1886); XVIII., 14-19 (September, 1894); C. D. Wright in *Forum*, XV., 323 (May, 1893); *Arena*, VII., 587 (April, 1893); *Quarterly Journal of Economics*, I., 497 (July, 1887); *Nation*, XLII., 354 (April 29, 1886); LIX., 42 (July 19, 1894), 376 (November 22, 1894); *Public Opinion*, XVII., 809-811 (November 22, 1894), 832 (November 29, 1894), 863 (December 6, 1894).

I. A national board of arbitration is not needed.———(*a*) Any legal claim can be enforced in the regular courts.———(*b*) If the regular courts have not power enough they can be given it by law.

II. Compulsory arbitration is impracticable.———(*a*) Arbitration must be voluntary: *Forum*, XVIII., 15.———(*b*) Attempts at compulsory arbitration have failed: *Quarterly Journal of Economics*, I., 497.———(*c*) Compulsory arbitration is unjust in its working.—(1) The decision can be enforced only against the corporation and not against the men: *Nation*, LIX., 376; *Public Opinion*, XVII., 842.———(*d*) The decisions would not be respected.—(1) The commission would not be a court, but a mixture of court and administrative board.—(2) It is likely that the personnel of the commission would deteriorate.—(x) That of the Inter-state Commerce Commission has.———(*e*) Many disputes cannot be arbitrated. —(1) The Chicago strike: *Forum*, XVIII., 16.

III. The commission would be opposed to business principles.———(*a*) It would be inquisitorial and meddling.—(1) It would give a share of the management of a business to others than the owners.———(*b*) It would be oppressive.—(1) Railroads are already interfered with enough by commissions. —(2) It would interfere with right of private contract.

IV. The commission would be opposed to progress.———(*a*) Workingmen should not be treated as children: *Nation*, LIX., 376.———(*b*) It would check the growth of trade unions: *Public Opinion*, XVII., 863.———(*c*) Is opposed by labor leaders: *Public Opinion*, XVII., 832.

LXIII.

THE CONTRACT SYSTEM OF EMPLOYING CONVICT LABOR.

QUESTION: '*Resolved*, That the contract system of employing convict labor ought to be abolished.'

Brief for the Affirmative.

GENERAL REFERENCES: *Second Annual Report of the Commissioner of Labor*, 1886; *Illinois Bureau of Labor Statistics, Fourth Biennial Report*, 1886. Part I.; *Michigan Bureau of Labor Statistics, Fourth Annual Report*, 1887; *Princeton Review*, V., 225 (March, 1880).

I. The contract system hinders the reformation of prisoners. ——(*a*) A diversity of employment suitable for the different capacities of prisoners and necessary for their moral well-being is made impossible.——(*b*) The comparatively innocent and the most depraved are kept in daily contact.——(*c*) New contracts bring new organization, and this destroys much of the benefit of industry.——(*d*) Prisoners are given routine machine work which little prepares them for a successful career when they leave the prison.

II. The contract system interferes with prison discipline: *Illinois Report*, pp. 88–92.——(*a*) The controlling authority of the prison is divided.——(*b*) The association of convicts with the outside employees of contractors is demoralizing. ——(*c*) The reporting of convicts by the agents of contractors gives rise to abuses.——(*d*) It is the intention of the law and for the best interest of society that the terms of the best prisoners be shortened, but it is for the interest of the contractors that the men be kept in prison.

III. The contract system injures free industry: *United*

States Report, pp. 325, 344, 365-366, 373-378; *Illinois Report*, pp. 92-124.——(*a*) It reduces the wages of outside laborers.——(*b*) It drives manufacturers out of business.—(1) Contractors have undue advantages.—(2) The whole effect of competition falls on a few industries.

IV. A system of work on public account without machinery is preferable: *Illinois Report*, p. 135; *Michigan Report*, p. 216.——(*a*) The entire management of the prison can be united under one head.——(*b*) Any change which public policy may demand is possible.——(*c*) Hand labor is wise.—(1) It gives prisoners a trade requiring intelligence and skill.—(2) It does not offer injurious competition to outside industry.

V. The contract system has been abandoned by leading states after a thorough trial: *Illinois Report*, pp. 137-142. ——(*a*) New York.——(*b*) Pennsylvania.——(*c*) Ohio.——(*d*) New Jersey.——(*e*) California.

Brief for the Negative.

GENERAL REFERENCES: *Second Annual Report of the Commissioner of Labor*, 1886; *Massachusetts Bureau of Statistics of Labor, Tenth Annual Report*, 1879, Part II.; *Princeton Review*, XI., 196 (March, 1883); *Forum*, VI., 414 (December, 1888); *Nation*, XL., 194 (March 5, 1885); XLV., 88 (August 4, 1887); *Science*, VII., 28 (January 8, 1886), 68 (January 22, 1886).

I. Convicts must be employed: *United States Report*, pp. 316, 328, 382, 383.——(*a*) To keep prisoners in idleness is cruel and demoralizing.—(1) It produces physical degeneracy and leads to insanity.

II. Four systems of employment are open: *United States Report*, p. 4.——(*a*) The lease system.——(*b*) The piece-price system.——(*c*) The public-account system.——(*d*) The contract system.

III. The lease system is objectionable: G. W. Cable, *The Silent South*, p. 115; *Century*, XXVII., 582 (March, 1884); *United States Report*, p. 381.——(*a*) It reduces to a minimum the chances of reformation.—(1) The only object of the lessee is to make money.—(2) Moral regeneration is completely lost sight of.——(*b*) Prisoners are treated as animals rather than as human beings.——(*c*) The system makes possible the infliction of greater punishment than the courts impose.

IV. The piece-price system is objectionable. —— (*a*) It offers more serious competition to free industry than the other systems.—(1) More goods are turned out and a lower price is paid for them.——(*b*) It is very expensive for the state.—— (*c*) It failed in New Jersey, where it had its best trial.

V. The public-account system is objectionable: *United States Report*, p. 380.——(*a*) It is not a legitimate office for the state to conduct manufactures.——(*b*) To manage the business industries and conduct the administration of a prison requires a degree of experience and tact which can rarely be found in a warden.—(1) Private enterprise is more attractive. —(2) Wages are not sufficient to tempt the best men.——(*c*) The system is costly: *Illinois Report*, pp. 31–34.—(1) The large amount of funds leads to speculation, mismanagement, and extravagance.—(2) The prison is likely to be run by incompetents who get places through the political machines.— (3) With the state for a master officers are careless and business is neglected.—(4) The state cannot buy and sell as well as an individual.——(*d*) The system is injurious to free labor: *United States Report*, p. 310.——(*e*) Prisoners are forced to be idle when trade is bad.——(*f*) The system has failed signally where it has been tried.—(1) In New York: *Princeton Review*, XI., 210.—(2) In Illinois: *Illinois Report*, p. 34.

VI. The contract system is the best yet devised.——(*a*) From a moral standpoint.—(1) The system is eminently humane.—(2) It has been very successful in reforming the lives of prisoners.—(3) It gives a means to the convict of earning a livelihood when he leaves prison, and thus prevents him from relapsing into his old ways.—(4) It does not interfere with prison discipline: *United States Report*, p. 311.—(x) Contractors cannot control or interfere with the prison management.

VII. The contract system is best from an economic standpoint.——(*a*) It is the most remunerative.—(1) It makes the prison self-supporting: *Nation*, XL., 194; *Illinois Report*, pp. 34–38.——(*b*) It is not so injurious to free industry as other systems.—(1) The conditions are more nearly normal. ——(*c*) It furnishes constant, regular, and diversified employment.——(*d*) It avoids all business risk for the state.——(*e*) It simplifies prison management.—(1) It is not necessary that the warden should be an expert manufacturer.——(*f*) Contractors do not make larger profits than other business men: *United States Report*, p. 345.

LXIV.

MUNICIPAL AID FOR THE UNEMPLOYED.

QUESTION: '*Resolved*, That in times of depression municipalities should give work to the unemployed.'

Brief for the Affirmative.

GENERAL REFERENCES: Stanton Coit in *Forum*, XVII., 276 (May, 1894); C. C. Closson in *Quarterly Journal of Economics*, VIII., 168 (January, 1894), 453 (July, 1894); John Burns in *Nineteenth Century*, XXXII., 845 (December, 1892); *Review of Reviews*, IX., 29 (January, 1894), 179 (February, 1894); *Forum*, XVI., 655 (February, 1894); *Fortnightly Review*, LX., 454 (October, 1893), 741 (December, 1893); *Arena*, IX., 822 (May, 1894).

I. In times of depression relief for the unemployed is necessary.——(*a*) To assist the individual.—(1) Great privation and suffering.——(*b*) To protect the state.—(1) A large number of destitute is a menace to public safety.

II. Relief should be administered through work.——(*a*) The danger of humiliating or pauperizing the recipient is thus avoided: *Forum*, XVII., 276.——(*b*) The worthy can be separated from the worthless: *Forum*, XVI., 660.——(*c*) Laws regarding vagrancy can be more easily enforced.

III. This work should be furnished by municipalities. ——(*a*) Private attempts are inadequate: *Forum*, XVII., 277. ——(*b*) Municipalities have more work, and work of a simpler kind, than have individuals.——(*c*) Municipalities have better facilities for ascertaining the number and circumstances of the unemployed.

IV. The difficulties attributed to municipal aid are not inherent.——(*a*) Money can be obtained by the issue of bonds: *Forum*, XVII., 281–282.——(*b*) Relief can be limited to members of the municipality.——(*c*) The administration can be intrusted to an outside non-partisan commission.

Brief for the Negative.

GENERAL REFERENCES: D. McG. Means in *Forum*, XVII., 287 (May, 1894); C. C. Closson in *Quarterly Journal of Economics*, VIII., 168 (January, 1894), 453 (July, 1894); *Review of Reviews*, IX., 29, 38 (January, 1894). 179 (February, 1894); *Nation*, LVII., 481 (December 28, 1893); LIX., 6 (July 5, 1894); *Public Opinion*, XVI., 121 (November 9, 1893); *Spectator*, LIX., 1473 (November 6, 1886); *Political Science Quarterly*, III., 282 (June, 1888).

I. Municipal aid is impracticable.——(*a*) Manual labor only can be furnished, and for this the majority of the unemployed are unqualified: *Nation*, LVII., 482.——(*b*) The work done is likely to be unsatisfactory: *Nation*, LIX., 6.

II. Municipal aid is inadvisable.——(*a*) It does not discriminate between the deserving and the undeserving.——(*b*) It injures those in regular employment.——(*c*) It furnishes too great an opportunity to distribute aid for partisan purposes: *Nation*, LVII., 482.——(*d*) It tends to develop the evils of socialism.—(1) By weakening self-dependence.—(2) By fostering pauperism.

III. Organized charity is the best means of furnishing the necessary aid.——(*a*) It is scientific in theory.—(1) It best ascertains the real needs of applicants.—(2) It exercises a personal and moral influence which tends to strengthen the laborer's self-dependence.——(*b*) It has been successful in practice: *Review of Reviews*, IX., 30.—(1) In Boston.—(2) In New York.—(3) In Chicago.—(4) In Baltimore.—(5) In Philadelphia.

LXV.

THE HOUSING OF THE POOR.

QUESTION: '*Resolved*, That the housing of the poor should be improved by municipalities.'

Brief for the Affirmative.

GENERAL REFERENCES: J. A. Riis, *How the Other Half Lives*; M. T. Reynolds, 'The Housing of the Poor in American Cities,' in *Publications of American Economic Association*, VIII., Nos. 2 and 3, Chaps. iii., iv. (March and May, 1893); *North American Review*, LXXIV., 464–480 (April, 1862); *Nineteenth Century*, XVII., 926 (June, 1885); *Fortnightly Review*, XL., 587 (October, 1883), 761 (December, 1893); XLIX., 284 (February, 1888).

I. The present tenement house system is disgraceful: *How the Other Half Lives*.——(*a*) Exorbitant rents are charged.

———(*b*) Houses are overcrowded: *Nineteenth Century*, XVII., 927.———(*c*) Sanitary conditions are bad: *Ibid.*———(*d*) Criminal classes are harbored: A. T. White, *Improved Dwellings for the Laboring Classes*, p. 4.

II. The necessity for improvement is urgent: *Publications of American Economic Association*, VIII., 159-175.———(*a*) On account of the harm to the individual.—(1) Sickness and mortality are increasing.—(2) Intemperance is fostered.—(3) Pauperism and crime are encouraged.—(4) Children are corrupted by bad surroundings.———(*b*) On account of the harm to the state.—(1) Infectious diseases are spread.—(2) Political corruption is made easy.—(3) The tendency toward socialism and anarchy is increased.

III. Improvements should be made by municipalities.——— (*a*) The general public would be benefited.———(*b*) Private schemes are inadequate.—(1) From lack of money.—(2) From lack of the power of expropriation.———(*c*) Municipal improvements where carried on have been successful.—(1) In Glasgow: *Century*, XXXIX., 731 (March, 1890).—(2) In Birmingham: *Fortnightly Review*, XL., 770-771.

Brief for the Negative.

GENERAL REFERENCES: W. G. Sumner, *What Social Classes Owe to Each Other*; Thomas Mackay, *A Plea for Liberty*, Chap. viii.; M. T. Reynolds, 'The Housing of the Poor in American Cities,' in *Publications of American Economic Association*, VIII., Nos. 2 and 3, Chaps. v.-viii. (March and May, 1893); A. T. White, *Improved Dwellings for the Laboring Classes*; Octavia Hill, *Homes of the London Poor*; *Forum*, V., 207 (April, 1888); *National Review*, II., 301 (November, 1883); *Westminster Review*, Vol. 121, p. 137 (January, 1884); *Nineteenth Century*, XIV., 934 (December, 1883).

I. Municipal housing is not wise in theory.———(*a*) It is class legislation.—(1) One class is taxed for the benefit of another.——(b) It is demoralizing.—(1) It causes dependence on the state instead of on self.——(c) It is unjust.—(1) The least worthy class is assisted.

II. Municipal housing is not successful in practice.——(a) The Glasgow experiments affect but a small proportion of the community.——(b) Experiments in London failed: *Fortnightly Review*, XXXVIII., 425 (October, 1882).——(c) Experiments in Naples were unsatisfactory: *Nation*, LII., 134.

III. A better solution of the problem is found in other ways.——(a) Private philanthropy in the restoration of existing buildings.—(1) The work of Miss Hill in London: Octavia Hill, *Homes of the London Poor*.—(2) The work of Mrs. Lincoln in Boston: A. T. White, *Better Homes for Workingmen*. p. 19 —(3) The restoration of Gotham Court in New York: *Publications of American Economic Association*, VIII., 193.——(b) Private philanthropy in the building of model tenements.—(1) The Peabody buildings in London: *Publications of American Economic Association*, VIII., 211–213.—(2) The buildings of Mr. A. T. White in Brooklyn: A. T. White, *Improved Dwellings for the Laboring Classes*.—(3) The work of the Improved Dwellings Association of New York.——(c) The building of suburban cottages.—(1) The workingmen's homes in Philadelphia.

LIQUOR.

LXVI.

PROHIBITION AND HIGH LICENSE.

QUESTION: '*Resolved*, That state prohibition is preferable to high license as a method of dealing with intemperance.'

Brief for the Affirmative.

GENERAL REFERENCES: *North American Review*, Vol. 143, p. 382 (October, 1886); Vol. 147, p. 121 (August, 1888);

Vol. 135, p. 525 (December, 1882); *Forum*, VII., 678–682 (August, 1889); H. W. Blair, *The Temperance Movement*; E. J. Wheeler, *Prohibition*; *Cyclopædia of Temperance and Prohibition*; *Popular Science Monthly*, XLV., 225 (June, 1894); *Annals of American Academy of Political Science*, II., 59–68 (July, 1891).

I. The use of intoxicants as a beverage is a great evil.——(*a*) Economically: *The Temperance Movement*, p. 210; *North American Review*, Vol. 147, p. 147.——(*b*) Politically.——(*c*) Morally: *North American Review*, Vol. 147, p. 124.

II. Prohibition is a legitimate remedy: *Prohibition*, Part I.——(*a*) It is constitutional: Stone *v.* Mississippi, 101 U. S., 818–819; *Cyclopædia of Temperance and Prohibition*, p. 473.——(*b*) No unlawful trespass on personal liberty is involved: *North American Review*, Vol. 147, p. 38.

III. Prohibition is an effective remedy: *Prohibition*, Part II.——(*a*) It can be enforced.—(1) This is shown by the experience of Massachusetts.—(2) Maine: *The Temperance Movement*, p. 370.—(3) Kansas: *Forum*, VII., 678–682.—(4) Iowa: *Cyclopædia of Temperance and Prohibition*, pp. 513–522.—(5) It has diminished the evils of intemperance in the above states.

IV. High license is wrong in principle.——(*a*) It gives to an evil the sanction of law.——(*b*) It strengthens the saloon power: *New Englander*, XLVIII., 127 (February, 1888).——(*c*) It tends to make drinking and the liquor traffic respectable: *North American Review*, Vol. 147, pp. 123–146.——(*d*) It debauches public sentiment.——(*e*) It is the plan of the liquor men.

V. High license is a failure in practice.——(*a*) It does not restrict the evil: *Forum*, VII., 681.——(*b*) The revenue obtained from it is more than counterbalanced by the cost of the pauperism and crime resulting from it.

Brief for the Negative.

GENERAL REFERENCES: *Lalor's Cyclopædia*, II., 384-385; J. S. Mill, *On Liberty*, p. 158; *Forum*, III., 152 (April, 1887); II., 232 (November, 1886); *Macmillan's Magazine*, LIX., 338 (March, 1889); *Nation*, XII., 353 (May 25, 1871); XVI., 365 (May 29, 1873); XXXVI., 35 (January 11, 1883); XXXVI., 168 (February 22, 1883); XXXVI., 272 (March 29, 1883); XLVI., 70 (January 26, 1888); XLVIII., 133 (February 14, 1889); XLIX., 470 (December 12, 1889); *New Princeton Review*, IV., 31 (July, 1887); *New Englander*, XXXIV., 663 (October, 1875); LI., 401 (December, 1889); *North American Review*, Vol. 139, p. 185 (August, 1884); Vol. 141, p. 34 (July, 1885); Vol. 144, p. 498 (May, 1887); *Popular Science Monthly*, XXVI., 787 (April, 1885); XLIV., 577 (March, 1894); John A. Andrew, *Errors of Prohibition*; W. B. Weeden, *The Morality of Prohibition Liquor Laws*.

I. Prohibition is bad in principle: *Forum*, III., 152; *New Englander*, XLIV., 706 (September, 1885); *On Liberty*, pp. 158-160.——(*a*) It infringes personal liberty: *Lalor's Cyclopædia*, II., 384.——(*b*) It is an unwarranted and extreme measure: *Forum*, VII., 674; *Andover Review*, IX., 22 (January, 1888); *Nation*, XII., 354.——(*c*) It is inquisitorial: *Nation*, XII., 353.——(*d*) Society is concerned with the abuse, not the use of intoxicants: *Forum*, VII., 674; *Nation*, XII., 354.——(*e*) All consumption of alcohol is not deleterious: *Andover Review*, IX., 20.

II. Prohibition does not prohibit: *Forum*, II., 234; *Popular Science Monthly*, XXVI., 795; *North American Review*, Vol. 141, p. 38.——(*a*) It cannot control appetite.——(*b*) It is not supported by public sentiment.—(1) It is not supported by many good citizens: *Nation*, XII., 353; *Journal of Social Science*, No. XIV., p. 90 (November, 1881).——(*c*) It has failed.—(1) In Maine: *Fortnightly Review*, XVI., 168,

174 (August, 1871).—(2) In Iowa: *Nation*, XLII., 52 (January 21, 1886).—(3) In Kansas: *North American Review*, Vol. 141, p. 41.—(4) In Massachusetts: *Macmillan's Magazine*, LIX., 343; *Journal of Social Science*, No. XIV., p. 90.—(5) In Vermont: *Fortnightly Review*, XVI., 169.—(6) In Michigan: *Fortnightly Review*, XVI., 175–176.—(7) In Minnesota: *North American Review*, Vol. 141, p. 39.—(8) In Rhode Island: *Nation*, XLVIII., 133 (February 14, 1889).

III. High license with local option is the most effectual method of dealing with intemperance: *North American Review*, Vol. 144, p. 500; *Nation*, XLVI., 71; *Popular Science Monthly*, XXVI., 790–792; Charles Nordhoff, *Politics for Young Americans*, pp. 110–114.——(*a*) It reduces the number of saloons: *North American Review*, Vol. 144, p. 499; *Nation*, XLII., 52; XLVI., 71.——(*b*) Licensed dealers defend their privileges against unlicensed dealers: *North American Review*, Vol. 144, p. 199.——(*c*) The fewer the saloons the less the political power: *North American Review*, Vol. 144, p. 500.——(*d*) It has all the good features of prohibition without menacing personal rights: *Nation*, XXXVI., 273.——(*e*) It tends to prevent use of spirits: *North American Review*, Vol. 144, p. 500.——(*f*) It can be enforced: *Forum*, II., 410.——(*g*) The argument that high license should be defeated because it indefinitely postpones prohibition is an admission of the efficacy of the method: *North American Review*, Vol. 144, p. 506.

LXVII.

THE GOTHENBURG LIQUOR SYSTEM.

Question: '*Resolved*, That the Gothenburg system of eliminating private profits offers the best solution of the liquor question.'

Brief for the Affirmative.

General references: 'The Gothenburg System of Liquor Traffic,' in *Fifth Special Report of the United States Commissioner of Labor*, 1893; Report of the Legislative Commission appointed by the Legislature of Massachusetts to investigate the working of the Gothenburg System. *Massachusetts Legislative Documents*, No. 192 (February, 1894); *Forum*, XVII., 103 (March, 1894); XIV., 514 (December, 1892); V., 281 (May, 1888); E. L. Fanshawe, *Liquor Legislation in the United States and Canada*; T. M. Wilson, *Local Option in Norway*; *Atlantic Monthly*, LXXII., 538 (October, 1893); *Review of Reviews*, VIII., 548 (November, 1893); *International Review*, VIII., 402 (April, 1880); *Spectator*, LXXIII., 40 (July 14, 1894); *New England Magazine*, XI., 785-797 (February, 1895); *Arena*, IX., 561 (April, 1894); *The Month*, LXXIII., 60 (September, 1891).

I. All methods of dealing with the liquor question, not involving the elimination of private profits, have failed to diminish materially the evils of the traffic.——(*a*) State prohibition does not prohibit: *Forum*, II., 232 (November, 1886); *Popular Science Monthly*, XXVI., 787 (April, 1885).—(1) This is shown by the experience of Maine.—(2) Kansas.—(3) Iowa.——(*b*) Prohibition by means of local option has only resulted in shifting the place of sale.——(*c*) High license has also failed to diminish the evils.—(1) It makes the few dealers more greedy and energetic for larger sales.

II. The Gothenburg system of eliminating private profits furnishes the best solution.——(*a*) It does not violate personal liberty by prohibiting a moderate use of intoxicants.——(*b*) It encourages the sale of mild drinks.—(1) By allowing dealers a personal profit on them.——(*c*) It takes away the incentive for large sales.—(1) No personal advantage is to be gained.——(*d*) It does away with the corrupting influence of the saloon.—(1) Stringent rules forbid sales to minors and to persons intoxicated.—(2) Everyone is obliged to leave the saloon as soon as he has purchased his drink.——(*e*) It takes the saloon out of politics.—(1) There is nothing to be gained from political favor.—(2) Saloons can no longer be the headquarters of corrupt politicians.

III. The Gothenburg plan is a practical solution.——(*a*) It has been tried successfully in Norway.——(*b*) In the case of the United States the same system can be extended to the sale of malt liquors.

Brief for the Negative.

GENERAL REFERENCES: E. L. Fanshawe, *Liquor Legislation in the United States and Canada*; *North American Review*, Vol. 147, p. 638 (December, 1888); Vol. 144, p. 498 (May, 1887); *Nation*, XLVI., 25 (January 12, 1888); XLIX., 470 (December 12, 1890); *Journal of Social Science*, No. XIV., p. 118 (November, 1881); *Spectator*, LXIX., 918 (December 24, 1892); *Review of Reviews*, VIII., 553-554 (November, 1893).

I. The best solution of the liquor problem must minimize the evils of the traffic with the least restriction on personal liberty: *Lalor's Cyclopædia*, III., 380-385; J. S. Mill, *On Liberty*, Chaps. iv., v.

II. The elimination of private profits is objectionable on political grounds.——(*a*) It involves extensive participation by the government in the liquor trade.—(1) The disposition of profits must be overseen.—(2) Minute supervision by officials is necessary.———(*b*) It interferes unreasonably with the liquor dealer's right to conduct his own business.———(*c*) It regulates unreasonably personal liberty in drinking.

III. The proposition is objectionable on economic grounds. ———(*a*) It prevents the indulgence of a natural social instinct. —(1) A dispensary is not sufficient.—(2) A shop conducted on philanthropic principles is not sufficient.—(x) Men do not like to be objects of philanthropy.———(*b*) A strong demand of human nature always leads to violations of an opposing law.

IV. High license is the best solution of the problem.——— (*a*) It reduces greatly the amount of drunkenness.—(1) By reducing the number of saloons and increasing the profits of saloon keepers it induces better men to go into the business. —(2) It makes a license too valuable to be risked by the sale of liquor to drunkards.———(*b*) It takes the saloon out of politics.———(*c*) Where tried it has superseded all other legislation.

V. High license is not open to objections raised against the method of eliminating private profits.———(*a*) While preventing abuses it leaves the desirable features of the saloon.——— (*b*) It involves no unnecessary interference with personal liberty.

EDUCATION.

LXVIII.

CO-EDUCATION.

QUESTION : ' *Resolved,* That co-education in colleges is desirable.'

Brief for the Affirmative.

GENERAL REFERENCES: Julia Ward Howe, *Sex and Education; Report of the Commissioner of Education,* 1891–1892,

II., Chap. xxvi. ; *Barnard's American Journal of Education*, XVII., 385 (January, 1868); *Forum*, III., 631 (August, 1887); XVII., 582 (July, 1894); *Westminster Review*, Vol. 100, p. 320 (October, 1873); Vol. 109, p. 56 (January, 1878); *North American Review*, Vol. 118, p. 140 (January, 1874); *Baptist Quarterly Review*, IX., 63 (January, 1887); *Scribner's Monthly*, II., 519 (September, 1871); *Bibliotheca Sacra*, XLVI., 443 (July, 1889); *Education*, IV., 427 (March, 1884); XIII., 259 (January, 1893); *Nation*, XLVI., 91 (February 2, 1888).

I. Co-education is desirable from the point of view of colleges.——(*a*) It is economical.—(1) The teaching force, libraries, laboratories, and other equipments are made available for a larger number at little extra expense.——(*b*) It raises the standard of scholarship.—(1) The presence of the opposite sex is an incentive to study : *Barnard's American Journal of Education*, XVII., 389. —— (*c*) It helps to secure good order.—(1) Offences against propriety are less common : *Barnard's American Journal of Education*, XVII., 390–391. ——(*d*) The quality of instruction is improved.—(1) Where men and women are educated separately education tends toward masculine and feminine extremes.——(*e*) It is a convenience to patrons.—(1) Brothers and sisters can be sent to the same institution.

II. Co-education is desirable for young men.——(*a*) It has a refining influence.——(*b*) It gives them better manners. ——(*c*) It gives them higher ideals.——(*d*) It leads to a truer and juster appreciation of the abilities of women.——(*e*) It causes broad rivalry.——(*f*) It banishes consciousness of sex.

III. Co-education is desirable for young women.——(*a*) It gives them a better education than is otherwise possible. ——(*b*) It strengthens their characters.—(1) It gives them greater breadth of view.—(2) It takes away capricious fancies and romantic ideals and substitutes sober judgment.—(3) It gives them more natural views of life.——(c) It gives them a fairer standard of measurement.——(d) It gives them courage.——(e) Women are not physically incapable of working wiht men: *Report of the Commissioner of Education*, 1891–1829, II., 841–842.——(f) Women do not become less womanyl: *Forum*, XVII., 587.

IV. Co-education has been successful in practice.——(a) In the common schools of this country: *Report of the Commissioner of Education*, 1891–1892, II., Chap. xxvi.——(b) In the universities abroad: *Westminster Review*, Vol. 109, pp. 56–90.—(1) France.—(2) Italy.—(3) Switzerland.—(4) Holland.—(5) Sweden.——(c) In the colleges of this country.—(1) University of Michigan: *Education*, IV., 433.—(2) Cornell: *Ibid.*—(3) Oberlin: *Bibliotheca Sacra*, XLVI., 443.

Brief for the Negative.

GENERAL REFERENCES: E. H. Clarke, *Sex in Education;* *Report of the Commissioner of Education*, 1891–1892, II., Chap. xxvi.; *Educational Review*, IV., 164 (September, 1892); *Popular Science Monthly*, V., 198 (June, 1874); *Critic* (old series), III., 153 (April 7. 1883); XI., 85 (August 20, 1887); *Nation*, XI., 24 (July 14, 1870); XVI., 349 (May 22, 1873); XVIII., 408 (June 25, 1874); XLVI., 52 (January 19, 1888).

I. Co-education is undesirable from an intellectual standpoint.——(a) Women need a special course of study which they can get only in a separate institution.—(1) They have different paths and different duties in life from men.—(2) In a co-educational college they are compelled to pursue a course framed primarily for men.——(b) Women are physically incapable of pursuing to advantage the same course with men.—(1) They are not so strong.—(2) Their brains are smaller and differ greatly from those of men: *Educational Review*, IV., 165–170.——(c) Co-education produces morbid rivalry.——(d) It retards progress.—(1) There are too many distractions.

II. Co-education is undesirable morally.——(a) It throws women into a critical atmosphere.——(b) It makes them the subject of unpleasant comment.——(c) It brings them into contact with common men.——(d) It leads to sentimentality and often vulgarity.——(e) It makes impossible that guidance and direction which is so essential.

III. Co-education is undesirable socially.——(a) It tends toward making men effeminate.——(b) It unfits women for domestic life.——(c) It fails to promote refinement and gentle breeding.——(d) It makes women free and careless in manner.——(e) It develops strong mannish women who are disagreeable and who do little good in the world.

IV. Co-education is unnecessary.——(a) There are good colleges for the separate education of women.—(1) Smith.—(2) Vassar.—(3) Wellesley.——(b) There are colleges for co-ordinate education.—(1) Radcliffe.—(2) Barnard.—(3) Western Reserve University.

LXIX.

A THREE YEARS' COURSE FOR THE A.B. DEGREE.

QUESTION: '*Resolved*, That some system ought to be adopted by which the degree of A.B. could be obtained from colleges in three years.'

Brief for the Affirmative.

GENERAL REFERENCES: *Majority Report of the Faculty of Harvard College to the Board of Overseers.* January 7, 1891; *Harvard Monthly*, X., 201 (July, 1890); XI., 127 (January, 1891); *Andover Review*, XIII., 75 (January, 1890); *Nation*, XLIX., 425 (November 28, 1889); LI., 12 (July 3, 1890);

Annual Reports of the President and Treasurer of Harvard College, 1886–1887, pp. 75–76; 1890–1891, pp. 1–9.

I. A change is desirable from the point of view of the general public.——(*a*) The proportion of college-bred men in the country has not increased in proportion to the population: *Majority Report*, p. 11.——(*b*) The four years' course keeps away from college many men.—(1) Those who are unable to meet the expense.—(2) Those who are unwilling to give the time.——(*c*) Our national problems need especially the minds of college-bred men.

II. It is desirable from the point of view of colleges. ——(*a*) The influence and the ideals of colleges would be more widely extended.——(*b*) The scholarship of the colleges would be improved.—(1) Much of the under-graduate's time is now wasted.—(2) A more earnest and serious class of men would be drawn to college.—(3) Many of the men who did not take a professional course would return in the graduate department.—(x) The influence of the graduate department is sobering.

III. It is desirable from the point of view of professional schools.——(*a*) The present system brings professional men into the practical work of life too late.——(*b*) The present system robs the professions of the best men and fills their places with those who have not had a liberal education.——(*c*) Both of these defects would be remedied by the change.—(1) Men would get into the professional schools earlier.—(2) More of them would be college graduates.

IV. It is desirable from the point of view of students.—— (*a*) The average age at graduation is now too high.—(1) It is nearly twenty-three years. —— (*b*) Opportunity to save a year would be welcomed by many men.—(1) Those preparing for professions. — (2) Those possessing little means. — (3) Those intending a business career.——(*c*) Those men who wished to continue a scholarly life could do so with greater advantage in graduate schools.

Brief for the Negative.

GENERAL REFERENCES: N. S. Shaler in *Atlantic Monthly*, LXVI., 161 (August, 1890); *Minority Report of the Faculty of Harvard College to the Board of Overseers*, December 23, 1890; *Educational Review*, I., 1 (January, 1891), 133 (February, 1891); *Harvard Monthly*, IX., 1 (October, 1889); XII., 1 (March, 1891), 77 (April, 1891); *Education*, XI., 585 (June, 1891); *Academy*, V., 441–448 (November, 1891); *Nation*, LI., 106 (August 7, 1890), 226 (September 18, 1890).

I. The present system of requiring a four years' course for the degree of A.B. is wise.——(*a*) The degree of A.B. should stand for more than a given amount of book learning.—(1) Great benefits come from continued residence under academic influences.—(x) Development of character and individuality.—(y) Culture and refinement.—(z) Breadth of mind and liberality of thought.——(*b*) It is folly to suppose that these advantages can be acquired in a course of three years as well as in a course of four years.

II. The proposed change is highly objectionable.——(*a*) It lowers the standard of college education.—(1) By degrading the degree of A.B.—(x) It makes the college simply a wedge between the preparatory schools and the professional schools.——(*b*) It is an unwise concession to the hurried, materialistic spirit of our time.——(*c*) Broad culture and not so much specialization is what we need: *Educational Review*, I., 140. ——(*d*) The curriculum is now crowded.

III. All experience is against the change.——(*a*) England has found it unsatisfactory.—(1) At Oxford the greater number graduate in four years: *Minority Report*, p. 7.——(*b*) It has not been popular in America.—(1) Johns Hopkins has not made a success with it: *Harvard Monthly*, XII., 3.—(2) Almost all of our new colleges adopt the four years' plan.

IV. If the course be too long it can be shortened better in some other way than by dropping one of the four years of college.——(*a*) The preparatory course can be shortened.—(1) Our present system of preparatory education is radically bad. ——(*b*) Candidates for a degree can be allowed to take professional studies.

LXX.

INTERCOLLEGIATE FOOT-BALL.

QUESTION: '*Resolved,* That intercollegiate foot-ball promotes the best interests of colleges.'

Brief for the Affirmative.

GENERAL REFERENCES: *Harvard College, Report on Athletics* (Cambridge, 1888); *Popular Science Monthly,* XXIV., 446 (February, 1884), 587 (March, 1884); XLV., 721 (October, 1894); *Atlantic Monthly,* LXVI., 63 (July, 1890); *Forum,* XVI., 634 (January, 1894); *Century,* XLVI., 204 (June, 1893); XLVII., 315 (December, 1893); *Lippincott's Magazine,* XXXIX., 1008 (June, 1887); *Harvard Graduates' Magazine,* II., 1 (September, 1893); *Nation,* XXXVI., 268 (March 29, 1883).

I. Athletics in colleges are essential.——(*a*) '*Mens sana in corpore sano.*'——(*b*) Youth is the time for physical development.——(*c*) Without athletics students do not get sufficient exercise.—(1) There is no necessity for physical exertion.—(2) We have no military training as is the case in European countries.

II. Foot-ball is a beneficial form of athletics.——(*a*) It is acceptable to the students.—(1) It is played by a large number.——(*b*) It promotes bodily health.—(1) Training teaches the importance of proper ventilation and wholesome food.

———(c) It promotes moral qualities.—(1) Self-control.—(2) Temperance.—(3) Courage.

III. Intercollegiate contests are advantageous.———(a) They are a stimulus to general participation.—(1) If there were no intercollegiate contests there would be less interest in the sport and fewer men would try for the teams.———(b) They develop college patriotism.———(c) They bring the different colleges into closer relation.

IV. The evils of foot-ball are not inherent.———(a) The number of injuries is greatly exaggerated and can be decreased by new rules.———(b) The time given to training is not excessive.—(1) The foot-ball season lasts only ten weeks.—(2) It does not interfere seriously with college studies.———(c) The lowering of students' ideals, if a danger, can be prevented.—(1) By requiring a higher standard of scholarship.———(d) The crowds of outsiders and the large amounts of money expended can be avoided.—(1) By limiting games to college grounds and reducing the price of admission.

Brief for the Negative.

GENERAL REFERENCES: N. S. Shaler in *Atlantic Monthly*, LXIII., 79 (January, 1889); *Harvard Graduates' Magazine*, III., 305 (March, 1895); *Annual Reports of the President and Treasurer of Harvard College*, 1892–1893, pp. 12–22; 1893–1894, pp. 16–17; *Nation*, LV., 406 (December 1, 1892); LVII., 422 (December 7, 1893), 444 (December 14, 1893); LIX., 399 (November 29, 1894), 457 (December 20, 1894), 476 (December 27, 1894); *Public Opinion*, XVI., 244 (December 14, 1893), 505 (March 1, 1894).

I. The evils of intercollegiate foot-ball are ineradicable.———(a) Foot-ball by its nature offers great inducements to unfair and brutal play.———(b) The intense excitement and rivalry of intercollegiate contests make such temptations inadvisable.

II. Intercollegiate foot-ball is injurious to the players.———

(*a*) Physically.—(1) There is great liability to overwork.—(2) The nervous strain is great.—(3) The liability to injury is great. —— (*b*) Intellectually. — (1) It takes an excessive amount of time.—(2) It takes an excessive amount of thought.—(x) Men are totally preoccupied before the great games. ——(*c*) Morally.—(1) It encourages extravagance.—(2) It leads to vulgar notoriety.—(3) It dulls the sense of honor.—(4) It dulls the feelings and has a brutalizing influence.—(5) It leads to intemperance after training.

III. Intercollegiate foot-ball is injurious to the students at large.——(*a*) It discourages men who cannot excel from engaging in athletics at all.——(*b*) It promotes general immorality.—(1) Betting.—(2) Little meannesses are condoned for the sake of victory.——(*c*) It establishes false ideals.—(1) Physical force is placed above intellectual and moral qualities. ——(*d*) Much time is lost in watching games.——(*e*) Hysterical excitement is provoked at times in the great games.

IV. Intercollegiate foot-ball is injurious to colleges.——(*a*) It draws men to college for the purpose of engaging in athletics.——(*b*) It gives occasion for unbecoming celebrations. ——(*c*) It affects the proper flow of pupils to college.—(1) Many choose a college for its athletic record and not for its real advantages.——(*d*) It leads to the development of athletic rather than intellectual ability in preparatory schools. ——(*e*) It gives a false idea of the college to the community. —(1) Represents it as a place of leisure and a training school for athletes, and not as a centre of learning.——(*f*) It causes ill-feeling between colleges.

MISCELLANEOUS.

LXXI.

IRISH HOME RULE.

QUESTION: '*Resolved*, That home rule should be granted to Ireland.'

Brief for the Affirmative.

GENERAL REFERENCES: James Bryce, *Hand-Book of Home Rule*; W. E. Gladstone in *North American Review*, Vol. 155, p. 385 (October, 1892); *Nineteenth Century*, VII., 406 (March, 1880), 583 (April, 1880); XIX., 424 (March, 1886); XXI., 19 (January, 1887), 165 (February, 1887); *Contemporary Review*, LI., 84 (January, 1887), 305 (March, 1887); LIII., 321 (March, 1888); LV., 462 (March, 1889); LXII., 305 (September, 1892); *Fortnightly Review*, XXXII., 224 (August, 1879); LII., 293 (September, 1889).

I. Ireland has a right to home rule.——(*a*) The Act of Union for England and Ireland was forced by bribery and intimidation.——(*b*) The union has failed.—(1) England has shown herself incapable of governing Ireland.—(x) The people are now more wretched, and disaffection is more widespread than at the beginning of the century.—(2) Coercion has proved a failure.——(*c*) The Irish are capable of governing themselves.

II. Home rule is wise in principle.——(*a*) Two nations having such diversity of temperament and ideas cannot be held together in harmony without self-government.——(*b*)

The unity of the British Empire is not placed in jeopardy.
—(1) The supremacy of the imperial parliament is maintained.——(c) There are good precedents for home rule.—(1) The federal system of the United States.—(2) The German Empire.—(3) The dual system of Austria and Hungary.

III. Home rule would benefit Ireland.——(a) It would do away with the discontent and ill-feeling.——(b) It would secure for the country suitable legislation.—(1) The laws would be framed by better informed and more sympathetic men.——(c) It would bring about order and respect for law.——(d) It would bring to an end the contentions regarding land tenure.——(e) It would sober the people.—(1) By giving them responsibility.——(f) It would give the country new life and would develop industry.

IV. Home rule would benefit England.——(a) It would facilitate legislation in the English Parliament.—(1) The obstruction of the Irish minority would no longer detain business.—(2) The legitimate discussion of Irish affairs renders proper attention to home and imperial affairs impossible.——(b) It would strengthen the Empire.—(1) Ireland's hatred would be turned into good feeling and support.—(2) The discontent in Ireland, which forms a serious military weakness, would be removed.——(c) Refusal to grant home rule means a continuation of the present difficulties and fresh menaces to England's prosperity and advancement.

Brief for the Negative.

GENERAL REFERENCES: A. V. Dicey, *England's Case Against Home Rule;* A. V. Dicey, *Why England Maintains the Union;* George Baden-Powell, *The Truth About Home Rule; North American Review,* Vol. 155, p. 129 (August, 1892); *Nineteenth Century,* VII., 567 (April, 1880); XXI., 397 (March, 1887); XXXIII., 545 (April, 1893); *Contemporary Review,* XLII., 66 (July, 1882); LXIII., 626 (May, 1893); *Fortnightly Review,* XVII., 16 (June, 1872); XLVI.,

78 (July, 1886); *Political Science Quarterly*, IV., 66 (March, 1889).

I. The Irish have shown themselves incapable of self-government.——(*a*) They have ruled Ireland badly in the past.—(1) The Irish parliaments of 1688 and 1782 were failures.——(*b*) The present leaders are unfit to govern a nation.—(1) They failed to execute the land laws, thus undoing much good already accomplished.

II. The Irish themselves do not want home rule.——(*a*) The Protestants comprising one-third of the population believe in union with Great Britain.——(*b*) More than one-half of the remaining population, consisting of boycotters and dynamiters, are nationalists and want complete separation from Great Britain.

III. Home rule would be disastrous to English interests.——(*a*) It would greatly weaken the Empire.—(1) It would be a step towards disintegration.——(*b*) It would dislocate the English Constitution.—(1) It is inconsistent with the working of the English cabinet system.——(*c*) It would weaken England's strength as a war power.——(*d*) It would destroy equality between England and Ireland.——(*e*) It would give rise to endless disputes and complications.—(1) A federation cannot be successful unless based on mutual good feeling.——(*f*) It would set a bad example to people in other English possessions.

IV. Home rule would not settle the Irish question.——(*a*) Political changes cannot settle social evils.——(*b*) Irish grievances do not arise from political causes, but on account of the false and vicious land system.——(*c*) The British government being bound in honor to protect the landlords cannot allow a hostile Irish parliament to settle the question.——(*d*) Home rule would only aggravate the question.

LXXII.

PARNELL AND THE IRISH CAUSE.

QUESTION: '*Resolved,* That the memory of Charles Stewart Parnell deserves the gratitude of the Irish people.'

Brief for the Affirmative.

GENERAL REFERENCES: Sir Charles Russell, *Speech Before the Parnell Commission;* Justin McCarthy, *Ireland's Cause in England's Parliament; Contemporary Review,* LX., 625 (November, 1891); *North American Review,* Vol. 144, p. 609 (June, 1887); *New England Magazine* (new series), I., 190 (October, 1889); *Review of Reviews,* IV., 437–438 (November, 1891); *Westminster Review,* Vol. 135, p. 1 (January, 1891); *Public Opinion,* XII., 30 (October 17, 1891); *Nation,* LIII., 289 (October 15, 1891); *Spectator,* LXVII., 484 (October 10, 1891).

I. Parnell was a worthy and effective champion of the Irish cause.——(*a*) He united the Irish people for a definite object: *Public Opinion,* XII., 30.——(*b*) He disciplined the Irish parliamentary party to act as a unit: *Nation,* XLI., 254 (September 24, 1885).——(*c*) He contributed to the cause his own unrivaled skill as a parliamentarian and leader of men: *Contemporary Review,* LX., 632.——(*d*) He contributed valuable criticisms and suggestions to all Irish legislation in Parliament.

II. Parnell's policy of obstruction alone entitles him to Ireland's gratitude.——(*a*) By this policy he compelled Parliament and the English people to pay attention to Ireland's interests.——(*b*) He played the two English parties against each other.——(*c*) He converted the Liberal party and the greatest statesman of the time to the Irish cause.——(*d*) He obtained favorable legislation.——(c) He made the Irish policy of the Conservative party much more lenient.

III. Nothing in Parnell's career can neutralize the lasting good he accomplished for Ireland.——(a) He substituted constitutional methods for violence: *North American Review*, Vol. 144, p. 624.——(b) He successfully opposed coercion. ——(c) He opposed armed insurrections.——(d) He was careful of the means used in attaining his ends.——(e) He made the Irish question the chief question in English politics. ——(f) He made the ultimate triumph of home rule possible and probable.

Brief for the Negative.

GENERAL REFERENCES: Sir Henry James, *The Work of the Irish Leagues;* Justin McCarthy in *North American Review*, Vol. 152, p. 234 (February, 1891); *Nation*, LI., 431, 434 (December 4, 1890); LII., 6–8 (January 1, 1891), 193 (March 5, 1891); LIII., 330 (October 29, 1891); *Contemporary Review*, LIX., 1 (January, 1891).

I. Parnell was personally unworthy of the gratitude of the Irish people.——(a) He was moved by personal ambition and not by patriotism.——(b) He was devoid of moral principle.—(1) He admitted lying when it suited his ends.—(2) The O'Shea divorce case.——(c) He was utterly unscrupulous in his dealings with men.—(1) He betrayed the confidence of the Liberal leaders, Mr. Gladstone and Mr. Morley.—(2) He denounced his own colleagues who had aided him in his successes.—(3) He risked his whole party for his own satisfaction and selfish ends.—(x) By refusing to withdraw from the leadership when every sense of decency and justice demanded that he should.

II. Parnell's political methods were inexpedient and wrong. ——(a) He absented himself from the House of Commons when his presence was most needed.——(b) He worked the policy of obstruction to such an extent as to imperil the English Constitution and the cabinet system.——(*c*) His opposition to the Land Act of 1881 was wrong.——(*d*) He made use of unscrupulous agents.——(*e*) He encouraged boycotting and resistance to landlords.——(*f*) He tacitly encouraged crime.

III. Parnell's acts have seriously injured the Irish cause.——(*a*) In Ireland.—(1) By arousing disorder and inspiring contempt for authority.—(2) By causing a division in the Irish party.——(*b*) In England.—(1) By alienating the Liberal party and Mr. Gladstone.—(2) By renewing in the English public the old distrust of Irish character.

LXXIII.

THE CHINA-JAPAN WAR.

QUESTION: '*Resolved,* That the victory of Japan over China was for the interest of civilization.'

Brief for the Affirmative.

GENERAL REFERENCES: Henry Norman, *The Peoples and Politics of the Far East; Forum,* XVIII., 216 (October, 1894); *North American Review,* Vol. 159, p. 308 (September, 1894), p. 529 (November, 1894); Vol. 160, p. 621 (May, 1895); *Contemporary Review,* LXVI., 305 (September, 1894); *Blackwood's Magazine,* Vol. 157, p. 501 (April, 1895); *Overland Monthly* (second series), XXIV., 524 (November, 1894); *New Review,* XI., 221 (September, 1894); *Public Opinion,* XVII. (see Index, China and Japan).

I. The victory of Japan means the progress of civilization in China, Corea, and Japan.——(*a*) China will be aroused from her social stagnation.—(1) By the introduction of modern political ideas.—(2) By advances in educational matters.——

(3) By social improvements.——(*b*) Corea will be benefited.
—(1) Material prosperity is sure to come.——(*c*) Japan will advance.—(1) In constitutional government.—(2) In commercial freedom.

II. Victory for China meant the retarding of civilization in China, Corea, and Japan.——(*a*) Had China succeeded, the conservative government would have continued without improvement.—(1) The people would have continued in ignorance and degradation.—(2) Material progress of any sort would have been impossible.——(*b*) Corea would have remained in obscurity.—(1) Suppressed by her own nobility.—(2) Subjected to the indifference of China.——(*c*) Japan would have been set back to her earlier conditions.—(1) The liberal progressive party would have been distrusted.—(2) A less liberal policy on the part of the government would have resulted.

III. The victory of Japan will promote the peace of the world.——(*a*) European nations will be restrained from mutual encroachments.—(1) Russia's advance from the north will be prevented.—(x) By a strong internal government in Corea. —(2) The advance of England and France from the south will be checked.—(x) By a more progressive policy on the part of China.

Brief for the Negative.

GENERAL REFERENCES: George N. Curzon, *Problems of the Far East; North American Review*, Vol. 159, pp. 300–308. 316–320 (September, 1894); *Contemporary Review*, LXVI., 609 (November, 1894); *National Review*, XXIV., 263 (October, 1894); *Nineteenth Century*, XXXVI., 612 (October, 1894); *Nation*, LIX., 250 (October 4, 1894); *Spectator*, LXXIII., 360 (September 22, 1894), 392 (September 29, 1894), 915 (December 29, 1894).

I. All admit that China is the mainstay of Eastern Asia. ——(*a*) Governs four hundred millions of people.——(*b*)

Has prevented French advances.——(*c*) Has held Russia at bay.——(*d*) Separates England and Russia.

II. The effect on Corea will be bad.——(*a*) On the government.—(1) Permanent and successful independence is unlikely.—(2) If Japan annexes Corea the result will not be happy.—(x) Japan's influence heretofore has not been good. ——(*b*) On the people.—(1) The people hate the Japanese. —(2) Continued rebellions will keep the country in a perturbed condition and destroy social life and progress.

III. The effect on Japan will be bad.——(*a*) Politically. —(1) The Jingo policy will have full headway.—(2) Buffer state.——(*b*) Economically and socially.—(1) The war will have an unfortunate effect on Japanese life and character: *National Review*, XXIV., 266.

IV. The effect on China will be bad.——(*a*) The present dynasty shaken.——(*b*) The delicately poised Chinese empire in danger of disintegration.—(1) Petty kingdoms.—(2) Long periods of readjustment.—(3) Absorption by European powers.

V. Russian ascendancy is likely to come.——(*a*) Russia is pushing her influence in the East.——(*b*) Corean ports make a basis for Russia's naval operations.——(*c*) The barrier between England and Russia is destroyed.——(*d*) English dependencies in Asia and Polynesia are endangered.

VI. Russian ascendancy would be a set-back to civilization. ——(*a*) The effect on England would be bad.—(1) Religious and commercial civilization.—(2) England is the best colonizer in the world.—(3) The champion of free government.——(*b*) The effect on Western Europe would be bad. —(1) The balance of power in the West would be overthrown.——(*c*) The effect on the United States would be bad.—(1) Our interests in international affairs are identical with those of England.

LXXIV.

NIHILISM.

QUESTION: '*Resolved*, That the efforts of the Russian Nihilists are entitled to the sympathy of a free people.'

Brief for the Affirmative.

GENERAL REFERENCES: Stepniak, *Russia Under the Tsars;* Stepniak, *Underground Russia;* Edmund Noble, *The Russian Revolt;* L. Tikhomirov, *Russia, Political and Social*, II., Bk. VII., Chap. vii., and Appendix B; 'An Interview with a Nihilist,' in *New York Herald*, August 2, 1881; *North American Review*, Vol. 128, p. 174 (February, 1879); Vol. 129, p. 23 (July, 1879); *Century*, XLVI., 461 (July, 1893); *Westminster Review*, Vol. 137, p. 268 (March, 1892).

I. The Russian political system is corrupt.——(*a*) Men are arrested, hanged, shot, and exiled on the least suspicion.——(*b*) The administration of justice is a farce: *Russia Under the Tsars*, pp. 94–121.——(*c*) Officialism, bribery, and corruption are rampant.——(*d*) The prison system in Siberia is terrible: George Kennan, *Siberia and the Exile System*.——(*e*) Liberal education and freedom of thought and action are not permitted.——(*f*) Vice and brutality are befriended by the government.

II. Ordinary methods of redress are impossible.——(*a*) The people have no voice in public affairs.—(1) No parliamentary discussions, no public meetings, no representation by popular vote.——(*b*) The press is under a rigorous censorship. ——(*c*) The Czar pays no heed to petitions.

III. The methods of the Nihilists are justifiable.——(*a*) All people have the right to rebel when oppressed.——(*b*) Secret violence is the only form of revolution possible.——(*c*)

The creed of the Nihilists is not destruction.—(1) They simply demand a constitution.—(2) Violence is an incident, not an end.—(x) It is the only way the cause can be kept before the people.

Brief for the Negative.

GENERAL REFERENCES: John Rae, *Contemporary Socialism*. Chap. ix.: *Contemporary Review*, XXXVIII., 913 (December, 1880); *Nineteenth Century*, VII., 1 (January, 1880); *Revue des Deux Mondes*, XXXVII., 761 (February 15, 1880); *Fortnightly Review*, XXVIII., 149 (August, 1877); *Review of Reviews*, IV., 667 (January, 1892); *Baptist Quarterly Review*, VII., 185 (April, 1885); *Century*, XLV., 611 (February, 1893); *Nation*, XXX., 189 (March 11, 1880); XXXIII., 119 (August 11, 1881); *Spectator*, LV., 586 (May 6, 1882).

I. The aims of the Nihilists are unjustifiable.——(a) They wish to destroy religion, state, family, law, property, and morality.——(b) They offer no positive, practical remedy.——(1) Their demands are extreme and impossible.—(x) Radical socialism cannot be established by revolution.

II. The methods of the Nihilists are unjustifiable.——(a) Their methods are those of terrorism, secret murder, and underhanded conspiracy.——(b) They are regardless of the sanctity of human life.——(c) They adopt any means whatsoever to accomplish their purpose.

III. The result of the Nihilist agitation is only to make the condition of the Russians worse.——(a) Each outbreak causes the laws to be enforced with greater severity.——(b) The burdens of the peasants are increased.——(c) The educated class are driven from the country.——(d) The Czar is withheld from any reforms which he might wish to make.

LXXV.

THE INJUNCTIONS AGAINST THE CHICAGO STRIKERS.

QUESTION: '*Resolved*, That the injunctions issued by the federal judges against the Chicago strikers were unjustifiable.'

Brief for the Affirmative.

GENERAL REFERENCES: United States Strike Commission, *Report on the Chicago Strike; New-York Tribune*, July 3, 1894; *Albany Law Journal*, L., 140-151 (September 1, 1894); *Nation*, LIX., 22-23 (July 12, 1894), 190-191 (September 13, 1894).

I. The injunctions were illegal: *Report on the Chicago Strike*, p. 37.——(*a*) They transcended the fundamental purpose of injunctions: *Abbot's Law Dictionary*, I., 611.—(1) They were issued primarily to protect public rights: *Albany Law Journal*, L., 147.—(2) It is necessary to the obtaining of an injunction that there should be no plain, adequate, and complete remedy at law: *Bouvier's Law Dictionary*, I., 801.——(*b*) They infringed upon the rights of citizens: *Nation*, LIX., 190.——(*c*) They were without precedent: *Public Opinion*, XVII., 67, 68 (April 19, 1894).——(*d*) They could not be served personally: *Albany Law Journal*, L., 147.

II. The injunctions were unnecessary.——(*a*) There were adequate remedies at law.—(1) The enforcement of the Interstate Commerce Law, and of mail regulations: *Nation*, L., 22.—(2) The enforcement of insurrection laws: *Report on the Chicago Strike*, p. 16: *United States Revised Statutes*, §§ 5298, 5299; *Nation*, LIX., 22; *Public Opinion*, XVII., 330 (July 12, 1894).——(*b*) It would have been necessary in any case to employ federal troops: *Nation*, LIX., 191.

III. The injunctions worked positive evil.———(*a*) They established a dangerous precedent.———(*b*) They tended to incite disorder.—(1) They weakened the confidence of workingmen in the integrity of the courts: *Nation*, LIX., 191.—(2) The summary proceedings enraged the working classes.

Brief for the Negative.

GENERAL REFERENCES: *New-York Tribune* (and other leading dailies), June 22 to July 13, 1894; T. M. Cooley in *Forum*, XVIII., 5–13 (September, 1894); H. J. Fletcher in *Atlantic Monthly*, LXXIV., 534–541 (October, 1894); Injunctions in *New-York Tribune*, July 3, 1894; *Interstate Commerce Act*, February 4, 1887; Judge Grosscup's charge in *New-York Tribune*, July 11, 1894; *Public Opinion*, XVII., 306 (July 5, 1894), 330 (July 12, 1894).

I. The injunctions were legal.———(*a*) They were upheld by the federal executive.———(*b*) They were law unless set aside by a superior court.

II. The injunctions were just to the strikers.———(*a*) The federal courts have no bias against either laborers or railroads: Decision of Judge Caldwell in *Atlantic Monthly*, LXXIV., 535.———(*b*) The injunctions simply gave the strikers fair warning of what to expect from the law.

III. The injunctions were just in protecting the railroads. ———(*a*) The government compels the railroads to run for the public good: *Interstate Commerce Act*; *New-York Tribune*, July 4, 1894; *Atlantic Monthly*, LXXIV., 538.———(*b*) The strikers were injuring the railroads: *Forum*, XVIII., 6; United States Strike Commission, *Report on the Chicago Strike*. ———(*c*) The injunctions were the only peaceful means by which the government could lend help speedily.

IV. The injunctions were just to the general public.———(*a*) They were the best means for the government to adopt to protect the public.—(1) The strike was doing irreparable damage to innocent people: *Report on the Chicago Strike*, p. 14; *Forum*, XVIII., 5–13.—(2) The injunctions were the only means both swift and peaceable.——(*b*) The increasing magnitude of railroad strikes demanded a vigorous legal precedent which should check violence and protect the public: *Forum*, XVIII., 5–13.

ADDITIONAL TOPICS FOR DEBATE.

POLITICS.

1. The American Republic is likely to endure.
2. The present tendency in the United States toward centralization in government should be resisted.
3. The evils of party government in the United States are inherent.
4. A third party can never be effective in American politics.
5. The United States should annex no more territory.
6. The United States should annex Cuba.
7. A vigorous enforcement of the Monroe Doctrine is desirable.
8. Suffrage is a natural right.
9. Suffrage in the United States should be restricted by an educational qualification.
10. Voting should be made compulsory.
11. Criminals should be disfranchised.
12. Women should be allowed to vote in school elections.
13. Codification of the common law is unwise.
14. Judges should not be elected by popular vote.
15. Unanimity should not be required in jury verdicts.
16. Pensions once granted cannot lawfully be discontinued.
17. A court of arbitration should be established for the settlement of disputes between nations.
18. The English government represents the wishes of the people more truly than the government of the United States does.

19. A country is best governed by a single legislative chamber.

20. It is essential that the upper chamber of a legislature be chosen in a different manner from the lower.

21. Some method should be adopted by which minorities in legislatures can be represented.

22. Nations are best governed under a written constitution.

23. The compact theory of the Constitution is not defensible.

24. The Deity should be recognized in the Constitution.

25. It should be possible to secure amendments to the Constitution more easily.

26. All indirect elections should be abolished.

27. A national bankruptcy act should be passed.

28. Uniform usury laws are desirable.

29. The naturalization laws of the United States should be made more stringent.

30. Congress should take some action to prevent lynchings in the South.

31. An amendment to the Constitution should be secured prohibiting polygamy in the United States.

32. There should be legislation against speculation in futures and options.

33. Congress should subsidize a Pacific cable.

34. Congress has no power to regulate elections.

35. Congress should meet biennially.

36. The District of Columbia should be represented in Congress.

37. A majority only should be necessary to pass a bill over the President's veto.

38. The growth of the committee system in Congress is unfortunate.

39. Congress should assemble on the first Monday in January, and the terms of senators and representatives should expire on December 31st.

40. Members of Congress should be prohibited from speculating in stocks.

41. The contested election cases of members of Congress should be tried before the Supreme Court.

42. Congress should be forbidden to pay claims legally barred by lapse of time.

43. The practice of granting 'leave to print' should be discontinued.

44. The consent of the Senate should be necessary for the removal of presidential appointees.

45. States should be represented in the Senate in proportion to their population.

46. The House of Representatives meets too long after the election of its members.

47. Congressmen should be elected for three instead of two years.

48. There are too many members of the House of Representatives.

49. The desks should be taken from the hall of the House of Representatives and benches substituted.

50. The President and Vice-President should be elected by direct vote of the people.

51. No President should have a third term.

52. Presidents should be elected for a term of seven years and should be ineligible for re-election.

53. No President should be allowed to serve two consecutive terms.

54. Presidents should be allowed to veto items in appropriation bills.

55. The term of the President should end on the 30th of April instead of on the 4th of March.

56. The House of Lords should be abolished.

57. Members of the House of Commons should receive pay for their services.

58. A representative should vote according to the wishes of his constituency.

59. Rotation in office is undesirable.
60. The President, the Vice-President, and the cabinet should be prohibited from taking part in political campaigns.
61. The people should be able to initiate legislation.
62. The referendum should be adopted in the United States.
63. The governors of states should have the veto power.
64. The governors of states should not have the pardoning power.
65. State legislatures should assemble biennially.
66. State legislatures should be prevented from interfering by special legislation in municipal affairs.
67. Municipal elections should be held at different times from state elections.
68. Municipal misrule in the United States is due to the indifference of the better classes.
69. The degraded condition of American city governments is due to foreign immigration.
70. Immigrants should be compelled to be able to read and write.

ECONOMICS.

71. The most important question with which Congress has to deal is that of the currency.
72. The currency of the country should be regulated by the government so as to secure greater elasticity.
73. Governments should not undertake to regulate the supply of currency within their territory.
74. Stability in a currency is more important than elasticity.
75. It is not essential for a currency to have a metallic basis.
76. A double monetary standard gives a broader basis for a currency than a single standard.
77. There is not enough gold to transact the business of the world.
78. The price of gold has appreciated.

79. There has been a general fall in prices since 1873.

80. The currency of the United States has never been bi-metallic.

81. The history of France does not support the argument for bi-metallism.

82. An international bi-metallic agreement is feasible.

83. Congress should have the sole power to coin and issue money.

84. Convertible paper currency can never be depreciated by over-issue.

85. A government should confer on no coin the quality of legal tender.

86. The issue of legal tender notes during the war should have been declared unconstitutional.

87. The issue of legal tender notes during the war was expedient.

88. The government should retire all the legal tender notes.

89. The issue of the treasury notes of 1890 was inexpedient.

90. The emergency currency of 1893 was inexpedient.

91. The recent financial difficulties of the United States government have been due to a deficient revenue and not to defects in the currency system.

92. The methods of issuing bonds from 1891 to 1896 were improper.

93. The government should loan money at low rates of interest.

94. Savings banks should be operated in connection with the post-office.

95. People's banks, similar to those in Germany, should be established in the United States.

96. The United States should transact its business through a bank organized like the Bank of England.

97. National banks should be authorized to establish branches.

98. The system of banking reserves in the United States should be changed.

99. Our present system of bond security for bank-notes should be changed.

100. Our system of bank-notes is inferior to that of Germany.

101. The safety fund system of banking should be adopted in the United States.

102. An adequate bank-note currency could be secured by requiring each bank to pay out none but its own notes.

103. Foreign trade cannot be increased by legislative enactment.

104. Reciprocity is a wise means of encouraging commercial expansion.

105. Commercial reciprocity between the United States and South America is desirable.

106. A protective tariff benefits farmers.

107. A protective tariff is unconstitutional.

108. Trusts are the result of a protective tariff.

109. Trusts do not lower prices.

110. Taxation is the best method of raising revenue to carry on war.

111. Direct taxation is more advantageous than indirect taxation.

112. The internal revenue taxes in the United States should be abolished.

113. A personal property tax cannot be administered with fairness.

114. There should be a tax on expenditures.

115. Church property should not be taxed.

116. The national debt should be paid as rapidly as possible.

117. The wages fund theory is not sound.

118. The wages of women should not be lower than those of men in the same occupation.

119. The standard of living cannot be raised without raising wages.

120. Wages are not determined by demand and supply.

121. The economic advantages of production on a large scale do not outweigh the disadvantages.

122. General over-production is not possible.

123. The Interstate Commerce Act has been detrimental to the business interests of the country.

124. Railroad combination cheapens rates.

125. The supremacy of England as a commercial nation is not likely to last.

SOCIOLOGY.

126. The state should never undertake anything that can be performed adequately by private enterprise.

127. The state should have regard for the moral as well as the physical well-being of its subjects.

128. All large corporations should be regulated and controlled by the state.

129. The nationalization of land is desirable.

130. Every person has the right to employment.

131. The aged, widows, and orphans should be cared for by the state.

132. The blind and the insane should be cared for in state institutions.

133. Governments should grant old age pensions.

134. The German system of compulsory insurance should be adopted in the United States.

135. Free public employment bureaus should be established by each state.

136. Employers should be liable for the life and health of employees.

137. A law requiring industrial corporations to pay wages weekly is desirable.

138. Children under fourteen years of age should be prohibited from working in factories.

139. The amount of wealth transferable by inheritance should be limited by statute.

140. Convicts should not be employed in productive labor.
141. The plan of colonizing convicts is wise.
142. Colonization is the best remedy for city poverty.
143. Co-operation furnishes the most satisfactory solution of the labor problem.
144. Profit-sharing in the United States has not been successful.
145. Labor should be paid for by an equal amount of labor.
146. The use of new machinery is disadvantageous to the working classes.
147. The factory system has been a benefit to the working classes.
148. Strikes are productive of more harm than good to the working classes.
149. The boycott is a legitimate weapon of labor.
150. Blacklisting should be prohibited by law.
151. Overtime and piece-work should be prohibited by law.
152. Trade unions are the outcome of the mediæval gilds.
153. Labor organizations should be incorporated under federal and state laws.
154. Trade unions are not justified in restricting the number of persons allowed to learn a trade.
155. Members of trade unions are not justified in refusing to work with non-union men.
156. Trade unions cannot raise wages permanently.
157. Saloons should be permitted to open on Sunday.
158. The saloon is rightly called ' the poor man's club.'
159. Education should be compulsory.
160. The state should provide for technical education as well as for liberal education.
161. The state should furnish books and school supplies to pupils.
162. Sectarian institutions should not receive state aid.
163. Religious teaching should be given in primary schools.
164. The parochial school system is dangerous to American institutions.

165. Women should be admitted to local school boards.
166. College degrees should be required for entrance to professional schools.
167. Students should have a part in college government.
168. The honor system of conducting college examinations should be generally adopted.
169. Greek-letter societies are desirable in colleges.
170. Latin and Greek should not be required studies in colleges.
171. Admission to college should be by examination only.
172. College entrance requirements should be lowered.
173. Attendance at college recitations should not be compulsory.
174. College education does not unfit a man for business life.
175. Small colleges are preferable to large ones.
176. The faculties of colleges should supervise and control their athletics.
177. Intercollegiate athletic contests should not take place outside of college towns.
178. The results gained by college settlements do not justify their existence.
179. A national university should be established in the United States.
180. A university should be established in each state, which shall have no duty of teaching but which shall have the sole power of examining candidates and of conferring degrees.

MISCELLANEOUS.

181. The general disarmament of European nations is desirable.
182. The standing army of the United States should be increased.
183. The coast defenses of the United States should be strengthened.

184. The present administration of the Indian service is not satisfactory.

185. Appointments to the consular service should be made only after examinations.

186. The scheme of transporting the negro to Africa is practicable.

187. Service pensions should be granted.

188. Passengers' baggage should be exempt from duty.

189. The Australian system of registering deeds should be adopted in this country.

190. Child life insurance should be prohibited.

191. The metric system should be generally adopted.

192. Arctic exploration has not been justified in results.

193. The Elgin marbles should be returned.

194. The results of foreign missions do not justify their continuance.

195. Church unity is not possible.

196. National expositions do not benefit the countries in which they are held.

197. Vivisection should be prohibited.

198. Vaccination is inadvisable.

199. Cremation should take the place of earth burial.

200. The postage on letters should be reduced to one cent.

INDEX

A. B. degree, three years' course for, 181
Allegiance, party, 22; in municipal elections, 24
American Protective Association, 19
Annexation, of Canada, 59; of Hawaii, 62
Arbitration, national board for in railroad disputes, 162

BANK-NOTES, tax on state, 93
Bibliography of debating, xli
Bimetallism, 90
Booth, General, employment system of, 160
Bounties on sugar, 112
Bribery, English system for preventing in elections, 47
Brief system, xxv

CABINET, in Congress, 40; system of government, 37
Canada, annexation of, 59; reciprocity with, 102
Capital punishment, 57
Caucus system, 27
Chicago strikers, injunctions against, 197
China-Japan war, 192
Chinese, exclusion of, 73
Cities, executive power of mayor in, 49
Civil service reform, 44
Closure in Senate, 83
Co-education, 178
Colleges, co-education in, 178; foot-ball in, 184; three years' course in, 181

Commerce, state control of, 129
Congressional government, 37
Congressmen, district election of, 36
Contract system, 165
Convict labor, 165
Copyright law, an international, 80
Corruption, English system for preventing in elections, 47
Criticism of debates, xxxix

DAY, an eight-hour, 156
Debate, bibliography of, xli; criticism of, xxxix; importance of, xii; limitation of in Senate, 83; management of, xxx; practice before, xxviii
Disfranchisement of negroes, 6
Divorce, federal control of, 142
Duties, on ships, 104; on sugar, 110; on wool and woollens, 115

EDUCATION, state control of, 139
Eight-hour day, 156
Elections, federal control of national, 1; party allegiance in municipal, 24
Electors, choice of presidential, 30
Employment system, General Booth's, 160

FOOT-BALL, 184
Free trade, 96

GOLD standard, an international, 88
Gothenburg liquor system, 176
Governments, cabinet and congressional, 37

HAWAII, annexation of, 62
High license, 172
Home rule, 187
Housing of the poor, 170

IMMIGRANTS, tax on, 70
Immigration, restriction of, 68
Importance of debate, xii
Income tax, a national, 117
Independence in politics, 22
Institutions, danger to American, 52
Interstate Commerce Act, amendment of, 137
Ireland, home rule for, 187; Parnell and, 190
Irrigation works, government construction of, 144

JAPAN, war with China, 192
Jury system, 55

LABOR, convict, 165; organization of, 151; party, 154
Light, ownership of plants for supplying, 132
Liquor, Gothenburg system, 176; high license, 172; prohibition, 172

MANAGEMENT of a debate, xxx
Manufactories, state ownership of, 129
Materials, xviii; use of, xxiii
Mayor, executive power of in cities, 49
Ministers, cabinet, in Congress, 40
Monopolies, ownership of natural, 132; prohibition of, 134

NAVY, increase of, 78
Negroes, disfranchisement of, 6; federal protection of suffrage, 3
Nicaragua Canal, United States ownership of, 65
Nihilism, 195
Nomination by caucus, 27

OLEOMARGARINE, right to prohibit the sale of, 149

PARNELL, Charles Stewart, and Irish cause, 190
Party, allegiance to, 22; in municipal elections, 24; a labor, 154; Populist, 16; Republican, 13
Pensions, policy of Republican party regarding, 75
Persuasive speaking, xxxv
Pooling, prohibition of, 137
Poor, housing of, 170
Populist party, 16
Practice before debate, xxviii
Presidential electors, choice of, 30
Prohibition, 172
Property qualification for municipal suffrage, 11
Protection, 96; and wages, 99

QUARANTINE, federal control of, 146
Questions, selection of, xv
Quorums, the counting of, 85

RAILROADS, government ownership of, 123
Rebuttal, xxxiv
Reciprocity with Canada, 102
Reed's Rules, present quorum in, 85
Republican party, 13; pension policy of, 75

SENATE, closure in, 83
Senators, popular election of, 32
Ships, free, 104; subsidies for, 107
Silver, further coinage of, 90
Single tax, 120
Strikes, compulsory arbitration in railroad, 162; injunctions issued at Chicago, 197
Subsidies, shipping, 107
Suffrage, federal protection for negro, 3; property qualification for municipal, 11; woman, 8
Sugar, bounties on, 112; free, 110

TARIFF, free trade, 96; protection, 96; wages and, 99

Tax, on immigrants, 70; income, 117; on state bank-notes, 93; single, 120
Telegraph, government ownership of, 126
Transportation, ownership of plants for supplying, 132
Trusts, prohibition of, 134

UNEMPLOYED, General Booth's system, 160; municipal aid for, 168

WAGES, tariff and, 99
Water, ownership of plants for supplying, 132
Woman suffrage, 8
Wool, duties on, 115

STUDIES IN AMERICAN EDUCATION.

By Albert Bushnell Hart, Ph.D.   12mo, cloth, gilt top, $1.25.

Contents: Has the Teacher a Profession?—Reform in the Grammar Schools—University Participation, a Substitute for University Extension—How to Study History—How to Teach History in Secondary Schools—The Status of Athletics in American Colleges—Index.

"This volume consists of six essays, each one excellent in its way."
—*Public Opinion*, New York.

"Prof. Hart is a keen observer and a profound thinker; he knows what American education is, and he knows what it ought to be . . . his whole treatment of the subject is vigorous and original. . . . He has a most helpful article on the study of history, and another equally significant on the teaching of history in the secondary schools."—*Beacon*, Boston.

"The essays on 'How to Study and Teach History' are admirable. As education is a unit, the same methods can be applied in all grades. The relation of college curriculums to secondary schools is the underlying subject of the book, but it is still an open question whether secondary schools should justify their methods because they prepare for college, or whether they should assume the independent position, that they furnish such knowledge as is most requisite for boys and girls who can study till they are eighteen, but are not going to college. It is easily possible to take this attitude and yet have a preparatory class for Harvard in the same high school."—*Literary World*, Boston.

"As for the essays themselves, however, only words of praise ought to be spoken. The style is clear, concise, active, enlivened by apt illustrations; 'breezy' may perhaps be the word. The thought is practical and clear-headed, as Professor Hart always is, and the essays themselves have been 'brought down to date.'"—*School Review*, Hamilton, N. Y.

"This new volume from the experience and pen of Professor Hart is one of practical interest, and a valuable addition to the rapidly increasing collection of works on pedagogy. . . . While all the chapters are interesting, perhaps the one most interesting to the general reader is that on 'How to Study History,' and here Mr. Hart shows his decided preferences for the topical method of study. This chapter should be read by all students of history and especially by those members of private classes, of which so many are to be found in our villages and clubs all through the country."—*Transcript*, Boston.

"His studies have a decidedly practical tendency, and together constitute an addition to our steadily growing stock of good educational literature."
—*Dial*, Chicago.

"The author is especially fitted to write a volume which has the rare merit of treating current educational ideas not only from the standpoint of the teacher, but also of the pupil, the board of education and the public at large. The book will prove specially interesting and instructive to the general reader."
Post Graduate, Wooster, Ohio.

"Whatever Dr. Hart contributes to educational or historical literature is always worth reading, and teachers will find these essays very suggestive."
School Review, Monroe, La.

LONGMANS, GREEN, & CO., 91-93 Fifth Avenue, New York.

PRACTICAL ESSAYS ON AMERICAN GOVERNMENT.

By ALBERT BUSHNELL HART, Ph.D. 12mo, cloth, gilt top, $1.50.

CONTENTS: The Speaker as Premier—The Exercise of the Suffrage—The Election of a President—Do the People Wish Civil Service Reform?—The Chilean Controversy—A Study in American Diplomacy—The Colonial Town Meeting—The Colonial Shire—The Rise of American Cities—The Biography of a River and Harbor Bill—The Public Land Policy of the United States—Why the South was Defeated in the Civil War—Index.

"Dr. Hart demonstrates by this book, as we think no one else has so well demonstrated, the possible close connection between academic study and practical politics."—*Atlantic Monthly.*

"The book is a solid, substantial, and most satisfactory piece of honest work. The author has selected his sheaves with excellent judgment, and threshed the grain out of them to the very best of his ability. There is no eye-service in it—no paragraph written to round out an article or help fill the pages of a magazine. Prof. Hart has worked for his readers with a will, and there is no reader so well informed on the topics of the book that he will not find it interesting, suggestive, and instructive. . . . Take the masterly exposition of one of the most important—many people will say the most important—of American public questions, the exercise of the suffrage. It will astonish almost every reader that such a wealth of thought, research, and information can be compressed into the limits of such an article, and yet be interesting, clear, and indeed attractive."—*Nation.*

"As qualifications for writing the six articles that make up Professor Albert Bushnell Hart's new volume, 'Studies in American Education' . . . the author adds to general scholarship and successful experience in teaching a special interest in the subject of education, and particularly American education. . . . His studies have a decidedly practical tendency, and together constitute an addition to our steadily growing stock of good educational literature."—*The Dial,* Chicago.

BOSTON.

By HENRY CABOT LODGE, author of "Life of Alexander Hamilton," "Daniel Webster," "George Washington," "A Short History of the English Colonies in America," etc. (*Historic Towns.*) Second Edition. With two Maps. 12mo, $1.25.

"Mr. Lodge writes with the ease of one to whom the subject in its larger aspects is familiar."—*Atlantic Monthly.*

"Henry Cabot Lodge's 'Boston,' which was some time ago added to the 'Historic Towns' series, is, notwithstanding its limitations, a sincere and striking book. . . . Two excellent maps accompany the volume."
—*Boston Evening Transcript.*

LONGMANS, GREEN, & CO., 91-93 Fifth Avenue, New York

www.ingramcontent.com/pod-product-compliance
Lightning Source LLC
Chambersburg PA
CBHW032143230426
43672CB00011B/2429